Non-Clinical Careers for Physicians

Steven Babitsky, Esq.
James J. Mangraviti, Jr., Esq.

S•E•A•K, Inc.
Excellence in Education since 1980

Falmouth, Massachusetts

Contents

Acknowledgments

The authors wish to acknowledge the numerous faculty members, recruiters, and mentors from SEAK's annual Non-Clinical Careers for Physicians Conference (www.seak.com) who were gracious enough to allow us to interview them. We would also like to thank Karen Cerbarano and Dee Netzel for their invaluable assistance with this book.

Related Products by SEAK, Inc.

<u>TEXTS</u>
The Physician's Comprehensive Guide to Negotiating
The Biggest Legal Mistakes Physicians Make
Bulletproofing Your Medical Practice
The A–Z Guide to Expert Witnessing
How to Become a Dangerous Expert Witness
National Guide to Expert Witness Fees and Billing Procedures
Cross-Examination: The Comprehensive Guide for Experts
Writing and Defending Your Expert Report
How to Excel During Depositions
The Comprehensive IME System
Writing and Defending Your IME Report

<u>SEMINARS & CONFERENCES</u>
Negotiating Skills for Physicians
Finding and Landing High-Paying Non-Clinical Jobs
Non-Clinical Careers for Physicians
National Expert Witness Conference
Fiction Writing for Physicians
Non-Fiction Writing for Physicians
Advanced Cross-Examination Workshop
Advanced Deposition Skills Workshop
How to Be a Dangerous Expert Witness
Persuasion Skills Workshop for Experts
How to Start and Build a Successful Expert Witness Practice
Expert Report Writing Workshop
Testifying Skills Workshop
Law School for Experts
Expert Witness Practice Management Workshop
How to Be an Effective Medical Witness
How to Be a Successful Independent Medical Examiner

<u>DIRECTORIES</u> (www.seakexperts.com)
SEAK, Inc. National Directory of Independent Medical Examiners
SEAK, Inc. National Directory of Experts
SEAK, Inc. National Directory of Medical File Review Consultants

For more information, call SEAK at (508) 457-1111. Inquiries may also be addressed to SEAK, Inc. at P.O. Box 729, Falmouth, MA 02541. Fax (508) 540-8304; e-mail address: mail@seak.com; internet address: www.seak.com.

About the Authors

Steven Babitsky, Esq. (sbabitsky@aol.com), is the President and founder of SEAK, Inc., a continuing education, training, consulting, and publishing firm. He has trained thousands of physicians over the past 26 years. He is the co-founder of SEAK's annual *Non-Clinical Careers for Physicians* conference. He is the co-creator and a trainer for SEAK's *How to Find and Land High-Paying Non-Clinical Jobs* workshop. He also serves as a non-clinical career consultant. He is the co-author of *The Successful Physician Negotiator: How to Get What You Deserve* and is the developer and trainer for SEAK's *Negotiating Skills for Physicians* seminar. Steve is also the co-editor of the text *The Biggest Legal Mistakes Physicians Make and How to Avoid Them*. He trains physicians and others on negotiation strategy and techniques and acts as a consultant to medical societies and journals in their negotiations with medical publishers, other organizations, and individuals. Steve has lectured nationally on negotiation strategies and techniques. Steve is also an expert on medical-legal consulting and has co-authored numerous books in this field and trained thousands of physicians. He was a personal injury trial attorney for twenty years and is the former managing partner of the firm Kistin, Babitsky, Latimer & Beitman.

James J. Mangraviti, Jr., Esq. (seakincjm@aol.com), has trained thousands of physicians across the United States and Canada. He currently serves as Vice President and General Counsel of SEAK, Inc., a continuing education, training, consulting, and publishing firm. Jim received his BA degree in mathematics *summa cum laude* from Boston College and his JD degree *cum laude* from Boston College Law School. Jim is the co-founder and co-seminar leader of SEAK's annual *Non-Clinical Careers for Physicians* conference. He is the co-creator and a trainer for SEAK's *How to Find and Land High-Paying Non-Clinical Jobs* workshop. He also serves as a non-clinical career consultant and mentor. He is the co-author of *The Successful Physician Negotiator: How to Get What You Deserve* and is the co-developer of SEAK's *Negotiating Skills for Physicians* seminar. Jim is also the co-editor of the text *The Biggest Legal Mistakes Physicians Make and How to Avoid Them*. Jim is also an expert on medical-legal consulting and has co-authored numerous books in this field and trained thousands of physicians. Prior to joining SEAK in 1996 Jim practiced law in Boston.

Prologue

It was 1992. I was the senior partner in a very successful boutique law firm on Cape Cod. I was making lots of money. People in my office looked up to me. My colleagues considered me indispensable. I was well known and well regarded around the area, having represented thousands of clients over the years. My parents were very proud of me. There was only one little problem. I was 44 years old and wasn't happy. My job was stressful and repetitive. I didn't want to be doing it for the next 15 or 20 years.

That same year I hired a law clerk to help me out on a book writing project. His name was Jim Mangraviti and he was about to start his last year at Boston College Law School, which I had attended twenty years earlier.

I talked to my wife about leaving the practice of law. She was wonderfully supportive. I told my partners I would be retiring at the end of the year. They didn't take me seriously. When December 31 came and I never came back they were in shock. How could you leave such a successful practice?

My parents and other relatives were equally puzzled. You did what? Quit at the height of your career? Are you nuts?

I had started a part-time publishing and seminar company (SEAK, Inc.) in 1980. I decided to turn this hobby into a full-time business. In 1993, I hired Jim right out of law school to help me build the business. He wanted to work at a law firm, but he took the job with me because he couldn't find employment in a law firm in a bleak job market. In 1994, he found a job at a law firm. I counseled him about the practice of law and how he should consider staying with me to build SEAK. He left anyhow and joined the law firm.

Jim and I kept in touch. He quickly discovered many of the realities of practicing law in a law firm that I had experienced and that I had warned him about. In 1996, Jim came back to SEAK and completed his own career transition from practicing attorney to businessperson.

While working at SEAK, Jim met his wife Nancy, who was at the time practicing law at a large, prestigious law firm in Boston. Within a short time after meeting Jim and seeing his predictable hours and the passion with which he went to work each day, Nancy had completed her own career transition away from law firm practice and has never looked back.

We've grown SEAK to 10 times its 1993 size. We're having fun. We're being creative. We're helping our clients. Some of our most enjoyable days are when we hear from clients who tell us how we have changed their lives for the better. We're making money comparable to what a practicing lawyer would make. We've brought my two children into the business as partners. Now each day I have the pleasure of interacting with my adult children.

In 2004, we put together a seminar on non-clinical careers for physicians. It was our most popular physician seminar of the year and we continued to improve the program. In 2007, we expanded our seminar into the current National Non-Clinical Careers Conference, now featuring breakout sessions and numerous speakers, mentors, and recruiters. We have helped hundreds of physicians understand that they are not alone in their desire for career change. We've shown them what's out there and how others have successfully made the transition.

I truly hope this book can be of help to you. Many, many others have made career transitions. If we can do it and they can do it, so can you.

As always, your feedback is welcome.

Steven Babitsky, Esq.
stevenbabitsky@seak.com
Direct Dial 508-548-9443

James J. Mangraviti, Jr., Esq.
seakincjm@aol.com
Direct Dial 978-276-1234

Chapter 1 The Truth About Clinical and Non-Clinical Careers for Physicians

1.1 Executive Summary

- If you are dissatisfied practicing clinical medicine, you are far from alone.
- Typical reasons for leaving clinical medicine include:
  o Unhappy in practice
  o Disability
  o Near retirement age
  o Family concerns
  o Want to be an entrepreneur
- Long-term prospects for non-clinical compensation are in many cases superior to clinical compensation, although an initial pay cut may or may not be required.
- Compensation in a non-clinical career can be extremely competitive especially if you factor in hours worked, stress, lifestyle, and bonuses.
- Succeeding and advancing in a non-clinical environment will require hard work and adapting to your new surroundings where you will start in an entry-level position.
- Family members are generally supportive of career change.
- In a non-clinical position you can still make a difference and, in many cases, you can help far more people than you were able to in your clinical position.
- The culture at a non-clinical employer can often be radically different than at your clinical position and can involve unpleasant bureaucracy and office politics.

1.2 If You Are Dissatisfied Practicing Clinical Medicine, You Are Far From Alone

If you are dissatisfied practicing clinical medicine, you have plenty of company. In fact, according to the Massachusetts Medical Society's July 2005 Physician Workforce Study, roughly 37% to 45% of respondents were considering a career change.

The reasons we typically see for physicians wanting to leave clinical medicine are as follows. If you fit into any of these five categories, you are not alone:

1. Unhappy in clinical practice for many of the reasons discussed below.
2. Disabled. Can no longer practice specialty due to a medical disability.
3. Have the "business bug." Really excited to get into business and be entrepreneurial.
4. Want to spend more time with family—need more predictable hours.
5. Getting older. Do not want to practice medicine any longer, but want to do something of value for the next 5 to 10 years.

For several years we have been running seminars and conferences for physicians who are considering non-clinical careers. One of our teaching techniques is to find out, in advance, why people are coming and what they are looking to accomplish at the course. A sampling of the e-mail responses we received prior to our 2008 Non-Clinical Careers Conference follows:

Example 1.1: Why physicians explore non-clinical careers
- Because of a lack of personal growth, general fatigue, poor sleep, and health-related concerns attached to my current highly stressed clinical position.
- Briefly, dissatisfaction with the current practice of medicine, long hours with poor reimbursement, the hassle with insurance companies, and the need for a lifestyle change.
- Dissatisfaction with present position due to excessive hours, lack of quality of life, being forced to work in a manner which I do not feel is conducive to optimal patient care, high overhead, decreasing reimbursements, increasing regulation by government and third party payers.
- Find my passion. Both for my career and for time outside of my career. I constantly feel unfulfilled.
- Because of increasing dissatisfaction with clinical medicine—more work, lack of appreciable compensation/reimbursement, litigious environment, and over-regulation.

- I am burned out from 24 years of emergency medicine practice with its inherent circadian disturbance.
- I am burning out of my career and have only been at it for four years. The hours are tiring. I am a family practice physician who works for a large organization. We have had two pay cuts in the last year and while our pay is being cut, we are being asked to see more patients and our staff is shrinking in size. I do not feel like I can keep this pace up for much longer.
- I am tired of working 26 weekends a year (and holidays).
- I feel like I am on a sinking ship at times and have tried to make changes but when you say "Hey, we have a leak, we're sinking if we don't do something..." Whose fault is it to stay on that sinking ship? I want to help people and continue to learn but I'm also not interested in being a martyr.
- I find that my passions are increasingly in the non-clinical (non-patient care) arena.
- I have 4 children and am forty next year. The specialty and the current healthcare model make it harder every year to do my job in a sane way.
- I see the future of clinical practice in medicine becoming even more burdened with administrative requirements and regulations, skyrocketing overhead, and diminishing reimbursements.
- I want to drop out of clinical practice to have a life. I am in an intolerable clinic situation where the overhead is 85% and I am involved with patients and EMR and other paperwork 16 hours per day.
- I'd like to change [my] career without sacrificing my standard of living.
- I'm finding medicine overwhelming and frustrating, plus not as stimulating as I had hoped it would be. I feel as if I'm constantly being micromanaged.
- I'm sick of whining patients, drug seeking patients, Medicaid patients, paperwork, having to pre-authorize everything, formularies, coding, and Medicare's overwhelming regulations.
- In a word, I am tired. I am tired of increasing illogical and unnecessary government interference and regulation while at the same time constantly trying to decrease my reimbursement for any given service. I am tired of working 10–15 hours per day and not seeing my family. I am tired of having to defend myself against frivolous and unmerited lawsuits because someone is using the medical malpractice legal system as their personal lottery. I am tired of people who think nothing of ignoring their statements and having to write off their care, it is not like I can repossess the medical services provided and the time spent and resell it.

- Likelihood of increasing bureaucracy, increasing stress, and diminishing return of my current neurosurgical practice.
- Limited time with my family and no time for myself are big reasons for wondering what else is out there.
- Looking for a less-fast-paced, less hectic work life for the next 15–20 years, current 50–80 hour work week in very time-demanding radiology practice is wearing thin. I can be more available to my family and friends.
- Need a change, can't stand doing all paperwork, answering to insurance companies instead of the patient. Time is right for career change.
- Now I feel "stuck" as I have invested so much time and effort in my training and experience.
- Practicing has become more of a hassle than pleasure.
- Sadly, the reimbursement for all the stress of practicing pediatrics is practically unacceptable.
- Seeking completely different work environment that better suits my skills, passions, and desires.
- The demand to see more patients in a shorter span of time and the ever-increasing amount of time spent outside of office hours to complete paperwork, phone calls, etc.
- Thoroughly tired of practicing medicine.
- We are in a field that's goal is to help people, but is really quite dysfunctional.
- I am dissatisfied with my current situation.
- I'm tired of the "rat race" and daily grind of seeing patients.
- I'd like to have an occupation in or out of medicine with no night, weekend, or holiday obligations.
- Formulating an exit strategy.
- I am interested in having a more balanced practice than I am involved with at the time.
- To find the excitement medicine once held for me.
- Not satisfied with current job. Have accomplished as much as I can, looking for new challenge.
- I've become a bit weary of seeing 30–40 patients a day.
- I am getting fed up with solo practice in the environment.
- Professional burn-out.
- My days in the office are often rushed and unfulfilling.
- I would like to explore new ways to use my medical education that would fit better into my family life.
- Looking forward to where I want to be in 5 or 10 years.
- I have no desire to do clinical medicine but must do something.

- I am very unhappy practicing clinical medicine. I don't enjoy seeing patients at all. I really don't even want to deal with them at all. I am especially unhappy about my schedule and the long hours.
- Becoming frustrated with demanding selfish patients and my environment.
- To decrease (hopefully) my stress levels.
- I am tired of the stress in emergency medicine—I would like to do something new and interesting with regular hours.
- To utilize my talents but to do it in a setting where I have better control of the time commitments.
- To use my skills and learn new ones, with flexible hours that will permit me to spend time with my children.
- I am very concerned about the future of medicine and longevity of my career in this field.
- Career change, better hours (less nights and weekends).
- I don't like to be micromanaged, it seems like more work is expected for less pay.
- I no longer feel satisfied—I feel imprisoned.

These responses are echoed by an American College of Physician Executives 2006 Physician Morale Survey. That survey found that 34.2% of physicians had experienced marital or family discord as a result of their work as a physician, 32.2% had become depressed, and 66.7% had experienced emotional burnout. According to the same ACPE survey, 69.9% of physicians know a colleague who has left the practice of medicine as a result of morale problems.

The following quote from a SEAK faculty member gives a good summary of the reasons why many physicians leave clinical practice:

Example 1.2: Physician discovers allergy to direct patient care
The reason that I left clinical medicine was that I discovered that I had a condition. I first became aware of it in the latter part of my medical school training and realized that progressively, until I worked in the emergency room, that I realized I was allergic to direct patient care. I realized that I wasn't enjoying what I was doing. Therefore, I had a responsibility to respect that because I do believe that if you are not passionate about what you are doing, you are only going to get mediocre results. I thought my patients deserved better than that. I was just not in the right place.

The unpredictability of the call hours and endless fighting with insurance companies finally motivated one young surgeon to leave practice. Consider the following examples:

Example 1.3: Young surgeon's call completely disrupts family life
I was in practice as a plastic surgeon and as a hand surgeon and I was in a multi-specialty practice that focused on muscular skeletal problems. So I was the hand surgeon in the group. We were in private practice so I was on staff at 5 different hospitals. I was taking a lot of ER calls, both for hand injuries and facial injuries which are very common in the ER and happen at all hours. That was keeping me very busy obviously and also the work was very unpredictable. It was very difficult for me to schedule time with my family or schedule time with my friends. There are a lot of times where I had dinner scheduled or something like that and I was frequently called out of that and had to run to the ER. Then, after I treated the patient in the ER, often with complicated repairs of tendon injuries and nerve injuries, I would get back to my office and see them for follow up and find out that they weren't able to go to hand therapy because their insurance company didn't recognize hand therapy as a particular specialty. I constantly found myself in battles with insurance companies trying to get good treatment for patients in the way that I was trained to treat them. That was very frustrating for me. That was the primary reason.

A pediatric oncologist who left clinical practice to work for pharma recalls the need to spend more time with his family:

Example 1.4: Stressful clinical practice left no time for family
The pediatric oncology program that I was in last was a smaller program and I had to have vastly more calm. I had fewer physicians working with me. I knew that was going to be the case when I made the switch in my academic position and moved to a smaller institution to set up my third bone marrow transplant program.

The stress became very great. I had two teenage boys and I wanted to spend more time with my teenage boys and I wanted to have no qualm, and not be bothered anymore in the night and weekend. With the advent of e-mail, and the availability of cell phones all the time, people would not leave me alone. So I was bothered continuously.

Also, my career had taken off a number of years before, so I became quite an expert in a small niche, so people called me all the time for help and advice. It wasn't as if the physicians calling me or the other healthcare providers calling me didn't know what they needed to do. They just wanted confirmation, and so they always liked to talk to someone else and be able to explain to their colleagues or patients, "I spoke with this person or this person," and have confirmation of what we really need to do in this difficult clinical situation.

6

It was very difficult to go away on vacation. It was very difficult to have time by myself. It was very difficult even to go to a movie theater and be able to sit there undisturbed by a cell phone. I really needed to make a switch to preserve my sanity and also to be able to give additional time for my own personal and professional development. But most importantly, to give time to my children.

1.3 Compensation

There are three things to understand about compensation when considering switching to a non-clinical career:

1. Many, if not most, physicians are underpaid in their clinical positions.
2. Long-term, the compensation potential for a physician outside of clinical practice is usually far higher than what can be expected in clinical medicine.
3. You may or may not have to take a significant initial pay cut when switching to your first non-clinical career. This depends a lot on your specialty, location, and current earnings. A specialist doing procedures making $400,000 per year will find it very difficult to avoid taking an initial pay cut, but a pediatrician making $120,000 per year may see an initial pay increase.

One of the biggest mistakes physicians make when considering switching to a non-clinical career is assuming that such a career move will destroy the physician's long-term financial well-being. In other words, physicians typically ask themselves how much money they will lose by leaving their practice. This is precisely the wrong question to ask. Most physicians should instead ask, "How much money am I losing by staying in clinical medicine?" Take a hard look at how much money you are currently making for the hours you put in and the risks that you take. For many physicians, it will be easy to see that they're not making a lot of money in practice.

Some perspective is important here. First-year lawyers in large New York firms make $150,000+ per year. They never had to go through internship or residency. This is straight-out-of-law-school money.

As a practicing physician taking private and government insurance, you are severely limited in what you can earn. The payors, not your patients, dictate how much you are able to earn. These rates are the same as for your colleagues even if you are qualitatively different in the services you are providing. Physician reimbursements are only likely to get worse in the future. Consider how a neurologist who left practice to work for an insurance company analyzed his situation:

Example 1.5: Analyzing the practice of medicine—call and flat or declining income

[One of] the two biggest problems with clinical practice was the burden of being on call. I had to be available almost continuously. I only had partial coverage with one other person in the area. Your nights, your weekends, your evenings were tied up. It was almost impossible to go to a movie or a restaurant without having your beeper go off.

The other problem, which was becoming apparent later in my practice, is that my income had pretty much peaked and I had come to the point where my overhead was increasing faster than my revenue. I was looking at a point where it appeared that I was going to be facing a declining income over the years. So this became a source of concern.

From a financial standpoint, [the insurance company's] offer was actually slightly more than I was making in practice, but there were other factors that I had to consider. I knew my income in my practice had pretty much peaked. I knew if I stayed with the corporation then over time my income would actually increase. The other thing is if you figured out on a pro-rated basis, what they were paying over the course of the year for the amount of work I did, as opposed to what I was making in practice, they were actually paying more.

There are no such artificial limitations on compensation in the business world. In the business world you are paid for performance. Save an organization money and you will be worth money to that organization. Make them money by selling a new product or creating a new product and you will be worth money to the organization. The more you produce, the more you are worth.

Organizations are willing to pay for performance. In a business, the bottom line affects all decisions. If you have proven yourself as a performer you will be able to land a job with lucrative compensation. Your bonuses will reflect your value to the company.

Until you have proven yourself to be valuable, you are less valuable to an organization. As such, entry-level jobs may require a significant pay cut. If you have confidence in yourself and work hard you will succeed and you will soon be making far more money than you ever could have made practicing medicine. Please consider what one SEAK faculty member has to say:

Example 1.6: Initial pay cut, but path to long-term success
I think as you make a career transition, in most cases, you will end up earning less money; at least to begin with. I think that's an adjustment that people need to be prepared for. They need to make that financial preparation and assessment so that when they start in a new career they won't have the financial pressure as an additional distraction, in addition to being at a new job and in a new environment with new people. Those factors in themselves are stressful enough but I think that the financial part has to be figured out. In the long run, people can do very well financially, if they work hard, treat the job very seriously, and are very dedicated to it, they can do very well.

One of our faculty members who was a family physician and launched her own consulting practice experienced an initial pay cut:

Example 1.7: Launching own business can result in huge initial pay cut, but there is no limit to what you can earn
I made minus $11,000 in my first year but it's just grown steadily ever since then. There's no limit to it. I'm limited by my imagination and by figuring out how to build the team to the next level.

Depending on your situation, the entry-level job may not require a pay cut. Much depends on your specialty and the point in your clinical career you are at. Lower-paid specialties such as internal medicine, pediatrics, psychiatry, and family practice will have income that is much easier to replace than higher-paid procedure-oriented specialties. The physicians in the former specialties will often see their income increase, even with an entry-level job.

Also keep in mind that in the business world, employees who can produce are often rapidly promoted with a commensurate increase in compensation. Consider the following example:

Example 1.8: Clinical income exceeded by 20% within six months of transition
A solo pediatrician (working 60+ hours per week) sold his practice and went to work for a health insurer as an associate medical director. Within six months, he

was promoted to medical director and was making 20% more than he was as a practicing physician.

An internist who went to work in the health insurance industry after 10 years of practice now makes a larger income:

Example 1.9: No initial pay cut, now makes much more than would clinically
Initially, I would say I probably made about the same. I think there is opportunity to actually make more in the administrative role than there is in the clinical role. Of course it depends on what kind of clinician you are. But I'm a primary care clinician and although I started out making about the same, I would say over time my income has grown to where I would make much more now on the administrative side than I would clinically.

The physician head of a medical affairs department encourages others to consider the long-term financial possibilities of transitioning to a non-clinical career:

Example 1.10: Think long-term when considering compensation
If they're coming in to work for a year or so, I would say [compensation compared to medical practice is] probably not very good at all. I think that in looking at when people ask about compensation in industry, always tell them, "Did you go to medical school based upon how much money you would make or were there other reasons that motivated you to apply and become a doctor?"

Those reasons should still be inside you, number one. Number two, unlike clinical practice where the physicians are paid for doing things, a procedure or an interview with a patient, in industry there are three buckets of reimbursement. There's direct salary, there's bonus, and there are stock options.

In my experience, those physicians who have done very well financially are those who've been in industry for ten, fifteen years, who were working in companies that had products that did very well and their stock options appreciated. And so, with a long horizon of having a career in industry, and being with the right company with the right products, people can do very well financially. Probably better than in private practice in many cases.

An internist who is the mother of a young child left practice after 5 years. She now has a career in medical informatics and discusses her earnings:

Example 1.11: Industry can pay much more than clinical practice
So in coming to [large nonprofit healthcare system] I would say I'm certainly making on par as an internist. If I were in the vendor community doing what I was doing, had I stayed in that career track, I'd probably be making double, maybe more. But I think in life we always make choices that arise as work balance.

A chief medical officer for a medical device company urges others to think long-term also. He highlights industry compensation practices for non-clinical physicians:

Example 1.12: In industry, prospects for excellent long-term compensation are very good if you perform well—bonuses and stock options
In terms of pay, that's probably the hardest thing for many people to accept. They are going to go into these companies, often, at an entry-level physician job. Depending on what specialty they've been practicing and where in the country they've been doing it, they may take a substantial pay cut. Sometimes it can be one-third to one-half of their pay. I always recommend to people that they have some savings in advance of making that career change so their lifestyle isn't affected in the first year or two that they're in their new job. I think that just adds more stress if you are worrying about how you are going to pay your bills, kids' tuition, or other obligations that you may have. <u>That being said, once you get into those jobs and you demonstrate that you are going to be effective in that position, the economic opportunities within many companies are very good.</u>

In addition to the salary, there are usually bonuses. Those bonuses are largely in your control. If you do a great job, you'll get a great bonus. You can have opportunities for stock options and stock grants, and sometimes special stock awards, again, for high performers. As you look over time those all add up into a nice compensation package. It's just that first leap that's tough and after that your salary will grow with each succeeding position and the economic opportunities will actually be quite good.

Example 1.13: After a small initial pay cut, doctor promoted rapidly and now makes considerably more in industry
It turns out that I was paid at about the 99.9th percentile of pediatric oncologists and bone marrow transplanters. So I actually took a small pay cut in joining the pharmaceutical industry. [Of course, on a per-hour basis I was doing

much better in industry.] That would not be true for the vast majority of pediatric oncologists or those with a pediatric background going into the pharmaceutical industry. It would be a big bonanza—a big bonus in terms of salary and benefits.

However, I was promoted within about three or four months and with salary increases and additional bonuses, I make considerably more now than I did in my previous job. But I did take a [nominal] pay cut initially.

Even a position with the government can be competitive in terms of pay related to hours and stress. Please consider the following comments from a physician who spent 23 years working for the federal government:

Example 1.14: Salaries with the federal government
I think the salaries are very competitive...maybe not for some of the more invasive higher-paid specialties, but certainly for the range of specialties. When I started medical practice, when I first started being a physician, I think there was probably a larger range in medical pay in that private physicians who wanted to work 24 hours a day, seven days a week could make almost an endless amount of money, especially depending how they organized their practice. Where now as more and more physicians are salaried, I think that the federal government has become a more competitive place.

CONSIDER BONUSES, STOCK OPTIONS, AND EQUITY
There are two more points to keep in mind when considering clinical and non-clinical compensation. First, when evaluating a job offer, don't just look at the base salary. Substantial portions of compensation in the business world are provided via bonuses, equity awards (e.g., stock options and stock awards) and the like. You will want to factor this in when evaluating a non-clinical opportunity. On the downside you also should keep in mind that in many industries your employer will want to keep all the fruits of your labor and have you 100% solely dedicated to them. That means that you may likely have to give up extra income that you may be earning in practice from honoraria, expert witnessing, consulting, and the like.

An excellent resource for getting an idea as to what physicians in management make is the *Physician Executive Compensation Survey* published by the American College of Physician Executives and Cejka Search. Unfortunately, there is a charge for this survey. The recruiting firm Witt/Kieffer publishes a regular *Executive Placement Study* that contains non-clinical compensation information and is available online free of charge.

1.4 Succeeding in the Business World: Hard Work but Many Positions Offer Less Stress and Predictable Hours

Practicing physicians are used to hard work. The hours can be long and demanding. Call can be disruptive.

To succeed and advance in many non-clinical jobs also requires hard work. A great work ethic is a key to success in many non-clinical careers. Consider the following quote from one of our faculty members who has hired hundreds of physicians for industry over the last twenty-five years. He was asked what doctors are a good fit for non-clinical work in industry:

Example 1.15: Great work ethic required to succeed in non-clinical position
You have to have a great work ethic, too. I mean you really have to—it's interesting. Today's people that I interview, I love—and certainly the young ones, they sit there and they talk about, "Well this will be good for my career. This is a good start for me in my career, my career, my career."

Well I give everybody advice. I say to them, "Why don't you tell me what you're going to do for me or what you're going to do for the company? I mean we're going to give you a paycheck, and it could be six figures." It's refreshing to hear somebody young that may say, "If you hire me, I'm going to do a great job for you." You don't hear that anymore. I thought that's how you get a job, you say, "Hire me. I'm going to do a great job for you."

You'd be surprised how many don't say that to you. We like to coach anybody that goes on to interview to actually say that. It's a nice refreshing thing.

If you are expecting your non-clinical career to be a vacation where you can relax and take it easy, you are in for a great disappointment. Please consider the following words of a SEAK faculty member who cautions against taking such an attitude:

Example 1.16: The importance of treating your new work very seriously
Physicians need to be used to the fact that they are actually in a new area, they are, at least initially, no longer a true expert in the work that they are doing. They need to ramp up. They need to learn as much as possible. They need to

make the psychological adjustment to be able to do that. In addition to that, sometimes physicians come into a new job and have the attitude that because they're not treating life and death emergencies, that they don't take the work that they are doing with enough of a level of urgency. Sometimes in the process, and generally inadvertently, belittling some of the people around them because those people take the work very seriously and work very hard at it.

To advance and be at the top of your game may require very hard work. The difference in non-clinical careers is that your hours are generally much more predictable, which makes them more manageable. Consider what a former surgeon has to say about his hours as chief scientific officer for a boutique medical communications firm:

Example 1.17: Important positive lifestyle differences in non-clinical career

I'd say probably on the average I work about the same number of hours now as I did before when I was in practice. Part of that is because I'm running this company and growing the company. It keeps me very busy. But, what's very different about it is that when I decide it's time to go home for dinner, I go home for dinner and I stay with my family. When I make plans on the weekend I know I can fulfill those goals and those plans with my family and my friends. I have much better control over the free hours and that's really the biggest difference. I think in any career you can work a large number of hours, or you can work a smaller number of hours. Sometimes you have control over that and sometimes you don't. But I think that if you can at least control your free time and be able to enjoy yourself and do what you like to do, then that's extremely important and that's been great for me.

It's been great for my family. Like I said, on the weekends we make plans and I don't have to carry a beeper. It's very different. We're able to go away on the weekends if we want to; which was a big struggle when I was in practice, almost impossible really, when I was in practice. I can make my vacations when I want to make my vacations and spend time with my family. They know that. I think that the kids, they may not realize it, but when you are having dinner and then running out all the time, or trying to do certain things and then running out all the time, they probably wonder...They probably wonder where your priorities are. When you have better control it's more fair.

Here's how an executive medical director at a big pharma company described why he left medicine and why he chose the field of medical communications and approvals inside the pharma industry instead of running clinical trials:

Example 1.18: Regular hours and less stress working for industry
I had already run national and international clinical studies for years. I was not interested in doing that again, and also that...involves being on call...if you are involved in a large study. For example, this friend of mine...runs a breast cancer study—an international breast cancer study that's enrolled I think 3000 patients already for the drug company for which she works. And she carries her Blackberry and another cell phone and she frequently gets calls from people about eligibility for a particular study, adverse events that have occurred, how to handle them—it's a—I didn't want to be on call anymore. I don't want to carry those devices.

Here's what a chief medical officer at a large health insurer has to say about working hours for physicians in his industry:

Example 1.19: Entry-level jobs may be 8 to 5, advancement may well require longer hours, but you still have more control
I would say at an entry-level job, it's kind of—I would say 8 to 5, 8 to 6 type of job Monday through Friday. There's no heavy lifting. But it's an entry-level job. If you want to advance in these roles, you're going to spend more and more hours and you're going to spend weekends. And you're going to spend a lot of night meetings and morning meetings. So right now, as a chief medical officer, I actually put in more hours per week than I did when I was a full-time clinician. I'm out of the office three, four, five nights a week. I spend a lot of time on the weekends catching up just on stuff that I couldn't get to. So you can stay at an entry- or medium-level job and have more control of your life, but the higher you go—or if you want to advance—you're going to have to put in the time and the effort and the resources to do that. Of course, you're compensated for that but I quite honestly don't have as much control over my schedule and my life as I would like to, just because of the demands of the job and what it entails. You do have more control. There's definitely more control, although I will say the higher you go, unexpected things happen. Stuff happens where something comes up on a Friday afternoon that you must have done by first thing Monday for your boss, or a major catastrophe happened on Friday and you're going to be working all weekend to clean it up, if you will. And so it's not like it's strictly a predictable routine type thing. But overall, I would say you have more control.

His experience is echoed by the physician CEO of a large hospital:

Example 1.20: "You're a CEO 24 hours a day"
Well you're a CEO 24 hours a day. You never get off duty, so to speak. So I carry a beeper and a phone, too wired. But I usually come in around 7:00 and I usually leave around 7:00 or 7:30. A lot of times I'll have an evening meal or a dinner at a function. But I do group leadership meetings. I try to keep the meetings down to the things we really need.

I keep an open door policy, so I have lots of people coming in and out, but I want to have time to go walk the hospital. If you're the CEO and they get you in your corner office and keep you there, you can become very ineffective. You need to be out and about, walking, talking, and that's one of the benefits of having a physician CEO. When I took rounds for years teaching, I had every legitimate reason in the world not to be out checking up on people, but just to go out and do what the joint commission does. I was doing a tracer. I was taking care of my patients with my house staff, and so I would see how things really worked.

Here's the experience of an internist who went to work for a medical informatics vendor. She ultimately left for an 8 to 6 job at a non-profit, taking a substantial pay cut but still making a comparable salary to what she would have been earning in clinical practice:

Example 1.21: Hours in private sector can be long and hard as well
I realized that for me personally that I didn't want to stay in the vendor environment, because at that point my lifestyle had got to a point where I was on the road generally from Monday 'til Friday, and that was not an infrequent part of the work. I was consulting. I was in product design. I was the vice president at the company. So for me personally, when it came to that point in my life I decided to make a transition.

I can tell you when I was working at the vendor my hours were 6:00 to midnight and sometimes wee hours, putting out fires and so forth. So I think when you're in consulting, when you're working in a vendor community you can have very long hours, and because the sun never sets on any of your customers, if you're in a global company, there are around the clock issues that can emerge. When you're geographically-centric you can have more control.

I think in a hospital environment it's more 8:00 to 6:00, but there are times when you're online or on e-mail frequently or on the phone for various issues in the off hours as well. But it's definitely less, significantly not the same level of intensity as when I was working in the vendor world.

Consider the words of a primary care physician who became a Wall Street financial analyst focusing on pharma who experienced long days during the week, but almost never had to work weekends and was not on call:

Example 1.22: Long days and commute in non-clinical position, but no weekends
I was married with a family and with kids already and living in New Jersey so for me, it was very difficult in terms of physically, logistically getting to the job. I was getting up at 4:30 A.M. to catch a bus to go—or a car ride to go into the city. I had to take a bus or whatever to get to my job location in Manhattan. I think I started probably around a quarter to—I want to say 7:00 A.M. is probably a normal starting time. Maybe as late as 7:30 A.M. Certainly never later than 8:00 A.M. And typically my days would be, I'd say usually at least until 6:00 P.M., sometimes later, sometimes a little bit earlier. I never worked weekends. To be successful: 1. Park your ego at the door. You are an intern again and need to learn a lot. 2. Show you have endurance; stay late, produce the work that is needed. 3. Learn Excel. 4. Know how to write. 5. Maintain good relationships. 6. Form an opinion, back it up, and convert others to your viewpoint. 7. Be ethical.

Here are a chief medical officer's feelings concerning working conditions in industry. Bottom line is that they vary depending on your job, but that they are still much more predictable than practicing clinical medicine:

Example 1.23: Hours vary depending on the non-clinical position
In terms of hours, that really varies by the position. I think it's important to map out for yourself what kind of work lifestyle you are looking for. Are you looking for one that is going to require travel or do you need to be home every day? Do you need a job that's going to be as close to 9 to 5 as possible, although I don't believe that many jobs are 9 to 5 anymore. But still, one that has reasonable hours, then that's important to identify up front. That may preclude you from taking some medical director or medical science liaison jobs that require a lot of travel. Many of those jobs require at least 20–30% travel to medical meetings or investigator meetings or out to travel sites. So, if travel is not going to be an option then that may make somebody look more at say pharmacovigilance jobs, where they are going to be working in-house, in the office, and not have to be traveling a lot. The good thing is that, overall, I think there can be fairly good control of your hours. Weekends are much more, sort of, free than in clinical practice because you don't have call. There are times when you have to travel for medical meetings that take place over weekends.

But even sometimes with those you can bring family if you want to, to be there, so that you are not away from home as much. So I think that the opportunities are there for people to either have very tightly controlled hours or to have jobs that require extensive travel, if that's what they desire.

There are, of course, many non-clinical jobs out there where the hours worked are much less than in clinical medicine. A neurologist describes his position as a disability analyst for a large disability insurance company:

Example 1.24: Some non-clinical jobs are 8 to 5
[I worked from 8 to 5 Monday through Friday.] There was no call, there were no nights, and there were no weekends. In addition, they had a very generous vacation policy that included 6 weeks of paid vacation, plus 10 days of holiday, including 3 personal days, plus you are allowed 10 days for CME time with a $3,000 CME budget. In fact, the free time was so generous I couldn't even take it all. It was just more than you can use.

The ability to have regular hours and less stress can have an enormous impact on your health, lifestyle, and overall happiness. Please consider how two faculty members put it:

Example 1.25: Regular hours and vacation can change your life
[My new career is] great. I have free time. I don't have to worry about what's going to happen at night or on the weekends. We're able to do a lot more, participate in a lot more activities. We've done a lot more travel than I ever could do in private practice. When you are in private practice, you never turn your brain off. You are always worried about what's going on back there. Nobody dies. You don't have to worry about that kind of stuff. The phone's not ringing. Just in the last couple of years, we've been to Portugal, we've been to India, and we've been to Maui. I've been to Arizona a couple of times. We've had a lot more opportunity to do things.

Example 1.26: Non-clinical career makes a tremendous difference in young mother's family life
It is coincidental that I started my coaching business, gave birth to my coaching business right at the time that I gave birth to my daughter. So I've always had the luxury of being able to work from home ever since she was born. I can't imagine how difficult it must be, particularly for a woman but I would imagine even for a man to leave the house at 7:00 A.M., 7:15 A.M., 7:30 A.M. to be at work, do rounds, start in the OR or whatever it is and to not get back until 6:00 P.M. or maybe even 7:00 P.M. in the evening. Then to try and come back and make some sense out of family life. I can't imagine what that must be like. It must be so

tough. So for me, the greatest joy and blessing has been that I have clients all over the country. I've had clients in Canada. I have a client currently in South Africa. Thank goodness for technology, it's just pretty remarkable.

What I used—I used 10,000 square feet maybe when I was in clinical practice to earn my income. I can now earn that same income in 10 square feet—with my desk, my computer and my telephone. So it's a joy.

In some jobs, the hours vary depending upon which projects are in-house. A vice-president at a medical advertising agency describes the working hours for their medical directors:

Example 1.27: Your hours may ebb and flow
You could be in a pre-launch phase where there may be heavier hours, and people do work very hard—these are the smartest, brightest people I've ever known in my life and they enjoy working hard. So it could certainly be some long nights here and there, and if you're getting ready for a pitch or we have four weeks to completely learn a new therapeutic area down cold, there may be some extra hours and some weekend work in there. But typically, we recognize that there's a balance.

They also get three weeks vacation and four personal days and a community service day and their birthday off, plus we're closed the week between Christmas and New Years, so we understand the personal time and honor that and encourage people to take a lot of time.

Do not expect a non-clinical job to be stress-free. Your new non-clinical position will likely have different stressors than your current clinical position. The higher you advance in a non-clinical field, the higher the expected stress. Please consider what a health insurer chief medical officer has to say:

Example 1.28: Different stressors at non-clinical job—generally more stress as you advance higher in your non-clinical career
I actually thought, when I started getting into this, and many of my friends who inquire about getting into this field think, "Oh, this is much less stressful. It's much less—it's much more tolerable, I won't have to put up with all the nonsense that clinicians have to do."

I spend more time with our attorneys than I do with doctors, and you have bosses who in most cases are not physicians. Your skills and medical knowledge and expertise and degrees won't count for what you think [they] should count for, so there are a lot of different stresses on each side. And one, I wouldn't put as necessarily better than the other.

The entry-level job is probably less stressful but again, you have a boss—mainly in an entry-level job, your boss will probably be another physician. So on that level, it probably works out a little bit better, but even entry-level jobs, there are certain expectations you have to meet. You can't just kind of go in your office and do your own thing. There are certain assignments you're given. There are certain expectations. You're graded and evaluated every year. Your merit increase and your bonuses are decided on how you perform. Some doctors can't get used to that.

The other big difference is that you will often be handsomely rewarded for hard work in a non-clinical setting. This is a big difference between clinical and non-clinical work. For more on compensation, please see Section 1.3.

1.5 What Your Parents Will Think

What will my parents think? They are so proud of me. I'm the doctor in the family. They helped me pay for school and now I'm not going to be a doctor anymore? I can never face them.

These are all fairly typical concerns of a physician thinking about a career change. In our experience, parents usually come around to be supportive of a career change. If you are not happy, they genuinely want you to be happy. To get a better comfort level, talk to other physicians in non-clinical careers and let them tell you how things worked out with their parents. The story of one of our faculty members is fairly typical of what we've seen in terms of short-term shock and long-term pride and support. In his own words:

Example 1.29: Parents initially very disappointed when left residency for non-clinical career
I had a Jewish mother that put her head in the oven [when I told her I was leaving my residency for non-clinical work]. In fact, I told my parents when I left medicine, I told them at Angela's on Mulberry Street, 'cause it was a white tie restaurant, and I thought if there was bloodshed they could easily clean the walls. I mean they were devastated. They grew up in the Depression and they were, "My son the doctor," and the tears and all this kind of stuff. So they had no clue what a medical director in an advertising agency does.

You know, my parents, the definition of a doctor to my parents is a split-level house, a white coat, and a little shingle that hangs outside. My dad used to come home from his doctor and say, "Boy, Sid Weiss is making a fortune.

They're setting up bridge chairs in his waiting room." And that was success, a large waiting room.

I could have come home and said I won the Noble Prize of Medicine and that wouldn't be good enough. Their definition of doctor was the shingle. So when [my dad] passed away, his card playing buddies came up to me at the funeral and they said to me, "Your father was very proud of you," and I knew he liked me. I had a hint he liked me or was proud. But I said, "Well why do you say that?" They said, "Because he used to go to the card games and he used to brag about you that you loved what you were doing. You loved your job. He used to say, 'I'm so lucky to have a kid that loves his job and loves what he's doing.'"

And so that really was touching to me, because I realized I do love what I do. I did make the choice early, and he liked the fact. I guess that is rewarding. Of course you can say, "My son the doctor," but it's nice to say, "My son the doctor, who is so happy with what he's doing," and that meant a lot. And I guess that's advice to anybody.

Here's how a physician that left practicing internal medicine for a career in medical informatics described the reaction of her parents and how they became supportive and recognized the impact she was having on patient care:

Example 1.30: Can be difficult to explain switch to parents
It's difficult sometimes to explain to parents why it is that you would move beyond medicine into clinical systems. So I think for my family it was perplexing at the beginning, but I think they see now that my work has a huge impact on healthcare. I'm addressing the knowledge-seeking and knowledge processing of thousands of clinicians. At [non-profit healthcare provider where I work] we are considered leaders in how we do expert—implement expert systems for the improvement and care, and our systems are vastly improving safety and quality.

I think my family well understands that the work I do and my colleagues do has a vast impact on healthcare. It's just a different kind than the impact a clinician has in their office. And I think they also well understand that I couldn't do this work if I were not a physician, because in many instances there are many things we do as physicians in the informatics community that we're the bridge. We're the bridge between the clinical mindset and the IT mindset, and that bridge is essential for the technology to be designed in such a way that we actually both improve the quality of care and the quality of life for the practicing physicians, who are facing a lot of challenges and continue to do so.

21

Keep in mind that although your parents might be disappointed, they are not the ones living your life. They are not the ones living with the daily fear of potentially ruinous malpractice suits. They are not the ones working disruptive hours or being micromanaged. They are not the ones that have lost the passion for doing a highly repetitive job. Only you know your inner heart and soul. People are generally happiest when they live for themselves, not for their parents. If you are smart enough to become a doctor and make life and death decisions, your judgment should also be good enough for you to determine when a career change is right for you.

1.6 Finding the Passion and Enjoying Your Workday

The short answer is that there is no way to know how happy you will be in the non-clinical career you choose. Your happiness will depend on your own particular situation and the career you choose. What we can say with conviction is that the overwhelming number of doctors we have interviewed are much happier since transitioning out of clinical practice. When asked for their regrets, the most common response we hear is "I should have left practicing medicine much sooner."

Here's how your colleagues who have made the switch say it in their own words. A physician now serving as a full-time, self-employed consultant states:

Example 1.31: Very much enjoys non-clinical career
I do very much [enjoy my job]. I've been very fortunate. [If I had to do it over again] I would [go this way again].

An emergency room physician who left clinical medicine for a career in pharma agrees:

Example 1.32: No regrets
It's been a very rewarding career that I've had ever since I left clinical medicine. Medicine has been very good to me, so I'm glad that I went into medical school. Though, my original thoughts of how I was going to leverage that medical education is far different now because I thought I was going to take care of patients; the more traditional role. But it gave me a wonderful career. What I would do differently, I think, I really have no regrets. It's been part of the journey.

A family practice physician who became a work-from-home consultant focusing on coaching other physicians to succeed finds her new work creative and fun:

Example 1.33: New non-clinical work is so much fun that it is addictive

It's so wonderful to finally understand what people say when they—I heard it said yesterday—when you love what you do, you never do another day's work in your life. I work incredibly hard, and I'm very focused and I'm very dedicated to not only delivering the coaching but also building my business, to figure out this whole marketing piece. It's so much fun. It's the most creative thing I've ever done with my life because medicine is in a way the opposite of creativity.

I would never go back into clinical practice. Not unless my survival depended on it. And if I did, I would be in dire trouble because I'd have to go back and do a whole lot of re-training because medicine has changed dramatically in ten years. I walk about 15 feet to my job because I work out of my home, which is wonderful. I have a young child so it works for me, even though I put in nine hours between the hours of eight and five and I have full-time child care, I'm there. I'm able to sense what's going on with her. For me, I guess the question is more—let me answer you specifically—very easy. But here's the real test: How easy is it for me to stop working at the end of the day? [B]ecause *I'm having so much fun. And I have to actively shut myself down to stop at 5:00 P.M., go do some family stuff, come back up around 8:00 P.M., 8:15 P.M., haul myself away from the computer about—within the hour to go spend at least some time with my husband. Because this is addictive. It's so much fun.*

Working for the federal government can be a creative change of pace. Consider this physician who spent 23 extremely rewarding years working for the U.S. government:

Example 1.34: Always something new and different in non-clinical career

I think what I liked was the combination of very interesting challenges—there was always something new and different every day, as well as the ability to really have an impact on a lot of people. I think particularly my last assignment with the Coast Guard was just extremely well-suited to my personal interests and the things I enjoyed. I was responsible, as the surgeon general for the Coast Guard, for both health and safety. And one of my long-time hobbies and passions has been cooking, and I was also responsible for the cooks. I was able to even pursue that as a federal employee. I was really very happy in federal service.

After spending many years in industry, this physician thrives on being an entrepreneur:

Example 1.35: Couldn't be happier in non-clinical career

This work world of ours, it's five, six days a week, and if you're not enjoying it you've got to make a move. And when I made that decision right in the middle of ENT residency, it was like a cloud just lifted up over my head, because then there were so many possibilities to do. And in the world of medicine, there is a path already for you. I mean it really is. But when I stopped and put my beeper down and I said, "Now I'm gonna do something different," *I could have done anything, and it really does feel like the clouds have cleared and the sun was shining, and I couldn't be happier.*

The vice president of a medical advertising company describes the creative energy he finds in his work environment:

Example 1.36: Physicians so happy, ad agency has nearly 0% job turnover

We have nearly 0% turnover. People really are very happy in this job. They find the creative environment, and it certainly is a very different environment than even a medical director on a pharmaceutical side of the business and it's very exciting. You walk in the door, there is a completely different vibe there and people really enjoy the work. We've had 17% growth for the last eight, nine years and no end in sight, so there are certainly opportunities.

Finally, a primary care physician who went to work in the financial services industry describes the pleasure he finds in his job as a wealth management advisor and drug analyst:

Example 1.37: Since switching careers almost 10 years ago, bored maybe 2 days

The number one reason for me getting out of clinical medicine was I was bored. I was bored with what I was doing. And since I've made the transition over the last several years, being a drug analyst and being a wealth management advisor, I've maybe had two days total that I've ever been bored. So that problem has been taken care of, which I'm very happy about.

Of course, nothing's perfect and there are other stresses in the job as well. But a typical day? No two days are the same. That's one of the beauties of the job. There are some days I'm going out and meeting new prospects who might be clients, there—a lot of time I'm spending on the phone talking to my existing clients, looking up different investments or different retirement plans or different estate planning services, learning about my practice and my business. Dealing with companies, dealing with my clients who also have companies and their issues and so on and so forth. I've got clients who are physicians who are business owners who currently are selling their companies. I'm involved with that. No two days are the same. Every day is different. There are some days I'm on the phone a lot, some days I'm traveling. Every day is different, which to me is a pleasure. I enjoy what I do very much.

1.7 You Can Still Make a Difference

If you got into medicine to make a difference in people's lives, don't despair. No longer directly seeing patients in no way stops you from making that difference. In fact, many physicians in non-clinical careers make even more of a difference in their new roles. In the words of one of our faculty members who was a medical TV reporter:

> **Example 1.38: Medical reporter makes a difference in lives and it is rewarding**
> I can tell you that as a medical reporter you definitely make a difference in people's lives. I get numerous phone calls, e-mails, and faxes. People who had no idea there are certain procedures or a test available and they have a family member or friend who could benefit from this. It's really rewarding too, and a privilege to give this information to people and to interview the experts and interview the people who are willing to share their stories.

Consider the feelings of a former ER physician now working for pharma:

> **Example 1.39: Greater impact on safety in industry than with direct patient care**
> Well, my ultimate career choice was drug safety, medical product safety, and I got exposed to that. One of the things that I had a lot of guilt about was leaving clinical medicine. After all I went into medicine to take care of people, and I didn't enjoy directly taking care of them, but what I realized and was so happy about was that it really leveraged my clinical skills. All my training was not wasted. I was finally able to understand that if I could work in ensuring safe drugs get out there, or understanding the risk profile of the drug, then potentially I had an impact on patient safety; more so than I would have had in a career in a private practice. I could potentially impact hundreds of thousands to millions of people...understanding the risk of the product and ensuring that that information was out there for patient protection.

One thing to consider as you struggle with whether to make a career transition is the people you are treating. One SEAK faculty member recommends that the question to ask is not are you being fair to your patients by leaving, but rather, are you being fair to your patients by staying in a role where you may have lost your passion? Here's what an ER physician who became an inventor and entrepreneur has to say:

Example 1.40: Non-clinical work making a big impact
We always look at products that are not me-too products. We always look at products that could make a big difference in people's lives. For example: the easy IO, this last product we developed, has made a huge difference for paramedics, makes it easier to treat our patients. We've had documentation of several thousand lives that have been saved because they've been able to get intravenous fluids into patients when they would not have been able to otherwise. This is especially true in Baghdad and with our armed services but also with our emergency rooms around the country. It's very satisfying to me to know that the device that I helped develop has been able to help in saving the lives of patients. It's made a big impact on the desperately ill people, on how we treat them.

You can and will make a difference. Consider the words of a chief medical officer in industry:

Example 1.41: Adding value to overall healthcare system
Once [you]'ve decided it's a route [you] want to take, just enjoy it. Find the best possible job [you] can for [yourself] that fits [your] interests and needs, be enthusiastic about it and realize that [you] are not selling out. [You] are not not going to be a doctor anymore. [You] are still a doctor. [You'll] be a doctor every day that you go to work and you'll be adding a lot of value to the overall healthcare system by developing new products, by ensuring that current products are safe and effective, and by expanding the knowledge of a lot of physicians out there by sharing new information with them. I think it's a role that is very respected and very necessary in the current medical environment.

There will, of course, be tradeoffs in terms of job satisfaction. Consider what a pediatric oncologist who went into industry has to say about what he misses most:

Example 1.42: Miss immediate satisfaction of patient care, but industry work benefits thousands more people
There are certain things, of course, that I miss. I miss terribly the looking after patients and the immediate satisfaction of doing something good for them. I

was on the frontier of my special team, and so I looked after patients who were very sick and oftentimes I was their last stop in terms of what could be done for them. And so if I succeeded and they survived and they survived well and had good quality of life, it was very satisfying.

In the pharmaceutical industry, there's no question that the work that I do and that my colleagues do will benefit thousands more people than we could ever see on an individual basis in a clinic, but these are patients we don't know. They don't come back and thank us. We don't get that warm, fuzzy feeling that we've done something good for people as we did when we refilled someone's prescription or gave them some advice that was very helpful.

1.8 Culture Shock and a New Pecking Order

As you consider a non-clinical career you need to be comfortable about no longer being the center of attention and the person in charge. In business, you will likely start off as a junior member of a team. As one SEAK faculty member put it, you will move from being a clinical veteran to a business novice.

You will also have to be prepared for the culture at your new employer and for the inevitable office politics. Physicians considering a non-clinical career need to be prepared for this. Consider the experience of an emergency room physician who transitioned to pharma:

> **Example 1.43: Need to get used to taking orders and office politics**
> Well, you know, if there's more than one person, politics exist and I'm not a political person. It's just human nature that there's politics and there's turf wars and things like that. That never interested me. Also, in the emergency room I was the leader, I was the head of everything. When you join big pharma, you typically come in at a lower rung and you have other people that you have to report to, such as in the military. I wasn't the commanding chief there so you had to take your orders.

A neurologist who went to work for a large insurance company concurs:

> **Example 1.44: Corporate structure may take some getting used to**
> The big disadvantage for some people might be getting used to working in a corporate setting. I didn't have that much difficulty adjusting. Some people might. I think because I had prior military experience, it helped me deal with that kind of structure.

A surgeon who went into medical communications cautions physicians about adjusting to their new role in a non-clinical work environment:

Example 1.45: Important to check your ego at the door
Something that I was able to deal with okay, but I think that some people have some difficulty with is that, for me in particular as a surgeon, you are used to walking into the operating room and telling about 10 different people what to do and they are all circling around you doing what you told them to do or what you asked them to do. There is an ego component of that and also I think a bit of a control component of that. People may not even realize it but as you step into a different situation in the workplace, where you are just one of the other employees and a part of the team. It's really important to check your ego at the door and be able to be a part of the team and function at that capacity. It's actually a fairly different role for a clinician going over to this side of the industry.

A pediatrician who formerly was in solo practice describes potential hurdles in a non-clinical setting:

Example 1.46: Loss of autonomy and dealing with large bureaucracy in non-clinical world
The loss of autonomy and having to deal with a large bureaucracy was the least satisfying aspect of my non-clinical position at the health insurance company.

An internist who became a managed care executive discusses the challenges of dealing with hierarchy and subordination:

Example 1.47: "It's a different world"
You need to be comfortable with change, it is a different world. Are you prepared to move, frequently change positions, get fired, always be on the lookout for other opportunities, answer to people who may not be as smart or educated or talented as you? Personal subordination is not easy [to] accept. Can you transition from a position of professional independence based on many years of training and experience to one of dependence based on hierarchy and superior authority?

Non-clinical careers often involve becoming a part of a team. An occupational medicine physician who runs a large department of medical consultants for a disability insurance company discusses this transition:

Example 1.48: Be prepared to be part of a team
Make sure you don't mind working in a teamwork environment. It's an important thing. Most physicians are trained for years to be the center of a

clinical team. If a patient is dying on the table, people look to the physicians to make those quick calls and those decisions. It's a responsibility they bear and they do very well with it. When you move out of the clinical setting and into a more collaborative setting, typically, the good news is, people typically don't die or live based on your immediate decisions. As long as you are conveying your clinical information properly, how that's used is often a matter of team consideration. Are we going to put it in this kind of report? Are we going to take the information and put it in another venue? The idea is that the physician, once they've done the clinical job, does not then have control over specific uses of it. It is very difficult for some physicians.

A chief medical officer of medical device company agrees:

Example 1.49: Culture shock
Be prepared for culture shock. Though [drug and medical device] companies really do care about doing the right thing, revenues drive companies more than doing the right thing for patients. You are the conscience of the company in this regard so you have to maintain a balance between two sometimes opposing forces...The transition is mainly that it's just a different culture than they are used to being in. As a physician, you are often looked at as sort of the revered person that the office or the department in the hospital revolves around. People don't routinely question what you are saying. You have this very autonomous role. When you move into a company, there are people that are going to question what you are saying especially if it impacts something that they want to do negatively. You are going to have to work on cross-functional teams. You are going to work with other people who have maybe more experience in the industry than you have. It can be a humbling experience. But if people approach it saying that this is just another learning opportunity, physicians have gone through lots of education and training, they can just look at it as another educational and training opportunity, then the transition is a lot easier.

A pediatric oncologist who went to work for big pharma urges physicians to consider the autonomy they will give up in a non-clinical setting:

Example 1.50: You will leave a lot of independence behind
I think they need to be very clear and have a good understanding of what they want to do and why they want to do this and also what they're going to leave behind. There's a lot of independence I left behind, now I'm part of this big corporate structure and I don't always have control over a lot of things that happen, whereas even as an academician, I had a great deal of control over my life and my day-to-day basis. And I don't necessarily have that now in the sense

29

that if the corporation decides to drop a product on which I have been working, I have no choice. I have to move on to do something else for them.

1.9 Instability and Job Insecurity

Depending upon the field you get into, you need to be prepared for the fact that you may have far less job security in a non-clinical position. Non-clinical businesses enjoy booms and suffer busts. There can be and are massive layoffs. Businesses can change with emerging technology. New management will come in and clean house. In non-clinical careers you need to mentally prepare yourself for far greater job instability than you usually have practicing medicine.

> **Example 1.51: Industry changes—medical TV reporter laid off**
> One SEAK faculty member is a very talented medical reporter for a major market local TV station. Local TV news, unfortunately, is being negatively affected by falling ad revenues as more and more people get their news online. As a result, local TV stations have been pursuing aggressive cost-cutting. This cost-cutting led to the elimination of the position of the medical reporter.

> **Example 1.52: MD financial analyst laid off after 9/11**
> A SEAK faculty member worked for a year and a half positioning himself for a job as a drug analyst on Wall Street. This included substantial networking and starting an MBA and CFA program. He finally landed the job and then shortly after 9/11 was laid off in the series of layoffs that swept Wall Street. He was forced to adapt and later became a very successful financial advisor.

1.10 Advice for Physicians Considering Leaving Clinical Practice

Please consider the advice of physicians who have left clinical practice:

> **Example 1.53: Almost anything will be less stressful than practice—but you must be prepared to take risk**
> First of all, I think taking a course like [SEAK] offers is helpful. I think it gives people the opportunity to learn how to go about doing it and to realize that there are other options out there. I think people need to be somewhat introspective and try to figure out what their strengths and talents might be. In my case, I just kind of, over time, got more involved in medical legal work and I guess, because of that, got good at it. Other people might find that they have talents in other areas, you need to look. Maybe it's pharmaceutical; maybe it's communications; maybe it's a career that has nothing to do with medicine at all. You need to take a look. That's the first thing I would suggest. The other thing

is you need to realize, as a physician, you must have some talent. You don't get through medical school on nothing. You must have some basic innate intelligence. I think the other thing about being a physician is, at least in my experience, the stress of being a physician is so high that I think you find that just about anything else you might pursue is relatively stress free. It seems easier to do. One thing you have to be willing to do is to take risk. If you don't take risks, then you are going to stay right where you are. Actually, I think it's been kind of exciting to be able to pursue and do these things. Like I said, I didn't do it initially for the financial issue, I did it primarily to free up my personal life. I've found that it's been very beneficial in all kinds of ways. Those are the things that I would suggest.

Example 1.54: Carefully research where you want to go
If you're moving away from something you don't like, be very careful what you move to, because it will not be as good as it looks.

Example 1.55: Get ready for being low on the totem pole
Realize that when you change careers, you must almost always take a step back and you have to move down in the pecking order a bit.

Example 1.56: The importance of finding your passion
Really think about what you enjoy doing and want to do. You have to assess whether you are running from something or to something.

Chapter 2 How Hard Will It Be and How Long Will It Take?

2.1 Executive Summary

- Before deciding on a career change, it is wise to explore whether you can fix what you don't like about your clinical position (hours, malpractice risk, paperwork, etc.).
- Career change can be emotionally traumatic.
- How long your transition will take and how hard it will be depend upon many factors, including:
  o How quickly you decide on the jobs you want to focus on
  o How hard you work at your career transition
  o Your flexibility to move or commute
  o How much money you need to make short- and long-term
  o Your current financial situation and whether you have developed a financial cushion
  o Whether you have demonstrated leadership in your clinical career
  o Your skills and experience including your specialty, certifications or lack thereof, communications skills, personality, industry experience, interests, business experience, and advanced education
  o Economic and industry conditions
  o Your job-searching skills (such as networking, job hunting, and interviewing)

2.2 Should I Leave Clinical Practice?

One of the most gut-wrenching decisions you will face in your professional life is whether to transition from a clinical career in which you have invested so much time, training, and education. If and when to do so is obviously a deeply personal decision. Before you decide to leave, we suggest that you see if you can "fix" your clinical career to make it enjoyable again.

Please consider the words of one of our faculty members who left emergency medicine for a career in pharma:

Example 2.1: Try to fix what you don't like about clinical medicine before taking the leap

They have to understand why they are not happy with what they are doing now and they also have to have a game plan, I believe, in what they think they would like to do. It's ok not to have all the answers, but they have to understand at a conscious level why they are unhappy. If there's anything within their clinical practice that they can correct I would recommend them doing so before they take a leap. But, if they make the decision all I can say is come on board. It's been a very rewarding career that I've had ever since I left clinical medicine.

One of our clients, we'll call him Charlie, took this advice to heart and was able to fix his clinical career. In a nutshell, Charlie was a successful urologist in his early fifties who was looking to move out West and have more fun. He decided to start a continuing education company with his wife and base it near a ski resort. The new business sucked up a lot of Charlie's time, made little or no money, and stressed him and his wife out to no end. Eventually Charlie met a urologist who practiced in the resort town. Charlie negotiated a partnership for himself where he works one week on, two weeks off. He does some consulting on the side. Charlie now lives where he always dreamed of living and has the free time he wants to pursue his outdoor passions. In short, he was able to "fix" his clinical career to make himself happy.

A good way to approach the decision is to get out a piece of paper and put down on one side what you like about your clinical job. On the other side, put down what you don't like about your clinical job. If what you don't like grossly outweighs what you like and you are not able to fix what you don't like, it's probably time to get serious about getting a plan to transition into a non-clinical position.

One of the key questions for leaving clinical medicine when you are unhappy is: What is the cause of the unhappiness? Are you truly unhappy because of the demands of your job, call, hours, malpractice, or pay? Alternatively, are you unhappy for other reasons (such as family or health) and in essence blaming clinical medicine for this unhappiness? This self-awareness and honest appraisal may be difficult to come to grips with. Professional help may be of assistance in the decision-making process.

34

Once you determine that, in fact, your job/clinical medicine is the cause, or a major cause, of your unhappiness, the transition to non-clinical medicine makes a lot more sense.

Leaving clinical medicine is a big step that should not be taken lightly. Thorough soul-searching is wise. Here's the advice from one SEAK physician faculty member who spent 14 years in industry:

Example 2.2: Try to fix your clinical practice first
The first thing that I recommend is have a clear understanding as to why you are making the change. Are you really unhappy with your current job? Are you just looking for something that maybe is a little bit more interesting but you still like seeing patients on a day-to-day basis? Making any big career switch is going to be kind of a jarring move. It's often a little unsettling for most people so you really have to be sure that you dislike what you are currently doing enough to want to take that leap of faith. Once you do it, I think there are great opportunities. There are great ways to apply your years of medical training and knowledge in new areas, develop new treatments that affect thousands or hundreds of thousands, sometimes millions of patients versus just the patients you come in contact with every day. All the advancements in medicine today, whether it be for drugs, biotech treatments, or devices, have required the expertise of physicians working internally in companies. I think it's a great opportunity for doctors to use that knowledge to better the overall practice of medicine.

2.3 Emotional Trauma

If you are considering leaving non-clinical medicine, you can expect your transition to be a very emotional experience. Giving up your clinician identity, dealing with your family, and secretly searching for a job while employed can all be quite stressful. Please consider the words of one SEAK faculty member:

Example 2.3: Career transition can be emotionally traumatic
Wow. For the longest time I was very confused. I couldn't articulate exactly why I wanted to leave. That made me feel even more like a failure. I felt embarrassed that I wasn't doing what all my other colleagues wanted to do. I felt angry that I had spent so much time and energy investing in becoming a doctor. I was fearful of what people might say or think about me and I felt very guilty about wanting to leave, about leaving patients, about leaving my colleagues, and about having a great education and wanting to do something else. Because of this, I was very suspicious of everyone. There were just a variety of things that I went through.

2.4 Family Support

One of the key determinants for a successful transition from clinical to non-clinical medicine is the level of support of the physician's spouse or significant other. The physician seriously considering a career change needs to identify the needs and desires of their spouse or significant other early on. The spouse or significant other's financial, family, and social status may be immediately and adversely affected by the physician's transition to a non-clinical position. On the other hand, having a happy non-clinical physician will likely be more attractive than a miserable physician out practicing clinical medicine.

Physicians are well advised to explain and enlist the support (emotional and financial) of their spouse/significant other in the transition process. In addition, children old enough to understand should be consulted and, if possible, enlisted to help as well.

The bottom line is that physicians who have the support of their families are much more likely to make a successful transition to non-clinical medicine.

2.5 How Long Will It Take and How Hard Will It Be?

Career transition can be a time-consuming, difficult process. Exactly how long it will take and how difficult it will be depends upon a number of factors, some of which will be within your control and some of which will not be within your control. These factors include:

HOW QUICKLY YOU DECIDE ON THE CAREER(S) YOU WOULD LIKE TO PURSUE
It is difficult to get to a destination if you don't know what your destination is. In order to map out and effectively execute a career transition action plan, it is best to first spend time figuring out what you would like to do in your new non-clinical career. This is a crucial step because you do not want to end up in a career you like even less than your current career practicing medicine. Once you determine the new career(s) you would like to target, you can most efficiently devote time and resources to making your transition.

TIME COMMITTED TO CAREER TRANSITION

Researching and landing a non-clinical career can take a lot of time. Networking requires time. Building up your resume may take considerable amounts of time. Even drafting an excellent non-clinical resume will take time. Posting resumes takes time. Applying for jobs takes time. Interviewing takes time.

If you want to maximize your chances for a successful career transition, you must find and dedicate sufficient time to the process. We have seen many a physician's career transition flounder because he did not dedicate the time necessary to pursue the opportunities.

> **Example 2.4: No progress on career transition because no time committed to it**
> We recently sent a follow-up e-mail to physicians who attended a non-clinical careers conference we put on a year ago. "How is your transition going?," we asked. A number of people responded to the effect of, "I haven't had any chance to focus on this because I'm so busy with work. I need to get out soon, though, these hours are killing me." If you want to make a career transition, you need to find the time to commit to your transition.

FLEXIBILITY TO MOVE OR COMMUTE

It is understandable that many physicians are reluctant to move. They may like where they live. They might have to sell their home at a loss if they move. They may have children in school that they do not want to disrupt. Whether you are willing to move or commute are personal decisions that only you can make. If you are not willing to move or commute a sizeable distance, your transition will generally take longer and be more difficult.

> **Example 2.5: Rural doctor who is unwilling to move**
> We recently were asked to help a 55-year-old emergency room physician living in a very rural part of the country (it was six hours driving time to the nearest large city). She was unwilling to move and strongly preferred to work from home. This severely limited this physician's options in terms of the non-clinical work available and made her career transition much more difficult.

> **Example 2.6: Doctor unwilling to commute**
> We recently obtained an interview for a client with an insurance company located in the client's home state. Because the client was unwilling to move or consider a long commute, the client turned the interview down. This

physician's career transition will take longer and be harder than if the physician was willing to relocate.

Some industries (such as pharmaceuticals, the federal government, non-profits, and other fields) tend to be concentrated in certain parts of the country. See Chapter 3. Other fields (such as state and local government, administration, medical-legal, and insurance) exist in most parts of the country. If you are unwilling to move, you should take into account what is available in your own area before deciding on a viable non-clinical career path. There is no point in deciding to target a position that doesn't exist near where you live.

REQUIRED INITIAL AND LONG-TERM COMPENSATION
The amount of guaranteed money you need to earn in salary in your first non-clinical position will affect how long your transition will take and how difficult the transition will be. Although you certainly don't want to sell yourself short, you should be realistic about how much certain positions will pay at an entry level. If you are a surgeon or a highly paid specialist who does procedures, you may have to take a significant initial pay cut when taking your first job. If you are unwilling to do so, your career transition can be much more difficult and take much longer. Similarly, starting your own business is probably not a good idea if you absolutely need a decent salary for the first couple of years of your transition.

In some cases, a physician's compensation requirements can be so unrealistic as to make their career transition next to impossible.

Example 2.7: Physician looking for starting salary of mid-seven figures
We were recently asked to help a physician who had both an MBA and a law degree. He was willing to relocate if necessary, which helped. The only sticking point—and it was a huge one—was that he was looking for a starting salary in the mid-seven figures. We politely told the client that this was not realistic.

You also want to take into account what your long-term compensation requirements are. If you need large potential long-term compensation, consider jobs in industry or starting your own business. Non-profits and government jobs should not be in the mix, unless such a job is taken to position you for a move to industry (say, working at the FDA for two years and then going into regulatory affairs in industry after that).

CURRENT FINANCIAL SITUATION

If you are considering a career transition, it is usually a good idea to start living within your means as soon as possible. The less debt you carry and the less income you need just to make ends meet, the easier it will be to find a job that will support you and your family. In addition, if you are able to save some money, you will be able to use this to support your lifestyle during the early part of your career transition where you might have to make a financial sacrifice.

LEADERSHIP

We have asked a lot of people who hire doctors what they look for. One word we keep hearing over and over again is "leadership." If you have demonstrated leadership, are able to get things done, and people respond to you well, you will generally be able to obtain a non-clinical position faster than someone who has not shown leadership. Please consider the following:

> **Example 2.8: SEAK faculty member discusses how he looks for leaders when hiring physicians**
> I can hire managers, very good managers, but leaders, particularly physician leaders, what I'm looking for is somebody who will help try to build consensus, somebody who's not satisfied with the status quo. They want to see change and they're willing actually to create radical change if need be. I want somebody I call a servant leader, who is trying to make it better for the people who work with them, so at the end of the day their careers are enhanced.
> I want them to be collaborative. I want them to be people who listen deeply, who communicate well and have good interpersonal skills. But I also want people who will hold folks accountable. Servant leadership sounds warm and fuzzy. It's anything but that. I mean Southwest Airlines, the Container Store, there are a number of major businesses that use that technique, but they also put the discipline with it. So I have to have the discipline to delegate responsibility and hold people accountable.
> That's the most important thing. A lot of people have good ideas and good vision, but implementing, execution is the key. So you want folks who can actually get the vision, build a plan around that vision and execute it.

SKILLS AND EXPERIENCE

The skills and experience levels of physicians vary widely. Different entry-level opportunities will be open to you depending upon the skills and experience you bring to the table. Variables could include your specialty, clinical experience/certification, communications skills, personality, interests, business experience, leadership experience, industry experience, and advanced education. Let's discuss each of these briefly:

SPECIALTY

In many "traditional" non-clinical fields, you will use your medical knowledge for the benefit of your employer. Your specialty often matters. If you have the specialty the particular employer is looking for, your transition will be easier. Keep in mind your specialty when targeting careers. Certain specialties are in demand in certain industries. For example, oncologists are in high demand in the pharmaceutical industry and orthopedists are in high demand in the medical-legal field. Please see Chapter 3 for more information. When networking or researching a particular industry, it is always a good idea to ask what opportunities there are for physicians with your specialty in the field.

> **Example 2.9: ER physician not suited for medical-legal work unless physician returned to active practice**
> We recently were asked to help a 55-year-old ER physician who was interested in doing medical-legal (expert witness) work from home. The physician spent 20 years in the ER and had retired a year previously. We explained to the physician that medical-legal work for ER physicians is mostly malpractice-related and, as such, the physician would need to return to active practice (at least part-time) to have credibility in the field and to meet qualifications laws in some jurisdictions. We were informed that returning to the ER part-time was not an option and this effectively ended most career options in medical-legal for this physician. Note: Had this physician been a neurologist or orthopedist, there would have been medical-legal work doing IMEs available. Bottom line, your specialty affects your job options in many cases.

CLINICAL EXPERIENCE AND CERTIFICATION

Some employers, positions, and careers require certain amounts of clinical experience, others do not. Some require board certification, others do not. It depends upon the employer and the position. Many physicians leave clinical medicine during their internships and residencies and go on to *extremely* successful careers. See Section 9.5. This is a viable career path, but the number of traditional entry-level non-clinical jobs available to physicians without practice experience or board certification are fewer.

COMMUNICATION SKILLS AND PERSONALITY

For the vast majority of positions, employers are looking for candidates with communication skills and a likeable personality. Personality is important because the employer will want you to be a good fit for the company. The employer will also want their internal and external customers to be pleased to deal with you.

Communication skills are *crucial*. Employers need physicians who can persuade and explain. If you possess and can demonstrate strong communication skills, your career transition is likely to be easier and take less time.

Example 2.10: Snippets from job postings for non-clinical careers discussing communication skills

- Regional technical director for medical device company: "Must have excellent communication skills and be very polished and experienced in giving presentations to all size groups."
- Bayer Healthcare medical science liaison: "Communicate complex scientific data..., skillfully influence and persuade people..., possess strong interpersonal and communication skills."
- Blue Cross/Blue Shield, VP and chief medical officer: "Must possess solid written and oral communication skills and be able to articulate issues in a concise manner."
- Medical director, The Physician Advisor Company: "Good communication skills."
- Swiss Re Insurance vice president and medical director: "Effective written and oral communication both with formal and informal groups."
- Tyco Global, senior product clinician: "Strong oral and written communication and presentation skills."
- Medtronic medical science liaison: "Effective interpersonal and communications skills..., advanced presentation skills."
- Boston Scientific, director of scientific communication: "Effective written and communication skills are essential in order to communicate with key opinion leaders, senior management, and cross-functional business partners."

- Unum Provident, medical consultant: "Excellent oral and written communication skills."
- Aetna medical director ($200K base + 20% bonus): "Strong public speaking skills, engagement of audience, and relationship building are a must."

Note the last bulletpoint listed above. When employers are looking for strong communications/speaking skills they are not referring to a physician who can deliver a standard PowerPoint presentation. These companies are looking for a physician who:

- Understands how to use presentations as a sales/business development tool,
- Can develop and lead continuing education programs,
- Knows how to size-up an audience,
- Understands adult learning principles,
- Has an engaging, energetic, dynamic style,
- Uses stories, analogies, and demonstrations to make his points,
- Encourages interaction and questions,
- Is an excellent teacher, and
- Truly enjoys speaking and communicating with others.

INTERESTS

Employers are looking for employees who are interested in their field. Employers want their employees to show a passion for their work because they will generally perform better when they are passionate. In addition, they don't want to spend time and money training a new employee who will leave after a short period of time. If you can demonstrate interest in your field and that you have relevant experience, you will have a distinct advantage during your interview.

Example 2.11: Show interest in the field
You are interested in a job doing disability consulting for an insurance company. You show your interest in this field by highlighting the IME work you have done on your resume and by enthusiastically discussing this IME work during your interview. You have also joined the relevant professional groups and read their publications. You are also prepared to intelligently discuss the field of disability consulting during your interview.

BUSINESS AND LEADERSHIP EXPERIENCE

The more business and leadership experience a physician has, generally the easier and quicker the transition will be. To ease your transition, seize career opportunities to gain business experience and leadership experience. This is often done by working part-time non-clinically and serving on committees.

INDUSTRY EXPERIENCE

Industry experience is obviously a plus. An employer prefers an employee who requires as little training as possible. The more industry experience you have, the faster and easier you can expect your transition to be.

Example 2.12: Industry experience—pharma
A physician in academic medicine who has worked on numerous clinical trials is going to be familiar with how these trials are run. This experience could go a long way when looking for a job in the pharmaceutical industry.

Example 2.13: Industry experience—insurance
You are targeting a career switch to the health insurance field. Previously doing utilization file reviews for independent review organizations may be considered a certain kind of industry experience and set you apart from other candidates.

ADVANCED EDUCATION

Having an advanced degree such as an MBA or MPH may help your career transition. The downside, of course, is that obtaining that degree will usually require substantial time, effort, and money. For more on the pros and cons of obtaining an advanced degree, please see Chapter 6.

TIME REQUIRED TO POSITION YOURSELF FOR A NON-CLINICAL CAREER UNDER YOUR ACTION PLAN

You may choose to position yourself for your new non-clinical career. If so, the time required for this positioning must be built into your expectations of how long your transition will take. Please consider the following examples:

Example 2.14: Medical reporter goes back to school
You want to become a medical reporter. Your plan is to work part-time in clinical medicine and go back to school to get a degree in journalism. This will obviously take some time.

Example 2.15: Expecting a pay cut, surgeon takes time to save up money
You are a successful surgeon hoping to go to work for a non-profit. You know this will require a significant pay cut. Saving up enough money to maintain your desired standard of living after your transition may take some time.

ECONOMIC AND INDUSTRY CONDITIONS
Your career transition timeline will be greatly affected by economic conditions. The easiest and fastest transitions will be in fast-growing fields. The hardest and slowest transitions will be in shrinking fields or fields experiencing distress. For example, the fall of 2008 was not a good time to be looking to switch into the financial industry and become a financial analyst for a Wall Street firm. A great way to get a sense as to which industries are growing and which are under pressure is to subscribe to and read *The Wall Street Journal.*

NETWORKING, RESUME WRITING, JOB HUNTING, INTERVIEWING, AND NEGOTIATING SKILLS
Your job-searching skills matter. The better you are at job searching, networking, resume writing, interviewing, and negotiating, the faster and easier your transition will be. For further information in these areas, please see Chapters 4, 5, 7, 8, and 10.

Chapter 3   Traditional and Non-Traditional Non-Clinical Careers for Physicians

3.1 Executive Summary

- It is critical to thoroughly research the potential fields you are considering. You do not want to end up in a career you like less than practicing clinical medicine.
- There are numerous traditional non-clinical fields you can consider, including:
  - Consulting
  - Running your own business
  - Industry (i.e., pharma, medical device, and biotech)
  - Marketing
  - Advertising
  - Continuing education
  - Communications
  - Health insurance
  - Disability insurance
  - Life insurance
  - Workers' compensation insurance
  - Independent review organizations
  - Federal, state, and local government
  - Non-profits
  - Informatics
  - Inventions
  - Medical administration
  - Media
  - Occupational medicine/corporate health and wellness
  - Expert witness
  - Independent medical examiner
- The earning potential for physicians in many of the above fields is excellent, although an initial pay cut may be required.
- Familiarize yourself with the typical job titles non-clinical physicians have (medical director, chief medical informatics officer, medical science liaison, etc.). This will help greatly in job searching.

- Do not feel limited to the traditional fields. There are numerous examples of physicians succeeding in other areas as well.
- Consider if you would prefer to work in a large or small organization. There are advantages and disadvantages to both.

3.2 Where Am I Going?

To have a successful career transition to non-clinical medicine, it is best to thoroughly research what you may like to do next. You do not want to end up in a new career that you find even less satisfying than your current one. Also, in order to land your first opportunity in a new career, you will most likely need to demonstrate that you are running toward your new career as opposed to running away from your clinical practice.

The following section provides an overview of the traditional areas that physicians get into when they leave clinical medicine. If you find any of these areas of interest, your next step should be to find out as much as possible about these fields through networking, research, and other techniques.

3.3 Traditional Non-Clinical Careers for Physicians

CONSULTING

There are many physicians who have become consultants. Consulting can usually be done from the physician's home office, but significant travel may be required. The advantages of becoming a physician consultant include:

- control over each assignment,
- diversity of tasks,
- ability to arrange own schedule,
- ability to locate where you chose,
- not having to work for an employer,
- ability to be creative,
- ability to leverage your time and expertise,
- opportunity to travel,
- better lifestyle,
- low overhead,
- small start-up cost,

- high hourly rates, and
- ability to work part-time so you can ease into this while practicing clinical medicine.

There are, of course, potential downsides to consulting as well. These include:

- you are not leveraged,
- difficult to build value in your business,
- you are dispensable,
- paycheck is not regular,
- you may eventually lose your "real world" expertise,
- always chasing down new work or paying someone to do this for you,
- time pressures, and
- the necessity of travel.

Physicians are sometimes hired by large consulting firms as employees. These positions typically involve a large amount of travel. As one of our faculty members put it:

Example 3.1: Consultant describes required travel in field
Right now, I would say 25 to 50 percent of my time [is spent on the road]. I think one of the key messages here is you are at the mercy of the client, and so if you need to be somewhere the next day you have to find a way to get there, whether you hop in your car or you get on the airplane. I live right in the middle of the country, which makes that a little easier. So I can get to either coast if I need to by driving less than 20 hours. So if there's some emergency, I can be onsite within 24 hours generally.

Finding or Building Your Niche: Physicians with clinical experience can have a lot to offer as consultants. Generally, what do physicians bring to the table?

1. **Content:** Clinical knowledge is probably the most common consulting value, particularly for physicians who can translate this knowledge into product specifications for companies developing healthcare products.

2. **Expertise:** Many physician consultants have particular expertise that transcends industries or healthcare settings. For example, strategic planning can be done for practice groups, hospitals, health systems, and health plans.
3. **Knowledge:** Broader than content, knowledge here refers to understanding of *processes*. Physicians consulting in practice management, for example, have broad experiences in understanding clinic flow dynamics, billing and receivables efficiencies, and personnel management.
4. **Behavior:** The value-add here is interpersonal. Physician consultants who work as facilitators, for example, bring skills to assist in conflict resolution, large group facilitation, and change management.
5. **Special skills:** Some consultants find they have a special talent or gift that is highly specialized and not easily reproduced or found either within an organization or large consulting firm. Patch Adams is a good example of a physician consultant/speaker who uses humor and drama in motivational speaking and training.
6. **Contacts:** The ability to introduce clients to key contacts in public or private life is another value of some physician consultants. Examples include physicians engaged as "lobbyists" for government, medical societies, or industry.[1]

When looking for or developing a consulting niche, you will want to examine your:

- Expertise,
- Experience,
- Training,
- Credentials,
- Personal skills and abilities,
- Business skills and experience, and
- What do you like/love to do.

---

[1] "What Is Your Value-Add as a Healthcare Business Consultant?," *Daring Doctor Newsletter*, 2/24/2006.

The key question for you to consider is what are you so good at that companies/people will pay for you to give advice and share your expertise, experience, and judgment?

The traditional areas of consulting for physicians include:

- Business consulting (advising startups on bringing new products to market),
- Clinical outcomes,
- Coaching (other physicians in career improvement, business development, etc.),
- Coding,
- Compliance,
- Drug safety (pharmacovigilance),
- Hospital provider-strategy/operations,
- IT,
- Marketing (medical approval of marketing copy),
- Medical devices,
- Medical support,
- Medical-legal (discussed in more detail below),
- Payor,
- Pharma,
- Physician groups,
- Physician-hospital relations, and
- Think tanks.

Developing the right niche is a key to success as a consultant. Without a niche you are a jack of all trades who will not be perceived as an expert. You will also have difficulty branding yourself if you don't have a niche. Please consider the following advice from one of SEAK's faculty members on developing the right niche:

Example 3.2: Find a niche that you are good at and that is marketable
Especially earlier in your career, try different assignments and find out what you enjoy, and then also what nobody else does, and trying to do those simultaneously is really key. Especially as physicians, we have a very long train up time, and by the time we're done we just want to work somewhere, get a decent job, support the family. While you're doing that you want to think about which of these skills is marketable, and take notes internally or otherwise. You

will find something that is unique, that you are uniquely good at, as long as you're receptive and you're thinking along those lines. I think that's the key.

You know, a lot of life is not according to plan. So the key is how quick on your feet are you when you get strange little career things that happen to all of us? Sometimes we are instrumental and sometimes the forces are external to us, but either way you have to adapt, and that's what I think makes a successful business person, especially a successful client, a successful consultant.

Paths to Becoming a Consultant: There are many different traditional paths to becoming a consultant. One of our faculty members, a surgeon, went back to business school after he was laid off from his job at the V.A. He was then hired by a small consulting firm where he gained valuable experience and was able to then launch his own independent practice. Another left his surgical residency and was hired by Booz Allen Consulting (a very large consulting firm) in March of 2001. He now runs his own consulting practice. His initial experience in consulting is something all physicians considering getting into consulting should take into account:

> **Example 3.3: Consulting, like many non-clinical career options, may have significantly less job security than clinical medicine**
> I actually got a job at Booz Allen in March of 2001. A lot of physicians say, "Oh I want to go into all this. That sounds great, the outside world and consulting and a nice office," all this kind of stuff. I started in March of 2001 and I did not have a job in November of 2001, because of 9/11. I mean thousands of consultants were laid off.
> So that's something, just to be open-eyed for physicians thinking of going outside of medicine. You can have a job one day and don't have a job the next day.

Work from Home: A nice thing about being a consultant is that the work can often be done from home. This means that you can be located anywhere (a major requirement for many physicians seeking a career change) and still be a consultant. A physician consultant notes:

> **Example 3.4: Much consulting work can be done from anywhere**
> I think given electronic capabilities with e-mail and videoconferencing or Web conferencing, absolutely [you can be located anywhere and do it]. I'm a big believer in personal contact with clients. I'm at my client company at least once a week, seeing people, interacting with them, and I think there's a value to that that just is really amazing.

But I know people who work for companies, where they have never, literally never met the person they've working with. They've spoken to them on the phone. They've gotten the work assignment. They work on it. They complete it. And they still never have seen that person live. So it's doable, but I think you do miss something in terms of actually interacting with the person.

Successfully working from home requires discipline, however. Please consider the following examples:

Example 3.5: Working from home a "double-edged sword"
Working from home, it's a double-edged sword. You run the risk of doing neither of your tasks, dad or consultant, at 100 percent when you're at home, because everybody expects that you're there 100 percent for them. So you have to make some real clear rules, "This is work time. This is not work time," almost as if you were in the office, because you really are in the office, and if you have to do something during the day you mark that time out. If you've got to stop your work during office hours or something, say, "Okay, from 10:00 to 2:00 I have this task I need to do," and vice versa. Again, the flexibility is you don't have to commute, so there are some efficiencies gained out of that, and you do have control over your work environment.

Example 3.6: Advice and insight from a physician who works from home 2–3 days a week in her non-clinical position
I think that you need to set up your schedule in the same way that you would set up your schedule from the office, and have a true work office, home office environment. I don't think working off your kitchen table is necessarily going to be productive. I have a home office with my fax machine and the computer set up in the same way that I do at the office, and I connect with the servers so I'm accessing all of the same information.

I try to schedule conference calls on the days that I'm working from home in the same way that I do on days that I'm in the office, because it provides a little bit of variety. I frankly think that the variety of home and office makes me more productive, because five days in the office can get pretty dry as well. So switching that and working from home one day a week, I'm not getting as many door knocks. I'm not getting as many questions from people passing by my office. So I might be able to focus a little bit more on writing projects or on researching than I am when I'm in the office, and it's easy for somebody to grab me really quickly and ask me a question.

Fees: If you talk to consultants through networking, you can expect many of them to be cautious about disclosing what they charge. This is often because they charge different rates to different clients and a disclosure of rates could be very problematic. Suffice it to say that of the many physician consultants we have interviewed none of them has ever told us that they are not earning a good living. Our sense is that fees are typically in the range of $200–$500/hour.

Conclusion: One Physician's Experience as a Consultant: One SEAK faculty member left his surgical practice during his internship to go work for pharma (finding this first position through a recruiter). He worked on research and development for two different companies over 4 years and then launched his own solo consulting practice in the niche of marketing products currently undergoing phase IV clinical trials to physicians (medical approval of advertising copy). In his words:

> **Example 3.7: Reflections of a self-employed physician consultant**
> I'm making a good living that I am very happy with. My overhead [home office] is very low.
>
> [One issue is that consulting income can be feast or famine.] I've had situations where I've had a major client that I'm doing a lot of work for, who turned around and said, "Our upper management has told us, 'No more consultants.'" So a big chunk of my income just disappeared. Partly that is under the consultant's control, because if you have a good portfolio of clients and you're not just getting down to one or two, you help to kind of indemnify yourself and protect yourself from that.
>
> One of the really difficult things is the isolation. I'm in my office, by myself, with my computer. You'll hear this from people who have home-based businesses and who work alone, it gets very difficult. There are things that I do. Obviously I spend time with my clients and I'm part of teams at my clients, which gives me some social contact in a business setting, and I also am in contact with other freelancers and consultants who are out on their own, and I'll go to lunches with them. I'll set up business lunches, so that I'm out interacting with other people as part of business, and then of course a social life besides that. But the isolation can be very difficult to deal with.

ENTREPRENEURSHIP

Many physicians become successful entrepreneurs. The most successful chain of bagel shops in our area is owned by a physician. One of our faculty members started and runs a specialty food company. Another faculty member launched and runs a business developing and selling his inventions. Yet another SEAK faculty member runs a series of weight loss clinics (he bought franchise rights to these).

The typical paths we see to physician entrepreneurship are as follows:

1. Starting the business from scratch. This is the most typical path. Most often, the business starts as a part-time venture with the goal of transitioning full-time from clinical medicine to running the business.
2. Buying an existing business. You would need the financing to do this. Are you sure of what you are buying? Why would you run it better than the previous owners?
3. Launching a business after buying franchise rights. This gives you a business in a box and tremendous support, but it could be very expensive both up front and with continuing franchise fees.

There are many advantages to being an entrepreneur. These include:

- The ability to be creative.
- Setting your own rules, working conditions, and culture.
- Being able to work with who you want to work with (for example, family members).
- Building an organization with inherent value that can later be sold or passed on to children.
- Creating wealth and jobs.
- The satisfaction of building and leading a winning team.
- No limit on earning potential. You are rewarded on your own merits. You make as much as you can make—nobody else arbitrarily sets your compensation.
- You don't need an MBA or other advanced degree that costs tens of thousands of dollars and many years of time commitment to start your own business.
- Intellectual stimulation.
- You can give yourself as many perks as are legal, including: favorable retirement plans, jobs for relatives, frequent flyer points, travel, and expense reimbursement.
- You can leverage yourself.

- You have the satisfaction of creating wealth.
- You don't have to work with anyone you prefer not to work with.

That said, there are also many drawbacks to becoming a physician entrepreneur. These include:

- There is no guarantee of financial success.
- You may actually lose money instead of making money.
- There is no limit to the amount of money you can lose, especially if you have high overhead.
- Lack of support. When your computer freezes, you can't just call the hospital IT department. You're on your own.
- Married to the business. Depending on the type of business and the team you have helping you, it may be difficult to get away and not run the business.
- It may be difficult getting the financing you need to run the business.

Starting a business is usually a good fit for extroverted, younger, self-starters who have been bitten by the entrepreneurial bug. It is generally a poor fit for physicians who are mentally exhausted, need a steady income, and are more looking to escape clinical medicine instead of having a real passion for starting and growing a business.

Consider the story of a practicing occupational medicine physician who followed a dream and started his own specialty food company. In his own words:

Example 3.8: The story of a physician-entrepreneur
I do occupational and environmental medicine at a clinic in Philadelphia. I'm also a clinic director. I'm also a regional consultant for five clinics in the area. In addition, I'm also very fortunate that I had the opportunity to help develop a business outside of medicine manufacturing, flavoring and roasting almonds for the natural food industry.

Finding a Unique Niche
Part of [the reason I got interested in starting my own business] was because of some dissatisfaction of what was going on in regular medicine. The fact that I was going to an MBA course was a very exciting inspiration to be around people who are in actual businesses. I think timing, it was slightly after 9/11. In fact,

my first business class was two days after 9/11 and we were in Connecticut so the whole idea that life can be very short and very cruel crossed my mind. I really wanted to pursue an idea that I had and that was rooted actually in medical, even though this is a food business, the idea is actually rooted in very sound and very deep medical research. Research that was done regarding the health benefits of various nuts while I was on a plane going to a conference and I was just shocked at how [in 2002] there really wasn't anything being done with this commercially.

Ideas Can't Be Licensed
Initially, I thought I would license my idea and the more I read about that was that big companies really don't want to pay inventors, typically for ideas. Typically, what they like to do is to see companies grow on their own with the understanding that many of them will fail. But [at] a large company, it's a lot easier for them to go ahead and then buy out that little company rather than having the large company take the risk of deciding what's going to work and what's not. So, kind of several things: timing, my business school classmates, realizing that things weren't changing in medicine, a little bit of sand in the shoe if you will, the fact of just by happenstance running across this wonderful health research about the health benefits of the nuts; particularly almonds.

Using Medical Knowledge
The impetus was reading some research and quite frankly it started with walnuts, was the original article to be honest. It showed that by eating a certain amount of walnuts per day would help lower your cholesterol. This study was done in Italy. I went home to my mother's house to see how many walnuts that really was, because I was wondering if this was like the artificial sweetener study where you had to eat the equivalent of 8 trainloads of the stuff for it to have the effect. So, my mother being a perpetual dieter had a little scale and we went ahead and weighed the walnuts and we found out that it was just about a handful. I thought, wow, that's marvelous. So, I thought, boy I could market this idea and just give people the right amount of walnuts in a little package and put it in their lunch. If they ate it every day, their cholesterol could go down. Then I also realized that any big nut company is going to figure this out and I'd be out of business in two weeks. So, what can I do differently?

Distinguishing Our Company
How do I distinguish myself? How do we do something a little differently? Dave Thomas, for example, the founder of Wendy's, was asked one time, how did he have the gall to go up against the big companies like McDonalds and Burger King. It's daunting if you really think about it, but he said something I saw in an interview. He said, all you have to do is do something a little bit different and a little bit better. That's why Wendy's hamburgers are square. Originally, their slogan was "at Wendy's we don't cut corners." So you get something a little bit

55

different and a little bit better. That's what I tried to do. I tried to take that lesson to heart. I thought, well, walnuts sometimes taste better, if you ever had walnuts on a brownie, every once and a while some of the walnuts will tumble off the brownies, and they're on the cookie sheet, and they taste really good. I thought, wow, I could roast some walnuts and sell them that way. So I tried that and I was working on different various recipes and I was thinking, maybe if I flavor them or spice them in some way, but without adding oil or making them candy. The people, I almost said patients, but it is for my patients too. It came out from working with patients with their diets, knowing the people can't tolerate boring diets. What can we do that's a little bit different and exciting? I thought, ok, I'm going to roast and flavor walnuts. I was doing this, and then one night in my house in Groton, which as most people might know, it's famous for submarines. It's a very industrial town. It was late at night and I realized that it was about 1:00 in the morning and here I am roasting walnuts in my oven in my kitchen. It didn't seem to make sense. It was very time-consuming actually doing it this way. I could only do so much at a time.

Looking for a Better Way
I knew there had to be a machine that did this short of buying a factory, and there was. I found a place in Ft. Lauderdale that sold machines and I went to them. They showed me their machines and they showed me how they roast almonds. I thought that was very interesting. They never even heard my story. I just listened to their story. Their story is that they sell these machines to people who roast almonds and sell them at carnivals or Disney World-type places and they showed me some of the economics of what the product costs and how much you can sell it for. I thanked them very much. I went back to Connecticut. My only dilemma at that point was that I really wasn't interested in almonds, but just for the heck of it I went ahead and research[ed] what the health benefits of almonds were.

Eureka Moment
That was the eureka moment. There was just a flood of great research. These were sound medical experiments done by researchers in Toronto, Italy, California. I found there was just 5x the amount of research about almonds than there was about walnuts. Things like the ability to lower cholesterol, reduction in colon cancer risk, actually helping people to lose weight. I thought this was absolutely phenomenal. Really good, high quality research. That was the moment to latch onto the almonds, work with my classmates to see what flavors worked. The other idea about why do the specialty foods business at that time too was also to transition. I also knew that hopefully I would have another career. Being in business school you realize that businesses don't just pop up overnight. I knew that if I wanted to have a business that I could work in and

that my family could work in too, it would take time. That was the other reason for 9/11. You have to start now. Even if it's small, let's start now. That was the idea.

What I Enjoy about the Business
What I enjoy about the business is that it's actually a very creative process. I think it's the same enjoyment that people get from creating art and music. You get a lot of satisfaction when people actually enjoy your product. I think it's just the enjoyment of seeing a creation from idea to end product; but also the people that you meet.

Working with Family Is Great
It's magnificent to be working with my family. I actually have to confess that I started in a family business myself. My father was a diesel mechanic by trade. He had a very successful Goodyear franchise that I know he wanted me to take over. I was kind of pigheaded and wanted to go into medicine and I did. And I'm not going to say I regret not going into business with him but I do understand better now. Unfortunately, he passed away at a young age, which was another influence on why I started the business soon. His goal was that he wanted to retire at age 55 and unfortunately he passed way before that happened. He financially could have done it. Anyway, working with the family is great because, even though there are some strings attached to it, and there's certain cautions that have to be taken, it's wonderful because it's not only a question of working together but its very satisfying being able to provide opportunities for each other to grow. One of the most exciting things for me is actually my cousin lives with us, my wife and I, and he's been going to trade shows with us since he was 15 years old. Theoretically, you are supposed to be 18, he's 19 now, but he's been 18 since he was 15.

Starting Your Business and Still Practicing Medicine
[You can even start your business and hold down a full-time job practicing medicine], and like a lot of things in life, you can but it's not easy. For the reason that I stated, I didn't really want to wait 5 years to start the business that I had the idea for. It could be too late. The time to start is now. There are ways, creative ways, of doing it. One way is working with your family. Another way of doing it is you can hire people. One thing I might suggest to a prospective entrepreneur is to look up virtual assisting on the internet. You can see that there's a variety of people that can help you with specific chores and tasks who work by the hour. That's a great way to start.

Advice to Physicians
I would ask [physicians] to think about the reasons and look at their expectations of why they want to do that. I think that in most instances the answers will point the way as to how they should proceed. One of the questions

that comes up: should you get an MBA? I remember one of my professors telling us the first day of class, if you want to make money, don't get an MBA, open a cookie shop. In a lot of ways, that's kind of why I went into the food business. I think that physicians are very uniquely qualified for a number of careers and businesses outside of medicine. In fact, a lot of famous physicians have. I'll give you a couple of examples: peanut butter was actually invented by a physician, and cereal was invented by a physician, and Welch's grape juice was invented by a dentist. So we actually have a fairly long tradition, it's just that it's not well publicized that these inventors of food products were actually physicians.

Developing/Coming Up with New Business Ideas: New business ideas can come from numerous sources. Physicians looking for viable business ideas need to be well-read, flexible, and open-minded:

> Make it a practice to keep on the lookout for novel and interesting ideas that others have used successfully. Your idea must be original only in its adaptation to the problem you are working on.
>
> —Thomas Edison

> Coming up with new business ideas is the result of looking at what everyone else looks at and seeing something different.
>
> —Steven Babitsky

The best ideas have little or no competition; this is where the highest margins can most easily be made.

Thoroughly vet all ideas. Play the devil's advocate. *Not* pursuing a flawed idea is a very good thing.

Keep trying. You may have to try several business ideas before one takes off. Even ideas that sound ridiculous may work. Sometimes such ideas can be very good as no one else is doing them. Most times, though, these ideas truly are ridiculous and that is why no one else is doing them.

Turn Problems into Business Ideas: Many physicians encounter problems during their clinical practice. The entrepreneurial physicians see their problems as opportunities for inventions, products, and services. Where can physicians get good ideas for businesses in addition to solving problems they encounter in clinical practice?

Creative Idea Sources:
1. *Read, read, read.* Read *The Wall Street Journal,* junk mail, journals, everything. The physicians who read and are exposed to new and developing trends and concepts are in the best position to come up with successful business ideas. *The Wall Street Journal* is an excellent source of business trends and ideas. If you can't afford to take time off to get an MBA, reading the *Journal* each day is your next best bet.

   Many physicians throw out their junk mail without opening or reading it. The physicians looking for business ideas understand that junk mail and advertisements are excellent sources of business ideas. What is selling? What can you do better? What can you adapt, improve, modify, etc.? All may be gleaned by looking at your junk mail.

   Physicians looking for business ideas are generally voracious readers of journals, business books, and magazines. They understand that being exposed to many new concepts and trends increases the odds of finding or being able to spot or develop a new business idea.

2. *Ask what people need/want.* The authors have learned an important lesson over the past 30 years. Namely, do not sit around your office trying to divine what people might want. We have learned to directly ask them what they want through interviews, needs assessments, and questionnaires. When coming up with new business ideas, it is best to look for what people want as opposed to what you think they need.

3. *Look for trends in the marketplace.* When looking for business ideas, it is a good idea to try to anticipate the trends and the needs of your customers. A product or service they need now and will continue to need in the future is what you are looking for.

4. *Study industry leaders.* All viable ideas need not be new ones. Just because one or more companies or people are already providing a product or service does not mean you should not consider providing it. The question becomes: can you provide a better, higher quality product or service? Can you make it more accessible? Can you provide it at a lower cost?

5. *Expand a current idea that is working.* Very often, new ideas are expansions of ones that are already working. The authors developed a successful writing course called "Fiction Writing for Physicians." The expansion of the idea was simple and logical and worked, namely: "Fiction Writing for Lawyers."

6. *Find and fill niches.* Locating, identifying, or developing a market niche can lead to many successful business ideas. The niche opens the doors to the customers. For example, the authors identified physicians who perform independent medical evaluations (IMEs) as a niche. After the identification of the niche, the business ideas and products were easy and natural (for example, books, conferences, white papers, and directories).

7. *Study an industry and identify problems and needs.* The physician looking for viable business ideas needs to seek out industry problems. Generally speaking, the solution is the business idea that may be viable. In healthcare, there are no shortages of major problems and needs. The solutions to these problems/needs are an excellent source of new business ideas.

The physician seeking new business ideas should not be afraid to strike off into unchartered waters. He needs a passion for his idea and the ability to do it better than anyone else. These physicians talk to people/potential customers to find out what they want. They understand that they need a cost-effective way to:

- Market and sell the product or service,
- Line up distributors,
- Make sure there is a need or desire for the product or service, and
- That they can deliver a high-quality product or service.

Protect Your Idea: Generally, you cannot copyright, patent, or trademark an idea. There are, however, various ways to protect an idea. These include:

- Line up your ducks before disclosing your idea to the marketplace,
- Protect the business name or Web site (for example, flowers.com),

- Align yourself with established businesses who can serve as distributors,
- Corner the market, and
- Keep your mouth shut.

Physician Entrepreneurs and Venture Capital: What will venture capitalists look for in a physician entrepreneur to determine if they will provide financial backing?

> How does the sometimes elusive and high-stakes world of venture capital really work? How can physician executives with innovative ideas or new technologies approach venture capitalists to help them raise capital to form a start-up company?...The ideal physician executive is described as: (1) an expert in an area that Wall Street perceives as hot; (2) a public speaker who can enthusiastically communicate scientific and business plans to a variety of audiences; (3) a team leader who is willing to share equity in the company with other employees; (4) a recruiter and a motivator; (5) an implementer who can achieve milestones quickly that allow the company to go public as soon as possible; and (6) a realist who does not resent the terms of the typical deal. The lucrative world of the venture capitalists is foreign territory for physician executives and requires a great idea, charisma, risk-taking, connections, patience, and perseverance to navigate it successfully.[2]

PHARMA, MEDICAL DEVICE, AND BIOTECH ("INDUSTRY")

There are numerous positions available for physicians in industry. For some specialties with many unmet needs, such as oncology, neurology, psychiatry, endocrinology, and cardiology, there is great demand for physicians. For obvious reasons, physicians with experience in academic medicine and with clinical trials are in the most demand. Opportunities for growth and for eventual lucrative earnings abound in industry. Departments that hire physicians include medical affairs, clinical affairs, regulatory affairs, pharmacovigilance/safety, and research and development.

---

[2] "The Ideal Physician Entrepreneur," Bottles, K, *Physician Exec.,* 2000 Nov–Dec; 26 (6):55–8.

Medical Affairs: Job titles for physicians in medical affairs departments include medical director and medical science liaison.

Medical director: Medical director positions could consist of a mixture of:

- Advising product development teams
- Managing clinical development teams
- Helping design clinical trials
- Interfacing with scientific leaders
- Interfacing with representatives of professional societies
- Assisting in professional education programs for doctors and nurses
- Verifying compliance with applicable regulations and company policies
- Supplying clinical expertise and training to business people in research and development, sales, and marketing
- Making presentations to health insurance groups
- Interfacing with Medicare and Medicaid
- Reviewing documentation such as marketing materials, package inserts, instructions for use, and training materials
- Helping draft safety reports
- Performing literature reviews with customers
- Working on continuing education and marketing
- Undertaking new business development

Here's how an executive medical director at a big pharma company describes his position in medical affairs:

Example 3.9: Medical affairs physician describes his position
I have a variety of tasks. Probably about a third to 40% of my job is education. I'm educating not only our internal customers, meaning people in marketing and the commercial operations and even medical monitors and others working on protocols about various oncology subjects, but I am educating our external customers.

And our external customers could be patients. They could be nurses. They could be physicians. They could be payers of all kinds. Right now, I have an innovative program that I've started where I'm educating case workers at various insurance companies who often serve as the point of information for patients who are caught in a complicated network of trying to figure out what to do and how do things get covered and that sort of thing. That consumes a third to 40% of my time.

Everything in a pharmaceutical company has to be reviewed by a physician and a lawyer to make sure it's in compliance with all the FDA regulations, and also to make sure that we're not making claims that are untrue. It's—now that I'm in this position, I can see so often things that are advertised by other companies or in the newspapers that are misleading and false. So I have to be sure that our advertising is really true and not misleading.

Everything in oncology has to come through me to be approved from a medical point of view. I used to cover just the U.S., but now I am being transitioned in a position to cover everything around the world that we produce. And that's going to consume probably almost 50% of my time.

Here is how the chief medical officer at a specialty pharma company described the medical affairs department he set up:

Example 3.10: What medical affairs departments do

In the medical affairs department, we're responsible for the oversight of the medical activities around phase four clinical trials. Meaning, clinical trials of drugs that are already approved in the country. We're responsible for developing...the educational programs to train physicians how to use our products safely. We're responsible for developing publications around our products and how they are used. We're responsible for responding to regulatory agencies regarding the safety of our products. It's a very diverse, dynamic field.

[There are absolutely a lot of opportunities for physicians in medical affairs.] This wasn't the case ten years ago, but what has happened because of all the concerns in the country around drug safety, the FDA realizes there needs to be a greater scrutiny and scientific rigor in post-approval work. Which means there's more work for physicians to do in that area. I think this could be a huge area of growth over the next ten years.

Here is what one chief medical officer looks for when hiring physicians in medical affairs positions:

Example 3.11: What employers look for when hiring physicians into medical affairs departments

I look for physicians who have a curiosity about research, who realize that their learning starts when they finish medical school—that doesn't stop. They're looking for lifelong learning. I look for physicians who like working with other people, don't have to be the boss all the time. And the one thing that is absolutely, absolutely essential for a physician is they have to have a very strong ethical fiber.

If they are physicians who like to cut corners, or can think of ways of spinning something from a marketing perspective, they're not people that I want in my department because how the industry is changing, with all the scrutiny from the government and from the press, I want physicians who are great scientists, who understand science, who care for patients. And do things strictly by the rules—

Medical science liaison: Medical science liaisons (MSLs) are more of a sales support role. These can be entry-level positions and can often be home-based with a large travel component. As a rule of thumb, the larger the company, the smaller the MSL's travel territory will be. A great advantage of MSL positions is that they exist throughout the country. Most MSLs are not physicians, but some are. MSLs could do the following:

- Develop relationships and lines of communication with key opinion leaders such as department heads
- Develop relationships with the people who develop treatment guidelines
- Find innovative ways to get the industry's information distributed to the medical community
- Review advisory board recommendations
- Act as a clinical resource in an area
- Work to identify potential investigators
- Monitor research studies
- Interface with those seeking industry grants
- Review marketing material for clinical content
- Work closely with the sales and marketing team on business plans
- Help select sites for clinical research
- Follow-up on adverse event reports
- Help with CME content development

Here is how the role of a medical science liaison is described by the chief medical officer of a medical device company:

Example 3.12: Role of medical science liaison
The medical science liaison role is one that is more outwardly focused. It, typically, is dealing with products that are already on the market that have received their FDA approvals or clearances are being utilized by physicians. A medical science liaison will take the information that the company learned during the clinical development and they will share that with physicians, they will develop relationships with key opinion leaders, getting them to understand how a new product or treatment can benefit patients and why it might be superior to other treatments that they are currently using. The medical science liaison works very closely with the sales force in terms of educating potential buyers of the products that a company has developed, in terms of answering their questions on more a clinical academic level while the salesperson deals with the day-to-day sales processes. So the medical science liaison is working day-to-day with other doctors as they are educating them and sharing information with them, and also can take ideas back from those physicians about how a product might be used better; maybe in a different patient population or in a completely different indication. That medical science liaison may help oversee clinical trials that can show that indication works as safely and effectively as it was shown to work in the original trials.

A physician who has hired and trained hundreds of medical science liaisons recommends the following:

Example 3.13: Key qualities of a successful medical science liaison
Two things you have to have. One is you have to know the product that you're going to be out there with, in the therapeutic category, inside and out. You can't fake it. If you know it inside and out you're a value to your colleagues within your company and you're a value to the people that you're going to be talking to, which are key opinion leaders and chairmen of departments around the country. You have to know that.

And I don't say you have to even be in that specialty, though. I mean you can be a generalist, but we could train you in talking about glaucoma and Xalatan with an ophthalmologist, because you'll know the brand even better than the specialist will know. You have to know the product, the therapeutic category.

Number two, you have to have a personality. It's that simple. You have to be likeable. You have to be interesting enough that somebody wants to sit with you. How I judge that when I interview people, if I have to look at my watch and I can't wait for the interview to end, then I know why would a chairman of Mass General internal medicine want to sit there and look at you and talk to you, if you're just boring, you're boring or you're dreary or miserable, or you're just not interesting to be with. You have to have the interpersonal skills.

MSL positions are field-based, meaning that you may not need to relocate to where your employer is located. However, a fair amount of travel may be involved and you may still need to relocate. In the words of a physician who was a pioneer in developing MSLs:

Example 3.14: Travel requirements of medical science liaisons
If you're with a large company that has 40 MSLs out there, your territory will be smaller and there's not as much travel. But there are some small biotech companies, for example, that only have five MSLs and your territory is Maine to Virginia, and there's a lot of travel involved there.

Usually there's one home day a week, home office day a week. So you're out on the road four times a [week]. If you're lucky, I mean if you're living in a hub city, if you're living in New York City or Philly or Boston, I mean there's a lot of medicine there. You can cover a lot just by staying in that city.

I feel sorry for the one that says to me, "I'd like to be an MSL." "Where do you live?" "I live in Stafford, Virginia." Well there's not many hospitals in Stafford, Virginia. You're going to have to get over to Richmond and Charlottesville and Washington. You're going to have to be on the road a lot.

Pay for MSL positions: MSL positions can be relatively low-paying at first, *but* they can position you very well for advancement in industry. In the words of a physician in industry:

Example 3.15: Paying your dues as a medical science liaison can be an excellent long-term career move
Believe it or not, a few years ago you'd have to pay higher than you do now, because there are that many doctors looking for a job. So I mean you could—especially since we know that pediatricians right now are being offered $80,000 to join a practice. You could get some at $80,000, but it could range all the way up to $125,000 to start.

It is an amazing job, a wonderful job for entry-level into the pharmaceutical side or a medical education, medical advertising side and medical communications. The reason being is that if you look at presidents of a lot of big pharma, some were sales reps. They started out in the field.

I really learned that when I was on the pharma side, where, as a physician you [may not have] much credibility about knowing the customer or knowing the business side. But when you walk in now with the MSL experience, you were out in the field and you sort of carried the bag. You carried a better bag. You had interface with the customer.

So now when you come into the home office you have the sales experience or the marketing experience, the business know-how, and it's a given you know the medicine and you know the science. So you really have it all to go into various areas in pharma. You can go into the marketing department, and that's a great pathway to go, VP of marketing up to president. If you like the science of the medicine, you can go into medical affairs, the medical regulatory legal area, or you can go into the clinical research side there. You really have your choice of where you want to go.

Clinical Affairs: Clinical affairs positions deal with clinical trials. Job titles in clinical affairs include medical director, biostatistician, medical writer, and medical director. Physicians working in clinical affairs could do the following:

- Design and direct clinical trials
- Keep costs down and within budget
- Help choose investigators and sites
- Negotiate contracts with hospitals, consultants, investigators, and others
- Interact with other parts of the organizations (such as R & D and regulatory affairs)
- Help prepare documentation and reports (technical writing) for the FDA and for internal and external use
- Participate in strategic planning
- Develop and implement standard operating procedures for trials
- Keep up-to-date on competitive products and trials

Here is an overview of the role of a medical director as described by a chief medical officer:

Example 3.16: Description of clinical affairs
Typically, what a medical director does, is, it's someone who focuses more inwardly on the company. They oversee clinical trial development in terms of protocol development. What endpoints are being looked at? Are those endpoints clinically meaningful? Meaning, once they do a clinical trial to show that a product is safe and effective, will physicians actually appreciate the endpoints that they've proved or will they think that they are just good research tools? They also work on reviewing the safety and effectiveness data as it becomes available to make sure that a product is not going to hurt anybody. It will actually help them. Then, once the clinical trials are completed, [they] will

review that information for the regulatory submissions to get that product approved. They will also look at how that information is then reflected in the marketing materials and brochures and physician education programs that would be developed. On the phase 4, most medical directors will still be focused on product development, usually expanding the indications for a product that is on the market currently.

Regulatory Affairs: This department oversees regulatory compliance. Job functions here could include:

- Developing compliance and reporting procedures
- Technical writing—drafting required regulatory reports and other documentation
- Safety reporting

Pharmacovigilance/Safety: Job functions in this department may include:

- Monitoring drug safety during clinical trials or post-market
- Developing safety surveillance systems
- Complying with regulatory requirements and documenting this compliance
- Responding to inquiries from regulators
- Protecting the public health
- Protecting the developer from inappropriate liability
- Overseeing a staff of safety analysts and case managers
- Evaluating post-market safety reports
- Collecting accurate and complete information on adverse events
- Making risk/benefit decisions concerning a product
- Being the medical conscience of the company

Here's how a SEAK faculty member who is an industry chief medical officer describes the roles of physicians in pharmacovigilance/safety:

Example 3.17: What physicians do in pharmacovigilance
There are a couple of different roles. There's sort of an entry-level role, which is mainly as a pharmacovigilance or safety analyst. Or sometimes it used to be called safety officer. People are getting away, nowadays, from those military types of titles. What the safety analyst does is, they are the person that receives a complaint that's sent in by a physician or from a patient about say an adverse

affect or an adverse event related to a treatment. They then investigate whether or not that treatment was caused by the drug or the medical device that was used and they try to gather as much information as they can about that patient and what happened. Then they can evaluate to see whether or not there was an association with the product. Those individual events are then all compiled to look at trends in terms of what's happening, in terms of safety. To see whether or not there are any [adverse] effects that are happening that weren't anticipated before the product went on the market or that the rates or anticipated events are higher than were originally expected. Usually, those initial rates are based on clinical trials, and the clinical trials population is very controlled so that once you get into the general population sometimes those rates change. But, the analysts are the ones that are doing the in-depth investigation into the events, or maybe reviewing the individual case files that other analysts who are maybe nurses or PAs are investigating, but they are providing a level of clinical review.

Then there are more of the director and VP roles, which are essentially those positions in pharmacovigilance that are overseeing the whole operation. So, you have responsibility in that company for the entire pharmacovigilance group, in terms of developing their systems and processes as well as doing final review; looking at all the trends and epidemiology of the events that you are seeing, ensuring that proper reporting is happening with regulatory authorities, and then interfacing with your colleagues in the company when issues arise related to safety, in terms of sharing that information with them and coming up with a game plan for how to deal with it.

Research and Development: Job titles here include scientist, medical director, and phase I specialist. Job functions might include:

- Direct phase II–IV clinical trials
- Work with MSLs
- Provide therapeutic expertise in a scientific area
- Oversee clinical trials
- Conduct phase I trials

Earnings Potential: Although there is tremendous potential for a large financial upside in working for industry, many entry-level jobs (depending on your current earnings) may require a pay cut. Entry-level medical directors may start in the $170,000–$210,000 salary range, depending on qualifications. Some positions, such as medical science liaisons, will have much lower initial pay. As such, it is good practice to save money and adjust your lifestyle before making the switch. The tradeoff for this compensation is obviously the training and experience that you will receive. If you perform well, you can reasonably expect advancement in 18 months to two years with 7 to 10 years typically required to reach a very senior position. Sometimes advancement is best accomplished by switching employers—and this may require relocation.

What is the potential financial upside of a career in industry? Upper-level positions may pay in excess of $750,000 salary, large, almost guaranteed bonuses, stock awards, stock options, and sign-on bonuses. Such positions are highly accountable to performance and can easily be lost if management changes.

What You Need to Know: Industry is its own unique world with its own lingo. If you are seriously interested in this field you should gain as much knowledge as you can so that you are conversant with industry language and practices. Speak to other doctors who are in the field. Start reading industry-focused publications. Take continuing education on drug development and regulation. Experience in a clinical research position in an academic institution is a huge plus. Relevant continuing medical education and participation in institutional review boards and relevant hospital and medical association committees also help build a resume for a jump into industry. The basic knowledge one SEAK faculty member feels you should gain prior to applying for jobs in industry includes:

1. A general understanding of the clinical research process (protocol writing, approval, site selections, monitoring, publication, etc.).
2. A basic understanding of statistics.
3. A basic understanding of how patients and investigators are recruited and how studies are approved.
4. How generally the FDA and other regulators interact.

There are many recruiters who focus on industry. It is a good idea to get in touch with as many recruiters as you can if you would like to explore moving into industry. Section 5.9 covers more on recruiters.

Here's what a SEAK physician faculty member with 14 years of experience in industry recommends in terms of landing your first position:

Example 3.18: How to land your first job in industry

The first job is always the toughest. I basically recommend that people start networking with either friends or colleagues or friends of friends who are working in industry to understand what other job opportunities there are, what the roles are like, what they involve, so that they have an understanding of maybe the area that they would like to go into from a job perspective as a medical director, medical science liaison, regulatory affairs, or maybe as a scientist. Once they know that, then they can start looking at companies where maybe they can best apply their existing knowledge and skills. Usually, that's in the same therapeutic area that they are looking at, one that they've been practicing in for years. That way they can offer the company their knowledge and expertise of a given therapeutic area while the company will offer them an opportunity to learn how to work within the company and to fulfill their day-to-day job requirements.

Besides networking, going online to sites like medzilla.com, reading industry publications such as "The Pink Sheet" or "The Gray Sheet" or "Fierce Biotech" gives people inside knowledge of what the industry is involved in so they sound credible when they go on their first interviews. Also, taking a number of courses, say in regulatory affairs or new product development, again, so that they are familiar with the language of the industry so that when they go in to an interview they sound credible and knowledgeable, even if they don't have a lot of industry experience. Once they get that first opportunity, then it will be easier to parlay that into the next opportunity and start looking at going up in their career ladder.

Here's further advice from a chief medical officer of a medical affairs department in terms of positioning yourself for a career in industry and your first opportunity:

Example 3.19: Positioning yourself for your first job in industry

I think for physicians that have an interest in coming into pharma, they should definitely complete their boards and be board certified. It would help them if they had a fellowship in some research experience doing clinical trials at a university or at their private practices. It would help them if they were a speaker for a pharmaceutical company, so they could talk to a sales rep about getting their name considered to be on a speaker's bureau for a pharmaceutical company.

But what they need is to have some exposure to research and to industry before they apply for a position. If they come in totally naïve and have no knowledge whatsoever, the pharma says, "I have to train this person. I don't want that. I want someone who already has some experience or at least knows this is what they want to do."

I think it would also be useful—this won't help a lot of our established physicians, but if you're in the right specialty where there's a lot of drug development, it's also very useful. So for instance, if you are in oncology, neurology, or psychiatry, endocrinology, cardiology—these are areas where there are a lot of products in development and we're needing a lot of physicians with therapeutic expertise. So it's a good boost for you.

[You can also try to target the companies doing research in your clinical area.] There are various ways of doing it. One is obviously if you were doing clinical trials you'd be seeing the products [that] are coming in your therapeutic area. Another area that you can look at the literature and see what is being developed, there is a publication called *R and D Directions,* which is on the internet and every year, usually in the early summer they publish a bibliography of all the products being developed that they know of. And that would be usually several hundred products—where they are in research, which companies.

You can also go onto centerwatch.com, which is a company in Boston that publishes clinical trials to see what products are being developed.

To get a better sense of what employers are looking for and what you would do working in industry, please consider the following sample entry-level job postings for physicians:

Example 3.20: Sample industry job listing
Board certified MD with Infectious Disease experience. Preferred experience in hepatology research.

This position reports to the Director or Senior Director of Clinical Research. Provides high level and complex scientific and clinical guidance to Medical Affairs, Clinical Trials Management, Biomatics, Global Drug Safety, Regulatory and Project management staff to meet project deliverables and timelines. Primary responsibilities include: providing high level input to complex Phase I-IV clinical trial protocol design and clinical study reports as well as Health Authority inquiries. Provides ongoing clinical monitoring for clinical trials including but not limited to assessment of eligibility criteria, toxicity management, and drug safety surveillance. Adheres to strict regulatory requirements of study conduct and industry standards of Good Clinical Practice as well as [company] SOPs. Also manages the clinical research component in the preparation/review of regulatory documents. IND annual reports, IND safety reports, Investigator Brochures and development plans. Coordinates the collection and assimilation of ongoing data for internal analysis and review. Coordinates and manages the preparation and/or review of data listings, summary tables, study results and scientific presentations. Presents scientific information at scientific conferences as well as clinical study investigator meetings. Plays a leading role in the authorship of complex scientific manuscripts and abstracts to scientific meetings and conferences. Leads two or more specific components of departmental complex strategic initiatives.

Typically requires an MD degree with post graduate clinical training and minimum 8 years experience with clinical research and strong familiarity with good clinical practices and International Conference on Harmonization Guidelines is preferred. Excellent scientific written and oral communication skills are required. Must possess a proven ability to work highly effectively with multiple departments. Must be capable of working with attention to detail in a time sensitive environment.

Example 3.21: Sample clinical affairs job listing
AVP, Clinical Affairs

Summary/Essential Duties & Responsibilities:

This physician with expertise in oncology would be responsible for the medical monitoring of multiple clinical trials in all phases of study. He/she would lead cross-functional groups to generate and implement clinical development plans for [drug] and selected pipeline products. This individual would be responsible for design, execution and analysis and reporting of clinical trials both for internal and regulatory uses including pivotal and activity-finding studies in a variety of oncologic indications.

1. Provide medical monitoring for clinical trials
2. Work with biostatistics on trial design and analysis
3. Work with monitoring and contract research organizations on study conduct
4. Adhere to principles of good clinical practice
5. Work with medical writing on reports and presentations
6. Recruit and communicate with investigators
7. Make presentations at internal and external meetings
8. Provide support and advice on safety issues with candidate's compounds
9. Work with discovery on relevant experimental designs for new drug candidates
10. Provide strategic input and backup to other development programs and to the drug safety group and to support the company with external presentations at scientific and commercial meetings.

Essential Knowledge, Skill, Experience:
1. MD with >5 years experience in oncology
2. Excellent working knowledge of clinical oncology practice
3. Thorough familiarity with areas of investigation in relevant tumor types and with the regulatory landscape
4. Excellent communication and presentation skills
5. Ability to manage various functional groups productively

Example 3.22: Sample medical director job listing
Medical Director

Medical Director, Physician Scientist to lead projects in innovative therapeutics for inflammatory diseases.

Preparation of clinical development plans. Design and conduct of Phase I-Iib clinical trials. Participation in development alliance with corporate partners.

Candidates must be a Physician Scientist with MD, board-certified in Internal Medicine. Previous experience in basic or clinical research and at least 3 years of clinical medicine experience preferred. 1-2 years experience in the pharmaceutical industry in clinical development is a plus. Must be willing to work in various sub-specialty areas according to the needs of the project.

Example 3.23: Sample pharmacovigilance job listing
Pharmacovigilance Physician

Position Overview:

The Pharmacovigilance Physician will handle medical review and analysis of serious adverse event reports. He/she will act as responsible PV physician for designated development products for clinical trials and programs. He/she will participate in analysis and preparation of safety data for internal and external use. The Pharmacovigilance Physician will also interface with other functional areas on safety matters.

Key Responsibilities:
- Review medical content, coding, expectedness, company seriousness and causality and provide final follow-up requirements for serious adverse event case reports
- Review of case narratives for submission documents
- In collaboration with Data Management review and sign off of coding from clinical trials
- Facilitate and execute reconciliation of clinical and safety databases

- Perform activities required to serve as PV physician
- Represent Department on Study Teams (working groups, sub-teams) for assigned products
- Provide content and review study related documents including: protocols, Ibs, ICFs, CRFs, SAPs, CSRs
- Develop and implement safety process plans for regulatory reporting and safety letter reporting for clinical trials
- Contribute to preparation and review of periodic reports (IND/Annual Safety)
- Participate in the analysis of safety data from on-going and completed clinical trials
- Review of product complaints for adverse events
- Participate in departmental development activities including SOP and Work Instructions initiation and development

Minimal Requirements:
MD required. 1-2 years clinical experience following post-graduate training with significant knowledge of general medicine. Must have strong leadership skills, and be able to collaborate with several cross-functional teams. Good level of computer literacy with Microsoft applications. Excellent analytical and problem solving skills. Excellent oral and written communication skills. Clinical research and/or industry experience in Safety or in Clinical Development is essential. Knowledge of principles of epidemiology and statistics desired.

Example 3.24: Sample medical affairs job posting
Sr. Director
Medical Affairs

This is a position within the Department of Clinical Development & Medical Affairs, part of the Medicinal Development Group at [company]. This position will oversee Medical Science Liaisons (MSLs) in the US and two to three Associate Directors. The Director will report to and interact with the senior leadership of the Medical Affairs (MA) Department, i.e. the head of Global Medical Affairs and Director, Global MA Operations. The Director is responsible for the medical supervision and team development/management of the US MSL group. The Director will be expected to provide input on a variety of topics and participate in a number of working groups and teams. The Director will transform strategies and objectives into tactical goals for the MSL team. This position is thus responsible for direct reports, implementation and monitoring of the MSL operations budget and active participation in matrix teams in different therapeutic areas with a very heavy focus on hepatitis C. The Director will also conduct the annual performance reviews with two Associate Directors.

The Director will foster the culture of "we wins", innovation, and pursuit of excellence focusing on coaching and mentoring the Associate Directors. This position is focused on US operations.

To qualify for this position, candidates must have an MD (Internal Medicine, Gastroenterology/Hepatology/Infectious Diseases), Pharm D or PhD (with relevant education and experience). The candidate should possess strong leadership capacity, excellent interpersonal and motivational skills and the ability to work well in varied team settings. The applicant must have a strong knowledge of collaborative, investigator-initiated and phase IV study process, as well as excellent reading/writing and oral communication skills. Ability to write and review scientific data is required. The candidate should have demonstrated initiative and problem solving skills and a thorough knowledge of all relevant guidelines and policies (OIG, SOPs, GCPs). Position is based in [city], but requires national/international travel.

Example 3.25: Sample medical science liaison job posting
Regional Medical Oncology Liaison, Western U.S. (FT)

Responsibilities:
The holder of the position is a field-based professional with clinical and therapeutic experience/expertise in oncology. Responsibility for developing and implementing medical and scientific initiatives that support currently marketed laboratory testing products, new products in development and new indications for current laboratory testing products. As such, this individual will belong to the core of the medical professionals that will design and execute medical scientific approaches to [company] laboratories' products and services.

The holder of the position provides scientific information on products and disease state expertise to targeted Opinion Leaders, Healthcare Professionals and Key Decision Makers consistent with the objectives of the Medical Services, Marketing, and Sales.

Major Responsibilities:
- Continually monitor the medical environment to sustain expertise in disease state management and new therapies and analyze the clinical impact of existing and potential technologies relative to predictive and personalized medicine products.
- Identify and engage current and potential customers whose scientific expertise and business knowledge is important to the understanding of our predictive and personalized medicine products.

- Identify pre-clinical, clinical and post-marketing study investigators and selected national medical and scientific thought leaders in response to needs of clinical development, marketing and sales.
- Develop peer-level relationships with pre-clinical, clinical and post-marketing study investigators and selected national medical and scientific thought leaders consistent with the strategy and objectives Medical Services.
- Manage customer inquiries to ensure relevant and appropriate information provided in response to their area of interest.
- Collaborate with Sales to assess key accounts and develop and implement account management strategies for marketing products.
- Assist in the development of, in coordination with Marketing and Sales, teaching materials for Medical Service and Marketing/Sales Personnel relating to new and existing genome based personalized medical testing.
- Identify business and market opportunities that support Marketing goals.
- Provide clinical support and deliver data presentations for national or regional managed care accounts and organizations.
- Adhere to internal standard processes and comply with regulatory and compliance requirements.
- Provide scientific support for company at conferences and meetings.

Minimum Requirements:
- Doctoral Degree in Medicine or equivalent
- Clinical training in oncology
- Demonstrated expertise or experience in medical education process
- Excellent oral and written communication skills and interpersonal skills
- Thorough knowledge of FDA requirements
- Strong leadership ability
- Ability to travel

Preferred:
- Experience in basic or clinical research

Example 3.26: Sample industry job posting
Scientist II, Medical Info.

This position supports the Neurology Team in the Medical Information Department.

The primary focus will be the initial triage of Medical Information requests and the production of responses in accordance with industry standard and [company] policies.

Primary responsibilities include responding to call center inquiries by providing verbal and written clinical and technical information to incoming unsolicited requests for information as well as intake and documentation of adverse events as they relate to [company] products.

This position will also provide support as clinical consultant: Provide clinical support to Sales and Marketing and Medical Affairs; develop and/or participate in training programs and provide training presentations where appropriate; provide support to [company] customers at major scientific meetings; serve as a liaison between Medical Information and other departments.

The Medical Information Specialist will also be expected to contribute to the following activities: critically review and evaluate medical literature for use in developing responses to inbound inquiries; provide clinical support within assigned therapeutic area (Neurology) to internal business partners such as sales/marketing, managed markets, medical affairs etc.; review clinical slide sets and other educational material for accuracy and consistency; participate in clinical review of marketing/promotional materials for scientific accuracy; coordinate coverage and staff MA booth at medical/professional conferences; weekly, monthly, quarterly and annual performance metrics reports; lead ongoing internal training of Medical Affairs staff; conduct Medical Information Sales Training presentations; and participate in on-call responsibilities of the Medical Information Department. Additional opportunities for ad hoc projects expected, including support of a centralized information database, development of internship and fellowship program and other high visibility projects.

Job Requirements
- Understanding of the indications for marketed products and investigational compounds in late development to attempt to identify future topics of scientific interest.
- Knowledge of basic legal/regulatory issues involved with receipt of requests and dissemination of information in order to ensure appropriate acquisition of requestor information; perform initial triage, and construct written responses for requestors.

- Professional demeanor as the primary liaison between the requestor and the company.
- Good organizational and follow-up skills for the successful triage and coordination, and completion of Medical Information requests.
- Advanced knowledge of marketed products and investigational compounds in late development.
- Ability to independently coordinate and supervise all aspects of the fulfillment of a Medical Information request, including the coordination of written responses, de novo literature searches, searches of the post-marketing study database, adverse event searches and other information searches.
- Skilled at cross-functional interactions with members of the Medical Affairs Department, Sales and Marketing, Drug Safety, QA, Customer Service, Sales Training and Information Technology Groups.

Qualifications:
- Minimum of 2 years related experience in a Medical Information role strongly preferred.
- Knowledge of medical terminology and strong computer literacy required.
- Experience working with post-marketing regulations within the industry and their practical implementation preferred.
- Requires strong verbal and written communication skills, a professional demeanor, excellent judgment, and an ability to handle multiple projects and work independently in a dynamic environment.
- Travel to medical conferences, involving overnight travel and occasional weekend travel (20%) is required.

Education:
MD or PhD or PharmD required

Example 3.27: Sample industry job posting
Medical Director

Position Description
As a key member of our renal clinical development team, you will provide medical leadership to cross-functional areas conducting human clinical trials, phases 1 through 4. You will also serve as the main clinical representative for products in earlier stages of development including interpretation of pre-clinical data and development of a clinical development plan. You may perform due diligence review of external products and report findings to renal business unit as needed. Strong leadership, interpersonal and communication skills are essential.

Basic Requirements: The successful candidate will be a MD with clinical training in nephrology. Two to five years experience in clinical research, academic or pharmaceutical is required.

Example 3.28: Sample job posting for clinical research medical associate director
Position Description
We are looking for a board certified Oncologist to join our Clinical Research Team as an Associate Medical Director. This position establishes and maintains direction of the clinical development through strategic planning. Translates clinical research concepts into specific objectives and activities to effective achieve program goals. Ensures the design and conduct of valid clinical studies, generating data supportive of Regulatory application and business/marketing objectives. Directs and/or manages all aspects of the preparation of the clinical sections of regulatory submissions. Develops and manages clinical program budget, identifies and develops relationships with external consultants, investigators and vendors. Evaluates procedures for joint quality control and quality assurance activities. Participates in conferences, scientific meetings, and writing abstracts. Keeps abreast of current state-of-the-art developments relative to the medical program focus, and provides education to clinical staff and other project team members, as needed. The ideal candidate will have strong leadership and effective communication skills as well as a collaborative team work ethic. The ability to travel up to 25% may be required. [Company] offers an integrated global presence, significant expertise getting products to market, and a robust pipeline for the future. Our employees enjoy an excellent compensation and benefits package, including 3 weeks paid vacation, a 401(k) plan with company match, full insurance benefits, and an Employee Stock Purchase Plan.

Basic Qualifications:
MD
1 to 2 years of related experience

Example 3.29: Sample regional medical director job listing
Regional Medical Director

The Regional Medical Director (RMD) is a product and disease/ therapeutic area expert who engages in discussions with Managed Care organizations and healthcare professionals to help the physician achieve positive health outcomes for patients on [company] products. The RMD has a broad understanding of basic and clinical science in the therapeutic areas related to [company] franchises, including quality management and the business environment of medicine. He/she is a resource to the Medical Group Account Manager (MGAM) and Director of Commercial Operations (DCO) and develops and maintains relationships with health care providers, serving as an advisor providing information that is appropriately supportive of [company]'s interests in a balanced and credible manner consistent with the regulatory environment and [company]'s ethical standards. Additionally, provides clinical and scientific support to key decision makers in managed care organizations and state Medicaid agencies. Effects of decisions are long lasting and heavily influence the future course of the organization.

These positions will cover the Central Region of the United States including Illinois, Iowa, Minnesota, Missouri, and Wisconsin.

Qualifications

Educational Requirements:
- MD or DO, US residency/fellowship trained
- Board Certification in primary care or a subspecialty in a field(s) of importance to [company]
- Active US licensure
- 4 + years active practice experience in the United States

Required:
- Strong interpersonal and communication skills
- Proven leadership skills
- Breadth of knowledge in clinical medicine
- Ability to interpret complex technical data to match the communication needs of the recipient
- Understanding of Managed Care/Payer environment
- Understanding of quality management and performance improvement in clinical medicine
- Strong knowledge and understanding of legal and regulatory environment and [company]'s policies
- Experience in a medical business-related role (i.e. pharmaceuticals, managed care, practice management, clinical research organizations, consulting, diagnostics and devices)
- Active role in a scientific, medical or teaching institution.

Example 3.30: Sample job listing for drug safety
Medical Science Director-Pharmaceutical

Job Description:
Identify, assess and appropriately manage safety signals from Phase 1 through Phase 3a development. Effectively represent Global Pharmacovigilance on assigned products' safety review committee activities. Review and evaluate serious event reports and maintain all aspects of medical safety for product lines. Thoughtfully communicate overall safety assessments for assigned products to key stakeholders. Provide medical review for safety sections of protocols, study reports, labels and investigator brochures. Maintain liaisons with Quality Assurance, Document Management, Clinical teams, Legal, and Regulatory Affairs. Assiduously evaluate safety data involving INDs/NDAs and share findings with management. Assist in preparing safety responses to regulatory authorities. Skills-Medical Doctorate or Doctor of Osteopathic Medicine degree is required. A physician who is board certified in internal medicine or family medicine is preferred. Clinical pharmacology or clinical trial experience is also preferred. A minimum of 1 to 3 years of clinical experience within a private practice or academic medical setting. Exemplary medical judgment and analytical thinking ability. The ability to review safety reports and safety sections for labels. Possess familiarity with biostatistics and computer data processing techniques. Strong interpersonal and leadership skills, self motivation, integrity and ethics are required.

Skills/Experience
Requirements:
Medical Doctorate or Doctor of Osteopathic Medicine degree is required. A physician who is board certified in internal medicine or family medicine or ex-US equivalent is preferred. Clinical pharmacology and/or clinical trial experience is also preferred. A minimum of 1 to 3 years of clinical experience within a private practice or academic medical setting. Exemplary medical judgment and analytical thinking ability. The ability to review safety reports and safety sections for labels. Possess familiarity with biostatistics and computer data processing techniques. Strong interpersonal and leadership skills, self motivation, integrity and ethics are required.

Education Requirements:
MD or Doctor of Osteopathic Medicine degree is required.

Significant Work Activities & Conditions:
Continuous sitting for prolonged periods (more than 2 consecutive hours in an 8 hour day)

Percentage of travel: 10%

Example 3.31: Sample medical science liaison job posting
Medical Science Liaison

Job Description:
The Medical Science Liaison (MSL) will advance relationships with established and emerging Regional/National opinion leaders in the Respiratory arena. They will track various asthma and COPD treatment guidelines and interface with the allied health care professionals who shape them. They will be responsible for developing creative and innovative strategies for addressing the specific needs of key customers. Goals will be accomplished by participating in the development and execution of a regional business plan in concert with the business objectives of the commercial organization and appropriate internal customers.

Responsible for implementing and maintaining the effectiveness of the quality system. Work closely with internal customers to develop and execute a business plan designed to meet shared business objectives. Develop tactics for communicating complex scientific information to the healthcare community. Uncover data that may have the potential for publication and/or abstract presentation. Disseminate and convey complex medical and scientific information to professional audiences. Provide necessary clinical support for [company] products in prioritized managed care accounts when appropriate. Present scientific evidence in support of customers developing guidelines and protocols. Develop and maintain professional relationships with Key Opinion Leaders and academic centers in therapeutic areas of commercial and research interests. Provide appropriate scientific and technical support. Develop speakers through one-on-one clinical training on approved clinical slide sets. Act as a clinical resource with professional and advocacy organizations with the objective of developing relationships and identifying potential business opportunities. Identify potential investigators at the request of clinical development. Identify opportunities to partner with accounts on Respiratory initiatives and source as applicable through Medical Affairs. Serve as scientific resource to sales, marketing and clinical as appropriate. Assist with CME content development, medical content review and professional communication materials, and key advocate initiatives. Provide support for answering unsolicited medical questions, adverse event follow through and other clinically related medical information issues.

Skills/Experience Requirements:
Knowledge of applicable regulations and standards affecting Pharmaceutical Products (e.g. CFR 210/211, cGMP) specifically, 3-5 years of clinical experience required. Previous pharmaceutical industry experience preferred. Strong analytical, conceptual and administrative skills. Significant disease and therapy and market expertise. Exceptional communication skills both oral and written

as a need to deliver comprehensive presentations to small/large groups of health care providers and internal management. High level of sensitivity relative to the needs of patients and health care providers. Excellent problem solving ability in concert with strong negotiation skills. Flexibility in adapting/reaching to changing market dynamics and competitive challenges. Tenacity and perseverance to help overcome customer resistance. Teamwork is a mandatory requirement as it involves internal/external networking in the district, region, and across the commercial franchise. High sense of urgency and commitment to excellence in the successful achievement of objectives.

Education Requirements:
Required-Doctorate Degree (PharmD, MD, PhD) due to advanced knowledge required.

Example 3.32: Sample medical director job posting
Medical Director-[Company] Diabetes Care

Job Description:
Primary Function/Primary Goals/Objectives:
1. Establish and implement Medical Policy for [Company] Diabetes Care business
2. Ensure patient safety is designed into [Company] Diabetes Care products
3. Serve as medical representative for issues with regulatory agencies
4. Define medical specifications for product requirements
5. Serve as subject matter expert in medical practice and patient management
   a. Responsibility for all medical risk management decisions associated with on-market product performance issues
   b. Define medical severity ratings for product performance issues in product development
6. Provide strategic guidance through participation in key associations (medical, clinical, industry, regulatory) to influence policy and regulations regarding medical devices
7. May provide medical support for the commercial organization
8. May establish partnerships/consulting arrangements with key medical leaders in the field of diabetes to support business needs
9. In the event this position is in charge of Medical Device Reporting: The incumbent may ensure accurate and timely reporting of medical device reports in compliance with applicable regulations

Traditional and Non-Traditional Non-Clinical Careers for Physicians

Major Responsibilities: Describe the primary responsibilities of this position.
1. Global responsibility for all medical (and clinical, if applicable) affairs functions
2. Providing medical oversight and decision making for all critical product issues related to patient safety
3. Work directly with product development to identify medical requirements for new products
4. Ensure clinical research activities meet business goals (if applicable)
5. Participate in local, state, national and international medical/industry/governmental organizations with the objective of understanding the environment in which the business will operate and ensuring that the Medical Affairs organization can meet the business needs in this area
6. Identify key medical leaders to strategically serve [company] as consultants (if applicable)
7. Provide strategic leadership for the success and cost-effectiveness of Quality System in achieving the business objectives and compliance with current worldwide GCP and Quality System regulations
8. Manage group responsible for medical device reporting (if applicable)

Skills/Experience Requirements:
5+ years experience in direct patient care in the areas of:
[Company] Diabetes Care-Endocrinology, Internal Medicine, and Family Practice preferred.

High personal integrity and ethics required
Excellent communication/organization skills required
Knowledge of clinical research, medical risk management and/or medical device regulations is preferred

Education Requirements:
MD degree with board certification

Percentage of Travel: 10%

Example 3.33: Sample clinical research physician job posting
Clinical Research Physician

Job Description
For more than 130 years, [company] has been dedicated to meeting the health care needs of people in the United States and around the world. We address these needs primarily by developing innovative medicines—investing a higher percentage of our sales in research and development than any other major pharmaceutical company. If you are interested in being considered for employment with a "Best in Class" Pharmaceutical company, please review the following opportunity:

Clinical Research Physician-[Drug X]
Through application of scientific training, clinical expertise, and relevant experience, the US Medical Division clinical research physician (CRP) participates in: design and conduct of local clinical trials; development of local clinical, regulatory, and commercialization strategies; new product launches; and various commercialization activities. The CRP is an integral member of an affiliate brand team for strategic planning, launch, and commercialization support. The CRP may also work closely with corporate program and product team personnel in new product development activities over the entire spectrum from Phases 1-3. This position reports to the US Urology, Women's Health and Osteoporosis Medical Director.

Key Objectives/Deliverables:
- Lead registration pathway for new development program(s)
- Collaborate on ongoing new indication programs
- Responsible for primary regulatory submissions for new indications
- Interaction with external consultants, opinion leaders, and worldwide regulatory agencies
- Primary contact for medical questions and requests related to the studies or indications

Minimum Requirements:
- MD Board Eligible/Board Certified
- Experience in clinical practice, clinical research or pharmaceutical medicine, and the drug development process relevant to the US

Additional Skills/Preferences:
- Excellent communication (written and verbal), interpersonal, organizational and negotiation skills
- A urologist or internist with expertise in erectile dysfunction and benign prostatic hypertrophy would be highly desirable
- Travel: primarily domestic

Example 3.34: Sample drug safety job posting
Scientist Drug Safety (MD)

Description

Drug Safety Scientist: Medical Case Evaluator

Purpose: The Drug Safety Scientist: Medical Case Evaluator (DSS-MCE) is responsible for implementing and coordinating safety surveillance procedures for delegated products. Responsibilities of the DSS-MCE include ensuring corporate compliance with international adverse event reporting requirements; interpreting the medical significance of incoming safety information. In addition the DSS-MCE may participate in preparing assigned regulatory and ad hoc safety reports, and will support the lead DSS.

Responsibilities:
- Implementing safety surveillance policies and procedures for delegated products and/or projects.
- Provide oversight for the AE reporting activities for delegated products and/or projects.
- Participate in the preparation and processing of internal and external AE reports. Review incoming adverse event (AE) information to determine required action based on internal policies and procedures including identifying follow-up on clinically important adverse event reports, and providing medical assessment as relevant.
- Ensure corporate compliance with international adverse event reporting requirements for delegated products.
- Assist the project lead DSS in the preparation of relevant safety documents. This includes writing detailed safety analyses and summaries including signal evaluation reports; regulatory reports such as US periodic reports (USPR) and Periodic Safety update reports (PSUR). In addition may assist the lead DSS in the preparation of other relevant documents such as pharmacovigilance plans, clinical study reports and regulatory approval filing documents.
- Monitor the safety profile of delegated products and collaborate with the lead project DSS to assist in recommending action including labeling amendments and risk management programmes when warranted.

Requirements:
- MD
- At least 2 years clinical experience required
- Medical writing experience required

- Experience with computers required; computer data entry experience preferred
- Pharmaceutical industry experience and pharmaceutical industry safety surveillance experience preferred
- Knowledge of regulatory adverse event reporting requirements preferred
- Management experience preferred

Example 3.35: Sample medical science liaison job posting
Medical Science Liaison II-[Drug X] (Southeast)

We are seeking a Medical Science Liaison (MSL) for the Drug X group within the Immunology, Tissue Growth and Repair (ITGR) Unit. MSLs at [Company] are field-based, highly educated, clinically trained health care professionals who develop and manage Investigator-Sponsored Trials (ISTs) as well as maintain an interactive relationship with key opinion leaders and study investigators. MSLs serve as a link between [Company] and the clinical community by providing current research and education to clinicians and other healthcare providers.

Responsibilities of the [Drug X] MSL include the following:
demonstrating a thorough understanding of both clinical and commercial strategies and priorities; coordinating, maintaining, and facilitating the IST program for the product line; delivering high quality scientific presentations on the vascular products and the overall therapeutic area to physicians and other key external parties; identifying, developing, and maintaining advocacy with key investigators, representing [Company] and the vascular team to the outside clinical community and providing clinical and technical expertise in relevant therapeutic areas by staying current on the scientific literature, attending scientific and key technical meetings, and partnering with [Company] clinical, research and commercial teams; and proactively providing feedback on emerging clinical trends.

Requirements:
Bachelor of Science in a medically relevant discipline (e.g., Nursing, Pharmacy, Medicine, etc), advanced clinical degree required (e.g., MSN, PharmD, PHD, MD) with 3+ years clinical cardiovascular experience; clinical research and/or cardiovascular clinical experience preferred. Pharmaceutical industry experience as a field medical liaison or similar field-based position preferred with a proven track record of success. Experience in public presentation required and education program development preferred. Significant (at least 50%) travel expected.

Example 3.36: Sample medical director pharma job posting
US-OH, PhD-Medical Director 919-MZ

The Medical Director, Musculoskeletal, will provide medical leadership in the development of category and brand strategic positioning, clinical and technical data, professional education materials, and promotion and advertising materials that support the market preparation, launch and ongoing commercialization of prescription products. This involves membership and/or leadership on diverse multifunctional US or Global Teams that are involved in Licensing and Acquisition efforts, develop data, claims, advertising/promotion, and scientific exchange and education materials that respond to the needs of physicians, pharmacists, patients, managed care and/or retail customers. The Medical Director will (1) provide medical support for the development of category and brand strategies, (2) support the licensing and acquisition efforts for the category, (3) support the development of abstracts and symposia at professional and scientific meetings as well as the development of publications that support the brand, (4) provide medical oversight of scientific exchange and education program (SEEP) materials to address the needs of health care providers, (5) lead the design and/or conduct of clinical trials and IIT grants to support commercial and clinical objectives as part of the Life Cycle Plans for each brand, (6) provide medical support for development of advertising, promotional and public relations materials for health care professional, managed care, patients, (7) support medical training for Company sales, commercial and scientific (P&SR) staff, (8) provide medical support for regulatory submissions, product labeling, and post-marketing pharmacovigilance, (9) work with medical experts, key opinion leaders and professional associations to further the understanding and dissemination of knowledge about our products and our therapeutic categories, and (10) be "the face of the brand" to the outside world via leadership as a medical expert and spokesperson for the brand or category.

A MD with clinical specialization, preferably in Rheumatology or Endocrinology is required.

Physicians should not be intimidated or put off by the long list of requirements set forth in the example job listings. Many times, these consist of wish lists that may be difficult or nearly impossible to fulfill. Physicians who come close to meeting the requirements or bring special or unique training and experience should not hesitate to apply for jobs they could excel in. Positions in industry will often be filled by physicians who do not strictly meet the requirements of the corresponding job listings.

Example 3.37: Physician from "wrong specialty" fills position
When I was hired, it was as Vice President Medical Director. In *The New England Journal of Medicine* they were advertising for numerous doctors and various specialties, such as cardiology, psychiatry, orthopedics, oncology, physiatry. The one specialty they weren't advertising for was neurology, but I sent in my application with a cover letter explaining to them why they needed a neurologist but they just didn't realize it…a few days later they called me for an interview and shortly after that they offered me a position.

Marketing, Advertising, Continuing Education, and Communications: To a certain extent, jobs in marketing, advertising, continuing education, and communications can be considered part of the pharmaceutical and device industry. This is because so much of this work has been directly or indirectly funded by industry. The rules governing the influence of industry on marketing and communication are rapidly changing. As a result, there is a certain amount of risk associated with a non-clinical career in this field. The changes in rules may ultimately create more or fewer opportunities for physicians. It remains to be seen which will be the case.

Jobs in this field include working directly for a pharmaceutical or medical device company, working for an advertising agency, or working for a medical communications company. Medical communications companies may put on CME or non-CME promotional education and perform publication planning.

Physicians typically serve in this industry as medical writers or medical directors. A medical writer is self-explanatory. A medical director typically works with other team members to verify that content is medically accurate and clinically relevant. Please consider the following example in which a non-board-certified physician who is a young single mother describes her work-from-home job in medical communications:

Example 3.38: Description of day-to-day work in medical communications
I like the variety of the position that I have. It's a field that you're sort of doing different things from day-to-day. Some days I'm traveling and going to a meeting. Some days I'm working from home and writing a needs assessment or writing a manuscript of some sort. Some days I'm running conference calls with key opinion leaders, faculty members on various topics. I also switch from subject matter to subject matter on a very regular basis. And for me that's very interesting.

I liked the fact that while I was not going to be in clinical medicine anymore, I was still going to be using the information that I had learned as a clinician. So that was a positive for me as well.

As I mentioned before, a lot of it for me also went into work/life balance and figuring out a career that fit my needs in terms of work/life balance.

We asked SEAK faculty members who work in medical communications what they are looking for when they hire physicians for this field. Here are their responses:

Example 3.39: What communications companies look for in physicians
There are a few different things. In general, they're looking for expertise in a particular area. If that person's being hired for a specific type of account or in some cases they are looking for someone who has broad expertise. They are going to be working across several different accounts. In our company, for example, we really look for physicians who can communicate well, which is often a talent that many physicians have to begin with. We're looking for them to communicate both internally and with clients. A physician who can present well really is an asset. In addition to that, in our particular area we look for physicians who have strong writing skills and understand what goes into quality writing, and review other people's writing as well.

Example 3.40: Ideal physician candidate for medical communications company
I think an ideal candidate is interested in researching and able to write. A good communicator, because you're not only sometimes communicating with industry in the way of pitches or just in conference calls and whatnot, but you're also communicating with faculty members a lot.

In one day you might switch from having a conference call with nationally or internationally known oncologists or interventional cardiologists, and then that afternoon you might be having a conference call with somebody in a field completely different. And while they recognize that you're not a specialist and don't have the same knowledge base that they do, of course you do have to be able to have a conversation with them about the content of the materials and what's going to be going on, and you have to gain their respect in a way for the programs to go the way that you would like to see them go.

These opinions are echoed by another SEAK faculty member who recruits physicians for medical marketing:

Example 3.41: What a medical advertising recruiter looks for in physicians
The joy of science is very dear to our heart, but certainly there's got to be a business sense in there as well and they have to be very nice. One of our core

values is grace—substance, style, conviction and grace are our mantra that we'll hit you over the head with if you visit our website. Grace being very important to us—and finding the subset of these people with grace and science background and a little medical knowledge with the business knowledge is a very small subset of people out there. Finding that small talent pool is really where we focus.

Doesn't necessarily mean that they have to have an MBA, but certainly some business sense to them [helps]. But certainly, any other knowledge or background [showing they] have had some exposure to pharmaceutical companies, have worked with them in the past, or were in a speakers program. Some inner knowledge of pharmaceuticals [helps].

Here's what a vice president and talent acquisition partner for a New York healthcare marketing ad agency has to say about his industry and what its physicians do:

Example 3.42: What physicians involved in an ad agency do

We—from typically the pre-launch phase all the way through patent expiration are involved in marketing a product, in making sure that the doctor receives the information so that they have a way of aligning the physician, the product and the patient properly. Letting them know about safety and efficacy and the information that they need to be able to determine whether it's a product they want to recommend to a patient.

They are involved in the core product marketing team, just like an art director and the copy writer and the account person, which is the liaison between the client and the agency. We call it the quad—those four are the primary leads for the team, which can be another 80 people perhaps on the team.

[Our physicians focus] on setting the goals and objectives and on a day-to-day basis, what the person typically does is working within the quad, working with the core product team and very closely with the client. But also talking to key opinion leaders, developing that very fertile field out there for information, doing research and peer reviewed articles, understanding where the competitors are, what's in their pipeline, what could even be in our client's pipeline. Attending conferences that they probably would be attending anyway because of their background and their knowledge, and providing insights into the marketing team so that they can talk better to the client and determine where we want to head with recommendations for the next steps.

Compensation: Base salaries in this field can be in the range of $120,000–$150,000 not including benefits and bonuses for a primary care physician. This could be much higher if the candidate is in a specialized area or in an area that the agency has a particular need for.

Many jobs in this area are concentrated in the New York/New Jersey area. The best way to see what is out there is to network and potentially use a recruiter. The Web site www.shsinc.com is an excellent resource to explore and contains numerous job postings in the fields of medical communications, marketing, and advertising. To get a better idea of some of the opportunities available in this field, please consider the following sample job postings:

Example 3.43: Sample ad agency job posting
Position: VP, Medical Writer
Location: New York

Company Summary:
A full-service advertising agency specializing in the health-care industry. They provide a wide range of marketing, educational, media, and creative services directed at healthcare professionals, providers, business-to-business targets, and consumers.

Description:
Be a part of a team who thinks having fun and being creative are some of the key ingredients to your success. Join an organization that has experienced tremendous growth and doesn't plan to stop anytime soon. See how substance, style, conviction and grace are held as core values and recognized in you.

Our client is seeking VP, Medical Directors, and VP, Medical Writers to join its Medical and Scientific Affairs Department for roles in medical direction and strategy, medical intelligence, medical writing, and advocacy initiatives.

We seek applicants with an advanced degree (PharmD, MD, or PhD) and experience in oncology, cardiology, pulmonology, nephrology, diabetes or internal medicine.

Example 3.44: Sample medical education job posting
Position: Medical Director/Dermatology
Location: New Jersey

Company Summary:
The core of our client's pioneering effort in medical education is a thorough understanding of the current science that drives how physicians diagnose and treat, as well as an understanding of the market systems that influence decision making.

Description:
  Job Description:
  Provide scientific and clinical expertise at a medical
    education/communications company
  Dermatology experience preferred
  Build relationships with clinical and research executives in the
    pharmaceutical industry as well as academic opinion leaders
  Plan and manage scientific presentations and publications
  Help develop medical education programs
  Provide independent medical direction for ongoing and new business
    activities, with minimal day-to-day direction from manager
  New business pitch preparation activities
  New business presentations
  Manage publication planning activities for assigned accounts
  Problem solving
  Development of product positioning and messages for new products
  Balancing work quality with timelines
  Prioritization of multiple competing projects
  Managerial direction
  Make decisions on content and fair balance, in consultation with account
    management and program management
  Self-management to adhere to agreed-upon T&Es and budgets; alert team
    to potential deviations and overages
  Proactively work with program management and account management to
    ensure timely delivery of high-quality content

Requirements:
  2+ years experience in patient care or medical education
  Advanced degree in biomedical sciences (PharmD, PhD, MD preferred)
  Developing educational concepts and content through critical analysis of
    data, distilling complex technical information for a variety of medical
    audiences, working with opinion leaders
  Knowledge of CME procedures

Writing proposals
Editing documents
Clinical research and publication experience is a plus
Ability to provide independent medical direction
Strong written and verbal communication and presentation skills
Software: Microsoft Word, PowerPoint, reference database programs such
    as Refman
Familiarity or interest in pharmaceutical marketing
Must work well in a team-oriented environment
Ability to meet deadlines while working on multiple, parallel projects
Develop solid understanding of the market and goals advocated by the
    medical and marketing clients

Example 3.45: Sample continuing medical education job posting
Assistant Medical Director
Connecticut

Company Summary:
Full-service, continuing medical education (cme) agency that services strategic
development and implementation of long-term medical education programs.

Description:
The role of the Assistant Medical Director is to support the scientific creation
and development of medical education or commercial materials for distribution
as contracted by pharmaceutical clientele while under the supervision of a
senior-level medical director.

Responsibilities:
- To support single or multiple brand projects and programs in which the
  development of medical education or commercial materials is directly
  supervised by a senior level medical director
- To acquire academic/clinical mastery of product trends
- To become an expert in your assigned therapeutic discipline with
  respect to clinical development and literature regarding your products
- To become aware of product market share as well as marketing and
  medical communication strategies of the client
- To assist senior-level medical directors and their products as necessary
- To establish his or her director-related role
- The assistant director will attend staff and scientific services meetings
  and report on job progress and departmental inefficiencies

- Responsibilities include but are not limited to the production of product monographs, faculty slide kits, executive summary, and original and secondary articles for commercial or education purposes
- Other responsibilities may be delegated by senior level medical directors

Milestones to achieve for career advancement:
- Produces successful products that have been delivered to clientele.
- Acquires a level of independence consistent with advancement to the associate level. Managing your time, responsibilities, and client work effectively are essential for career development and quality of deliverables presented to clientele.
- Demonstrates proficiency, excellence, and consistency in the duties described above.
- Has established efficient working relationships with program directors.

Requirements:
- MD or PhD in biomolecular (e.g., Immunology, Genetics, Molecular Oncology, Microbiology) or biomedical (e.g., Neurophysiology, Physiology, Clinical Pharmacology, Oncology, or Medical Psychology) or sciences
- 0–2 years experience in the medical communication/education industry
- The candidate will have expertise in the basic science of the proposed therapeutic target area with the ability to rapidly acquire new information pertaining to the development and execution of medical marketing initiatives of the pharmaceutical industry
- A strong publication record should highlight writing skills

INSURANCE

Any type of insurance company whose business is affected by an insured's health will tend to employ physicians in non-clinical roles. One of the nice things about insurance companies is that they are located all over the country. Some industries tend to be located in a few areas. For example, jobs in financial services tend to be in New York, Boston, and Charlotte. Jobs in pharma tend to be concentrated in the Northeast, California, and a few other areas. Insurance companies, however, are regulated and licensed on a state-by-state basis and have positions for physicians throughout the country. As the chief medical officer of a large health insurer attests:

Example 3.46: Insurance jobs exist everywhere
[Non-clinical jobs at insurance companies] exist everywhere...Somebody asked me if I would go to Idaho to be the medical director of Blue Cross of Idaho, so they're all over the place.

Working for an insurance company is certainly not a good fit for every physician. The major disadvantage to careers in insurance is that dealing with insurance companies is a leading reason why physicians want to leave clinical practice in the first place. Also consider the advice of one SEAK faculty member who worked many years in the insurance industry:

Example 3.47: You should have a thick skin if you want to work in insurance
These are not jobs [where] you're going to make people happy and you have to have a very thick skin. I tell people you're going to—virtually any decision you make is going to upset somebody. It's going to upset a member, a doctor, a hospital, a purchaser, your boss, the CFO, someone is going to be upset. So if you think you're going to be liked, this is not the job for you. You have to have an incredibly thick skin because any decision you make might make somebody happy, but it's also going to make somebody very unhappy. You have to realize that. The difference between clinical medicine and—one of the differences is when you're a clinician, you're advocating for that single patient that's in your office at that time. As a medical director, one of the things we have to do is look at populations of patients and so instead of spending—there's a new drug out. It's $500,000.00 a year. Instead of spending $500,000.00 a year on one drug for one patient, should we be using that money to cover better immunizations or more immunizations for more people? So you have to make these kinds of trade offs, and they're very difficult.

Here's what a chief medical officer of a disability insurance office has to say about lifestyle, working conditions, and pay in his industry:

Example 3.48: Lifestyle, working conditions, and pay in disability insurance field
With respect to lifestyle, it is significantly better. There's no call in insurance medicine. It is typically defined by working hours. Malpractice litigation is almost unheard of. There is some liability with respect to errors and omissions, but it's significantly less than that for malpractice. With respect to supervision, generally, in a clinical setting you are supervised by a clinician. In an insurance

Non-Clinical Careers for Physicians

setting, you are supervised generally by a non-clinician. So, there are some medical things that you have to take time and explain, etc. with respect to your role, your role in a clinical setting, you are much more primary to the patient care activity. When you are in the disability setting, you are part of a team. So, you do not have the sole single voice. With respect to autonomy, you have much more autonomy in a clinical setting than when you are a member of a team. Your input is only one of many team members. It is actually one of the significant areas where they differ. If you don't have to be the boss, then it's a lot easier. Pay; it depends. Hourly pay is significantly better than for most clinical endeavors. Typical clinical pay for general practice, say in an emergency room or urgent care center, ranges from $50-$70. This is for 2007. Usually, insurance contractors that are doing disability insurance, either for workers' comp or for group disability insurance, earn about, anywhere, depending on specialty etc., between $125 and $200 an hour. The more experience you have, the better analysis you can provide with respect to your written opinions, the more you can earn.

If you are considering a non-clinical career in the insurance industry, it may be a good idea to check out the following organizations:

- The American Academy of Insurance Medicine: www.aaimedicine.org
- The American College of Physician Executives: www.acpe.org
- America's Health Insurance Plans: www.ahip.org
- National Association of Managed Care Physicians: www.namcp.com
- American College of Healthcare Executives: www.ache.org

The major types of insurance companies that employ physicians are health insurers, disability insurers, life insurers, workers' compensation insurers, and independent review organizations.

Health Insurers: There are innumerable non-clinical positions for physicians in health insurance organizations. The job responsibilities could include designing plans, performing utilization reviews, approving or denying services (e.g., pre-authorizations), physician relations (e.g., contracting), medical quality, medical informatics, provider affairs, pharmacy affairs, and professional affairs. Note that there are also related non-clinical positions available to physicians in large employers who self-

98

insure, medical management/utilization review organizations, hospitals, integrated delivery systems, and as a consultant to all of the above.

Some of the job titles available to physicians in health insurance companies can include:

- Medical Director of Clinical Affairs
- Medical Director of Quality
- Medical Director of Utilization Management
- Senior Medical Director
- Deputy Medical Director
- Associate Medical Director
- Regional Medical Director
- Medical Director of Medical Informatics
- Medical Director Provider Affairs
- Medical Director of Pharmacy
- Medical Director Medical Policy
- Medical Director Professional Affairs
- Chief Medical Officer
- Chief Operating Officer
- Chief Executive Officer

Entry-level positions for physicians in health insurers typically entail performing utilization reviews, setting medical policy for health plans, and working with physicians to improve the quality and reduce the cost of healthcare. The average tenure of a medical director in managed care insurance is 4 to 5 years. The tenures average out to be short because there are frequent mergers, acquisitions, and divestitures. Here's a recent job posting for an entry-level non-clinical position at a health insurance company:

Example 3.49: Sample health insurance medical director job posting
Medical Director Associate

Description: The medical director associate will be a member of the clinical leadership team. The individual will provide day-to-day guidance, support, and leadership for the clinical and quality activities. Essential duties may include, but are not limited to:
- provides support to nurse care managers in daily tasks

- performs utilization management review (prior authorization, appeal and grievance review)
- participates in peer-to-peer discussions
- identifies opportunities for improved quality of care
- reviews medical policy and technology assessments
- assists with implementing QI initiatives
- supports practitioner/provider credentialing
- performs other duties as assigned

Qualifications
- MD or DO with board certification required
- 5 or more years clinical experience with expertise in medical management required
- Excellent oral and written communication required
- Demonstrated effective negotiation and leadership skills required
- Excellent interpersonal skills required to interact with all levels of associates and customers

Disability Insurers: Disability insurance is a field that is growing significantly. According to the National Health Interview Survey, from age 30 to 65, 30% of the working population will have a disability incident of six months or greater. The Social Security Administration estimates that the number of disabled Americans will double in the next 20 years.

Private disability insurance carriers typically use physicians for disability assessment (is a claim medically supported under the policy language?) and for underwriting (is the applicant insurable and how much of a risk is the applicant?). The work in disability assessments and underwriting typically involves reviews of the claimant's or applicant's medical records and other documentation, for example, an insurance application or the insurance policy. The physician's medical expertise is utilized. Here's what a physician who hires entry-level physicians for a large disability carrier has to say about what disability insurers look for:

Example 3.50: What disability insurance carriers look for in physician employees
They really want you to be clinically expert. That [and...] board certification. If you don't have board certification, there's a number of lower level certifications, such as, in terms of the time commitment, pain management certifications,

100

sport medicine certifications, etc. that can in some way substitute for it, but board certification is the primary criteria besides clinical excellence. They are looking for decisiveness; that you can look at a complex patient with multiple conditions and give a clear answer as to whether you feel they are disabled or not disabled, what the degree of disability is, if they are currently disabled, when they might get better or not, and support your answers with rational arguments. Particularly, if you disagree with the doctor saying that the patient is disabled. You need to articulate your answers. Those would be the big criteria: decisiveness, clinical excellence, board certification, and ability to write a reasonable argument, and to support your argument.

In terms of specialties, disability insurers are generally looking for family practice, internal medicine, occupational medicine, physiatry, psychiatry, orthopedics, rheumatology, cardiology, neurology, oncology, and pulmonary-sleep medicine.

Private disability insurers (some of the largest include CIGNA, Standard, Unum, Aetna, The Hartford, Prudential, Sun Life Financial, Reliance Standard, Lincoln Financial Group, and MetLife) typically employ some physicians in-house and also utilize outside consulting physicians. Some disability claims are managed by claims management companies. The top organizations for this include Unum, DMS (Disability Management Services), Berkshire/Guardian Life, and Mass Mutual. There is also work available for physicians as employees for or as consultants to the Social Security Administration (http://www.ssa.gov/disability/professionals/) to help resolve claims for Social Security disability. Here's a recent job posting for an entry-level non-clinical position at a disability insurance company:

Example 3.51: Sample disability insurer job posting
Medical Consultant

Description
Come and share your professional expertise with a Fortune 250 Insurance company and marketplace leader in disability-based insurance products and return to work services. Our people truly make a difference, both in the lives of our customers and in the success of our company.

This position is responsible for providing expert medical analysis of complex claims files. This includes such matters as providing opinions on work capacity, on the presence or absence of pre-existing conditions, on diagnostic criteria and therapeutic approaches to medical conditions and other determinations.

Principal Duties and Responsibilities:
1. Provides timely and accurate written medical analyses and opinions to the Benefits Operations staff
2. Applies current medical knowledge to medical data regarding diagnosis, treatment, prognosis, and impairment, etc.
3. Participates in the various medical risk management activities
4. Conducts 1-on-1 and group training to improve the Benefits Operations staff's knowledge and efficiency
5. Communicates with the policy holders attending healthcare provider(s) through phone calls, letters, etc.
6. Manages special projects as required

Qualifications
- Professional Degree (MD or DO)
- Residency trained
- Board certified
- Active, unrestricted US license
- Greater than seven years clinical experience in Internal Medicine or Family Practice
- Experience in private disability insurance or other corporate environment preferred
- Analytical skills appropriate to private insurance environment
- Familiar with or willing to learn electronic medical recordkeeping systems
- Excellent oral and written communications skills
- Excellent interpersonal/negotiation skills

Offers competitive pay, relocation assistance and excellent benefits. Come join us if you're interested in working in an exciting and challenging environment for a company that is on the move!

Life Insurers: Entry-level physician jobs for life insurance companies typically revolve around underwriting—determining the risk to the insurance company of insuring an applicant's life. These positions are typically a good fit for primary care physicians such as internists and family practitioners. Life insurance is a fragmented industry with life insurance companies located throughout the country. In light of this, this could be a good fit for someone who is unable or unwilling to relocate. Here's a recent job posting for an entry-level non-clinical position at a life insurance company:

Example 3.52: Sample life insurance job posting
Medical Director

This position of medical director provides a unique opportunity for primary care physicians who enjoy medicine but would like a stimulating and challenging career without the erratic schedule of a busy medical practice. While better time control and work/life balance is a perk, the medical director position is a full-time, challenging career with many growth opportunities.

Our medical directors are no longer responsible for treating patients' individual diseases, but they continue to use their medical expertise to understand how diseases and the risk factors associated with these diseases affect and individual's mortality and morbidity.

Since medical directors usually encounter a broader range of pathology than practicing primary care physicians, their work is intellectually challenging and requires creative problem solving to deal with these complex, and sometimes ambiguous medical issues. Their underwriting work must also stand up to legal and clinical judgment so they must possess a broad medical knowledge. To maintain their expertise, medical directors keep abreast of developments in clinical medicine through ongoing review of the medical literature and regular attendance at continuing medical education meetings.

As a resource for the company, medical directors use their education and interpersonal skills when providing consultations to the multiple departments they serve. Medical directors also provide educational sessions to others in the company, including underwriters and claims analysts on a wide array of medical conditions.

The staff of experienced and skilled medical directors in the Underwriting Standards department is responsible for establishing medical underwriting standards that will maintain the company's favorable mortality and morbidity results.

Medical directors enjoy mutual admiration in the company and are supported by and collaborate with actuaries, lawyers and other business professionals. They also work to nurture relationships with the field, outside physicians and the community. In addition, they represent the company at industry-related activities, such as the American Academy of Insurance Medicine, and must retain certification by the American Board of Insurance Medicine.

This position requires an MD or DO degree, board certification in Internal Medicine, Internal Medicine/Pediatrics or Family Practice followed by at least three years of clinical experience. The candidate must also hold or be able to obtain Wisconsin State Medical Licensure. Excellent verbal and written communication skills are a must as are outstanding interpersonal skills. The ability to independently evaluate complex medical cases and produce medical standards, exhibit ethical behavior and demonstrate excellent judgment is also required.

Workers' Compensation Insurers: Workers' compensation insurers typically utilize physicians to perform disability assessments and conduct utilization reviews. They may utilize physicians as employees or as independent contractors. Workers' compensation insurers are based in many parts of the country so this is a good choice for a physician who may live in a state with less industry than the Northeast or West Coast. Since alleged work-related injuries typically involve musculoskeletal or mental injuries, physicians who specialize in these areas are generally the best fit for these positions (such as neurologists, orthopedists, neurosurgeons, occupational medicine physicians, physiatrists, or psychiatrists).

Independent Review Organizations: Independent review organizations (IROs) exist to perform utilization reviews for other organizations such as insurance companies. IROs employ physicians as both contractors and full- and part-time employees. Signing up first as a contractor performing peer reviews is an excellent strategy to see how you would like working for an IRO and to also gain and demonstrate experience in the field. If you would like to do contract work, contact the IRO and ask to be placed on their panel. Fees for contract work typically range from $85–$200/hour (potentially more). The work can be done from home in most cases, but many IROs will want you to continue "in active practice" (at least part-time) for you to be eligible to do contract peer reviews.

A list of accredited IROs and a job posting board can be found at URAC's Web site www.urac.com. (URAC originally stood for "Utilization Review Accreditation Commission." However, that name was shortened to just the acronym "URAC" in 1996 when URAC began accrediting other types of organizations such as health plans and preferred provider organizations.) IROs include Broadspire Services, Inc. (www.choosebroadspire.com), Concentra Physicians Review (http://physicianreview.concentrahealth.com/), Medical Review Institute of America (www.mrioa.com), and MLS (www.mls-ime.com). Here's an entry-level job posting from an IRO so that you can get an idea of the type of work involved:

Example 3.53: Sample independent review organization job posting
Medical Director

Position Schedule: Full-Time Employee
Salary Range: $134,814–$202,220

Job Responsibilities
Position Summary: This position is responsible for managing the medical review activities of the [employer].

Essential Functions:
40% directs medical review activities of the organization. Conducting critical peer reviews to ensure healthcare given is appropriate and necessary. Instructs other physician reviewers on critical reviews and improvement of healthcare.

30% assists [employer] staff with training physician reviewers regarding their responsibilities and functions. Serves as a technical expert on the peer review process.

20% represents [employer]'s policies and procedures to medical and non-medical persons. Participates in committee meetings representing the company.

10% performs miscellaneous duties as assigned.

Minimum Education & Other Requirements
Requirements:
Current medical license.
Positions working on specific contracts may require U.S. Citizenship.

Because of the nature and immediacy of the work, the ability to maintain regular and predictable attendance is essential.

Additional Comments:
10% local and overnight travel.

GOVERNMENT
There are numerous non-clinical positions available for physicians in federal, state, and local governments. If you are passionate about positively affecting the lives of many more people than you could practicing clinical medicine, the government might be a good choice for

your non-clinical career. As one SEAK faculty member who spent twenty years in federal service put it, "What I liked was the ability to really have an impact on a lot of people." The types of things you can make a difference with when working for the government include:

- Applied public health: Prevent and control injury and the spread of disease and ensure safe drinking water, food, and medications.
- Global health: Work with other nations and international agencies to address global health challenges.
- Emergency response (a growing field): Provide public health and clinical expertise in response to emergencies and disasters.
- Research: Research the prevention, treatment, and elimination of disease.

When exploring government jobs, consider how flexible you are in terms of relocating. Federal non-clinical jobs for physicians tend to be concentrated in Atlanta, Maryland, and the District of Columbia. Once in federal service, there is also the possibility of transfer to another state.

Jobs for physicians in state government will obviously be located in that state. Positions can involve public health, administration, utilization management, medical licensing, occupational health and safety, and many other functions. Compensation varies widely for these positions with some being relatively low. Some positions may also require part-time clinical work. Good places to start to research the available positions in your state are the state and local health departments, the state physician licensing agency, and the state workers' compensation department.

Government jobs may focus on public health, research, epidemiology, occupational health and safety, and other areas. Experience or advanced education in these areas may help position a candidate to land the right job. Keep in mind as well that positions in the government can also better position physicians to later go back to the private sector and launch a career. For example, a stint at the FDA could be invaluable experience for a candidate looking for a lucrative pharma position with tremendous upside earning potential. With this fact in mind, physicians may want to think long-term about the value of government employment experience. Here's how a physician who works in pharma describes how his employment at the NIH was invaluable to his moving to industry:

Example 3.54: How government employment can position you for a career in industry
The senior management at [big pharma company] were my former bosses at the NIH and when they left NIH and joined industry, they remembered this strange doctor who liked to work late at night and gave me a call and it was an offer I couldn't refuse.

The best thing I could ever have done was the NIH. I really struggled before going to NIH—would I go into private practice or NIH? The change in salary was a five- to ten-fold difference. The NIH salaries were very low, but I decided I wanted again to sort of follow my interest, and the money would come. And so I spent four years at the NIH—best four years of my life. It was terrific for making contacts, networking, developing a deep expertise in a certain area and then from that...I went into practice, used those contacts to continue research activity, speaking with my contacts at NIH and in pharmaceutical companies.

Numerous federal agencies employ physicians. These include the National Institutes of Health (research), the Centers for Disease Control and Prevention (epidemiologists—an MPH is helpful for these positions), the Food and Drug Administration (medical reviewers as part of drug approval process), and the Center for Medicare and Medicaid Services (policy development, medical reviewers, and administrators). The CDC provides on-the-job training in epidemiology through its two-year (paid) Epidemiology Intelligence Service entry-level training program. (Visit www.cdc.gov for more information.) If you are interested in searching currently available jobs with the federal government, an excellent resource is www.usajobs.com.

If you're looking for a government job, a good technique is to try to get in contact directly with the person who makes hiring decisions. As one SEAK faculty member who spent 23 years in federal service put it:

Example 3.55: Find the decision maker and contact that person directly
I think whether it's the government or someplace else, the more you can figure out exactly what it is that you want to do and exactly where you want to do it, the more you can focus your activities. For example, perhaps you're a cardiologist and you're interested in working for the Food and Drug Administration, one thing we might want to do is identify through the internet who is in charge of approving the cardiac drugs and then sending that person an e-mail with your CV attached or drop them a note. But these days, e-mail is probably best.

Compensation: Available compensation working for the government is usually more transparent than when seeking employment at a private company. Salary ranges are often posted right on the job descriptions. Depending on your situation, these salaries may be very competitive— especially taking into account lifestyle, hours, benefits (potentially a full pension) and lack of potential legal exposure. They are sometimes very poor, however. In any event, the potential financial upside for working as a government employee is limited. If you're looking to get rich, the government is not the place to work for the rest of your career.

Here's just a small sample of federal and state government non-clinical job postings:

Example 3.56: Sample NIH job posting
Department of Health and Human Services
National Institutes of Health
National Institute on Aging
Intramural Research Program
Clinical Research Branch

STAFF CLINICIANS
The Clinical Research Branch (CRB) of the National Institute on Aging (NIA) is recruiting for two Staff Clinician positions within its Intramural Research Program (IRP).

The NIA, IRP, CRB is a major research component of the National Institutes of Health (NIH) and the Department of Health and Human Services (HHS). The CRB, located in Baltimore's Harbor Hospital, is dedicated to research in areas including, but not limited to, longitudinal studies and interventional trials with a focus on cardiology, neurology, immunology, endocrinology and oncology disease areas and geriatric syndromes including frailty.

We are recruiting two Staff Clinicians: one in the area of Genetics and one in the area of Internal Medicine. These Clinicians will participate in a clinical and translational research program as an Investigator of research studies aimed at applying innovative basic research findings to patients. Candidates must have an M.D. or M.D./Ph.D. and be board certified or eligible in Internal Medicine. Previous experience in clinical research and clinical trials is desirable.

Salary is commensurate with research experience and accomplishments and a full Civil service package of benefits (including retirement, health, life and long-term care insurance. Thrift Savings Plan participation, etc.) is available.

Example 3.57: Sample state health department job posting
Position Opening: District Health Officer

The State Department of Health is seeking qualified candidates for the position of Physician, Senior, District Health Officer. This position serves as the county health officer of any or all counties in a public health district facilitating the health interests of the people of [state] and enforcing State laws and Board of Health regulations. This position will be responsible for the following areas:

- Providing oversight of activities within the assigned public health district necessary to comply with State law and Board of Health regulations regarding health protection of the State's citizens, and such other assignments related to protecting the public's health as may be delegated by the State Health Officer.
- Coordinating multiple projects, and other assignments related to the promotion of the public's health, as delegated by the State Health Officer and that require specialized medical knowledge and skills.
- Participating in the Bio-terrorism Preparedness and Response Program, including vaccination program for first responders who may be exposed to infectious diseases when sent to bio-terrorism or disaster locations.
- Assuring continuous quality improvement in medical services, regulatory monitoring and enforcement, health protection and health promotion activities.
- Carrying out such initiatives, programs, responsibilities or duties as may be assigned by the State Health Officer.

Position Availability: To build a list of qualified, interested applicants for a full-time position which reports directly to the State Health Officer. Position involves statewide travel.

Salary Range: Negotiable, depending on amount of time worked and in accordance with State Personnel Board rules and regulations.

Minimum Requirement: Licensed to practice medicine in [state].

Example 3.58: Sample state health officer job posting
State Health Officer

The State is seeking qualified candidates for the position of State Health Officer. This position is appointed by and serves at the pleasure of the Director, Department of Health and Human Services.

Salary to $152,216

Salary range reflects retirement contributions by employee and employer.
Employer-paid contribution plan is available with a reduced gross salary.

The Position: Working cooperatively with the State Board of Health and local boards of health, the incumbent is responsible for the enforcement of laws and regulations pertaining to public health. Responsibilities include interpreting, implementing and providing guidance on federal and state laws and Board of Health regulations; investigating causes of disease, epidemics, source of mortality and nuisances affecting the public health; directing the work of subordinate staff.

Qualifications: Licensure or eligible for licensure as a physician or administrative physician in [state] and U.S. citizenship. Prior administrative experience and experience collaborating with public or private entities is preferred.

NON-PROFITS

If you are financially positioned to be able to do so, working at a non-profit may be a good fit for you. There can be tremendous personal satisfaction in helping a non-profit entity succeed in its mission. Non-profits that tend to employ physicians include philanthropic organizations, professional associations (state, national, and specialty), and non-profit research organizations. Many positions at non-profits are part-time only, which further limits the physician's earning potential. However, for physicians seeking more free time or who would like to maintain an active part-time clinical practice, this could be an excellent fit.

A large employer of non-clinical physicians is the American Medical Association (www.ama-assn.org), located in Chicago, with smaller offices in New Jersey and Washington, DC. State and specialty associations may also employ physicians. The AMA maintains job postings on its Web site. Here's a sample job listing from the AMA:

Example 3.59: Sample job listing from the American Medical Association
Vice President, Medical Education

Join the American Medical Association (AMA), the nation's largest professional Association of physicians, and help doctors help patients by providing vision, leadership, direction, and managerial and budgetary oversight for AMA programs across the continuum of medical education, from undergraduate, through graduate, to continuing physician professional development. This includes: 1) providing input into AMA's policy development process and influencing AMA's advocacy on medical education issues; 2) developing and leading programs consistent with the needs of an evolving medical education environment; 3) overseeing AMA efforts to improve the interface among physicians, the medical education community, and the medical education accreditation, regulatory, and certification bodies; 4) providing physicians and the medical education community with scientifically sound information on medical education; 5) serving as an AMA spokesperson on medical education issues and as a liaison with other organizations involved in medical education; and 6) enhancing value for AMA members and the medical profession as a whole.

Requirements

Extensive experience in medical education and academic medicine is required. In-depth knowledge of current issues and ability to participate on a senior level in medical education forums are essential.

Excellent leadership skills, particularly a demonstrated ability to motivate and inspire an experienced professional staff to perform at a continually high level and skills in planning and prioritizing.

Exceptional interpersonal and communication skills appropriate for interactions with all levels of management, the Board of Trustees, Councils and Sections, the House of Delegates, physician members and nonmembers and leaders of outside organizations.

Exceptional written communication skills, including the ability to write articles for professional publications and reports for policy bodies (e.g., the Board of Trustees, Council on Medical Education, and House of Delegates).

Strong presentation and speaking skills to deliver AMA messages to a wide variety of audiences, occasionally with limited time for preparation and potentially including testimony before Congressional committees or other governmental agencies.

Polished analytical skills to identify emerging policy issues, review and evaluate literature, evaluate relevant AMA policies, and identify and recommend alternatives that are consistent with AMA policy.

Experience in evaluating and directing programs, including developing and managing budgets, grants, and contracts and experience in handling all aspects of human resource management, including staff development.

Strong planning and organizing skills and a track record of successfully managing a high-volume workload and coordinating a number of projects and programs at one time.

Strict adherence to medical ethics and organizational policies, sensitivity to association priorities and politics, respect for members and staff, tact, and ability to maintain confidential information.

MD degree required. Additional graduate training, eg, Med, MPH, MS, or MBA, an asset. National reputation in medical education. Polished negotiation and coalition-building skills. Extensive travel and representation required.

In return for your expertise, we offer a competitive salary, attractive benefits, and an opportunity to make a difference.

INFORMATICS

Medical informatics is where technology, people, and information merge. Examples include electronic health records, telemedicine (the use of information over telemetry to take care of patients), and artificial intelligence to support clinical decisions.

Medical informatics is a rapidly growing field. As such, it offers many opportunities for physicians. In the words of a physician with over ten years of experience in this field:

Example 3.60: "Medical informatics is what's happening"
Medical informatics is what's happening. It's the next technology. We know that medical informatics, particularly the electronic health record, has been shown to improve clinical and financial outcomes. There's some inevitability to this. In addition, there are increasing government drivers and legislation to make this happen because of those very reasons. Whether you like technology or not, it's certainly being used and it's being used for good. It's a great way for a physician, for any healthcare professional, whether that person be a pharmacist or physician or a nurse, to utilize their knowledge in a way that's helping the health of an entire population instead of one patient at a time.

There are roles for physicians at vendors such as Cerner Corporation (www.cerner.com), McKesson Corporation (www.mckesson.com), and Eclipsys (www.eclipsys.com) who develop and market informatics products. In the words of a SEAK faculty member with vast experience in this field:

Example 3.61: Non-clinical careers with informatic vendors
There are vendors, like electronic health record companies or clinical decision support companies that want to hire physicians for a number of reasons. They need physicians to help design systems, to give advice as to how work flow should go, and of course to help sell. It doesn't mean that these physicians or healthcare professionals need to sell per se, but they need to support the sales process because the end user or the client is usually another physician.

A good resource for those interested in the industry side of medical informatics is the Healthcare Information and Management Systems Society (www.himss.org). Bigger vendors will typically involve more structure and stability and you will be allowed to focus on a niche. Decision making can be laborious and can require numerous meetings. Small start-up vendors tend to be less structured and need their employees to dabble in different areas at different times.

Hospitals and other large healthcare providers/systems typically employ chief medical information officers who report to either the chief information officer or the chief medical officer. Because there are jobs in informatics in health delivery organizations, these jobs will exist throughout the country. As such, medical informatics can be a good fit for someone who does not wish to relocate. These jobs also typically pay less than those in industry but are more family friendly with far less travel and shorter hours. One SEAK faculty member describes the role of an informatics physician within a hospital or healthcare provider as follows:

Example 3.62: Informatics opportunities within hospitals and other healthcare providers
Another role for a physician to play is in his or her hospital or healthcare system. That person could be the chief medical information officer. Usually that person is someone who has earned the respect of his peers and can "herd cats" so to speak and kind of help everybody get onboard with one idea, and make decisions together, and help with the adoption of new technology. So, the choosing of technology from a vendor and then helping people implement and execute that plan. Perhaps starting with a user group and rolling out to the greater physician population is the role of the chief medical information officer. That person would interact, probably, with the CIO or the director of information technology as well as other members of the executive team at that healthcare system.

Here's how a SEAK faculty member who works in informatics for a $5 billion healthcare system describes her job and what she feels is needed to succeed in it:

Example 3.63: What a physician working in informatics for a healthcare system may do
Most of what I do is provide leadership in the design and strategy for how we deploy clinical systems in the clinical care environment. These are clinical systems for, for example, the medication use lifecycle, electronic health records,

patient computing and the like. And in my particular area, I manage a team of about 20-some-odd folks, and about 20 developers, project managers, analysts in the design and deployment of knowledge-based for the clinical support systems.

I spend a lot of time in meetings, providing direction, managing people, designing budgets, and providing strategic plans and vision for how these clinical systems need to evolve in order to meet the needs of personalized medicine and the changing demographics in the market.

You have to have very strong people skills. First of all, you're always selling, because you're selling your ideas. You're selling your designs. You're also always listening. The selling includes enormous listening to your business sponsors, to your users, who are often not your sponsors, and to the market in order to help educate everyone about what you think they need in order to succeed in the way they deploy technology. It requires enormous people skills to be listening and selling all the time.

At the top level [of my organization] there's enormous sponsorship for dissemination of clinical systems, and I think that the majority of the conversation actually focuses on what's the best way to do that. And there are a lot of competing ideas, a lot of competing opinions, competing priorities, and shrinking dollars or at least the dollars sometimes become flat, particularly in the current economic environment. It's very much a marketplace of ideas construct, where it's very important to be very clear about what the business value is, of what you're proposing to do, and why it's going to really greatly improve the business performance and the quality performance of your health care organization.

Informatics Consultants: There are also opportunities for physicians to become consultants in the area of medical informatics. Many large consulting firms such as CSC, IBM, Deloitte, and Accenture employ physician informaticists. Assignments can focus on change management, implementation design, return-on-investment, and strategic alignment. These positions are not good fits for those who do not like to travel as significant (more than 50% of the time) travel may be required.

A common misconception is that a physician needs to be a techno genius to be successful in this field. This is simply not the case. What hiring managers look for from physicians is someone who is good with people and understands how technology can solve business problems. They actively try to avoid "propeller-heads." As the physician CEO of a large hospital put it:

114

Example 3.64: Don't be afraid of informatics if you are not a geek
We're looking for a chief medical information officer today, and they don't have to be a techno-geek, but they need to be a user, an end-user, somebody who actually understands what an electronic medical record is supposed to do for them.

A good transition approach for those interested in medical informatics is to obtain a fellowship, degree, certificate, and continuing education in the field. Stanford and Columbia have excellent programs in this field. For further information on available training and a listing of job postings in the field, please check out the American Medical Informatics Association (www.amia.org). Another great resource for information, training, networking, and job postings is the Association of Medical Directors of Information Systems (http://www.amdis.org). Here is a recent job posting from the AMDIS Web site:

Example 3.65: Sample informatics job posting
Chief Medical Information Officer
Memorial Hospital

[Recruiting firm] has been retained to identify candidates for the position of CMIO, a newly created position for Memorial Hospital.

The chief medical information officer (CMIO) is responsible for advising and monitoring the planning and implementation of clinical systems and performance improvement. The strategies and initiatives should be consistent with the values, mission and long-term strategic plan of Memorial Hospital. The CMIO works in conjunction with the chief medical officer (CMO), chief information officer (CIO) to represent the medical staff and other healthcare team members in relationship to information technology.

The CMIO will serve in a consultative role to the physicians and liaison to information technology. The CMIO will act as an advisor to the CEO and CIO and other IT staff with regard to physician issues and the impact that information technology has or may have on medical practices at Memorial. The position will be responsible for recommending alterations and designs for clinical systems material that will affect quality and safety in patient care. The CMIO will chair any physician advisory committee and lead in defining ideas and initiatives in improving patient care through technology. The CMIO will become nationally visible in representing Memorial through publication, presentation and attending relevant conferences. The position reports to the chief information officer with a dotted line to the chief medical officer.

An M.D. with pediatric specialty is preferred; family practice with a strong pediatric component will be acceptable. Informatics training is preferred and three to five years of experience in clinical systems and process redesign. A clinician who understands trends in healthcare, point of care technology products and informatics is desirable. Please send resumes or nominations (with preference for email communication) to [contact name].

Volunteering to take the lead on technology issues and transitions in your clinical practice is another way to build your resume and position yourself for a career in this growing field. Consider volunteering to assist in electronic health record implementation in your group practice or hospital. Don't look at this as giving away your time, look at it as a less expensive way of gaining knowledge and experience than going back to school.

Another good approach if you feel you may be interested in this field is to begin talking with the chief medical information officer of your local hospital.

INVENTIONS

Many physicians become inventors. In 2005, Dr. Gary Michelson, a spine surgeon who has invented and patented numerous spine implants, surgical tools, and techniques settled with Medtronic for $1.35 *billion*, the largest one-time intellectual property award in U.S. history. Dr. Michelson is not alone. Jim Langer developed Kinetic Concepts (KCI) which has sales of over $700 million per year. Dr. Langer has a net worth of over $500 million. Dr. Julio Palmaz developed a cardiac stent and gets a very healthy invention royalty.

One of our faculty members, an entrepreneur and inventor of numerous products has some advice for physicians considering becoming inventors:

Example 3.66: Advice for aspiring physician inventors
The first thing you do when you have an invention is to protect your idea because otherwise somebody will steal it from you, for sure. You protect that by getting a patent. A provisional patent is a good way to start out. It doesn't cost a lot. You always sign an NDA. That means non-disclosure agreements with people you talk to. You have to be very protective of your idea. Beyond that, you have to start developing it, so, sooner or later you are going to have to get some money to help develop it; unless you are independently wealthy. You also have

to develop relationships with other people. You have to get the engineering involved, manufacturing, you need FDA approval. There are a lot of other steps you have to go through. So, the first thing is to get your idea perfected and protected. Then you take it and get it developed further through engineering. You have to raise money for that. At that point, then you can take it and commercialize it.

Raising Money
The best way to raise money is to really develop a very good executive summary. You don't have to have a full-blown business plan, but you need an elevator pitch. You need to be able to give your ideas to the investor in a very clear and concise manner; the so called elevator pitch. But, you really need to be able to give that story in a matter of a minute or two. You also have to have thought through things. You need to have a prototype that actually works [and articulate] where your competition is, how much money is it going to cost, what are your projections, and what's your exit strategy? You need to think things through, and you need to start out by getting an advisory board that can help you, of people that are smarter than yourselves. You need to put together a management team to get that off the road.

Any physician who wants to bring a product to market acts very noble. They need to have a lot of persistence to get it done and it can get done if you have enough persistence and time. I would suggest that they not delay because there is a window of opportunity and if they just let it sit on the back burner it will never get done. Just do it. You have to get out there and get moving the people together, get the money together, and make it happen. It takes some energy, but I advise them to go ahead and move ahead. Work with folks who have done it before and I think they will be successful.

ADMINISTRATION
If you are looking for a non-clinical career where you can make a tremendous impact on patient care, you should consider working as a medical administrator of a hospital, group practice, or other large healthcare provider. These jobs are never boring and involve something new each day. In the words of a physician hospital CEO:

Example 3.67: Administration can be very rewarding
But what happens that's really refreshing and rewarding is that we're creating better systems of care for patients. You can see better care. You see better training. You see better and more relevant research. You see more community service. And if you can do that and every day be creative, you just don't get tired of this.

Communications and interpersonal skills are a must if you want to be a successful medical administrator. It is essential to be able to lead an effective meeting, make presentations, be a great listener, and write well. If you are not a "people person," this is not the non-clinical career for you.

Medical administration jobs exist in all parts of the country. As such, they are a good fit for someone who does not want to or is not able to move. A good way to start to explore the opportunities available in this field is to ask for some mentoring from the medical director of your local hospital.

Many entry-level administration positions often involve a mix of clinical and administrative work. As such, this field is a great fit for someone who wants to test the waters before diving into a new career. Here's how the physician CEO of a large hospital describes how he finds new physician leaders:

> So we have other people who might be working at a department level or a division level, division being smaller, or down in a section, which is even smaller. We hire people there and we pay them for their administrative time, maybe 20 percent or so, but I'm watching all those folks for leadership capabilities. Hopefully they'll use those opportunities as a stair step to more advanced work later on in administration.

Positioning Yourself: Entry-level positions in this field include medical director and vice president of medical affairs. What employers will generally look for is someone with a minimum of three to five years in clinical practice, board certification, and leadership experience. Examples of leadership experience include serving on committees such as long-range planning, quality improvement, utilization review, and credentialing. Other ways to demonstrate leadership experience (and position yourself for a move into administration) is to chair task forces on patient care issues, serve on medical executive committees, be an elected officer of medical staff, be involved in healthcare legislative issues, and be active in state, local, and national medical associations. "Paying your dues" with this service can be a great way to get your foot into administration. As one physician hospital CEO put it:

> If they're coming in to work on a committee, are they willing to pay their dues and come in and serve? Are they willing to start out with 20 percent

time and work their way up until they impress somebody? 'Cause that's usually what happens. On anything we do, we do some work. It impresses somebody and they give us more to do. The busy guy always gets more to do.

Helpful qualifications also include an advanced business degree such as an MBA or Masters in Medical Management or a certificate from the American College of Physician Executives. Although helpful, advanced training is certainly not a requirement for success in this field. In the words of a physician hospital CEO who does not have an advanced degree:

Example 3.68: You don't need an MBA to be a successful physician administrator
I think it would have helped me to have an MBA, if I'd have had the time. If I had a degree I'd probably get a Masters in Public Health, because I'm so interested in community medicine and preventative medicine. I wish I had the epidemiology skills, the statistics and that sort of thing, but I'd rather do on the job training and do a lot of reading. And it's risky, because people might not give you, I guess, the benefit of the doubt. Because you're a physician, they don't think you're a very good business person.

I found that not to be true in many cases, but in general a lot of times it's something that doctors get in trouble with, because they have the vision, they have the idea, they have the service ethic, they have the curiosity and intellect, but they may or may not have the jargon. I mean you've got to be able to stand toe-to-toe with the CFO. You don't need to be a surrogate CFO. **You don't have to have an MBA, but you've got to be conversant. You can't let people intimidate you with knowledge.**

Physician medical administrators can work on wide variety of issues. These include:

- Being a bridge between the administration and the medical staff, community organizations, governmental agencies, and other healthcare organizations
- Credentialing
- Peer review
- Continuing medical education
- Strategic planning
- Quality assurance

- Utilization review
- Overseeing clinical research
- JCAHO accreditation
- Developing practice guidelines
- Measuring and improving patient satisfaction
- Recruiting, evaluating, and supporting physicians
- Negotiating with insurance companies
- Resolving grievances
- Budgeting and cost control

One upside of medical administration is that there is room for career advancement for medical administrators. Many hospitals have a chief medical officer. In many organizations the chief executive officer, chief operating officer, chief information officer, and vice president for quality are physicians. The keys to success are having the right attitude, being true to yourself, and showing leadership. In the words of one physician hospital CEO:

Example 3.69: Keys to success as a medical administrator
I think if you go in with the right attitude you can. Attitude is 99 percent of it, right, but you've got to have that attitude. You've got to deal with frustration. You've got to sometimes be courageous. You've got to live your values. If you talk about your values and you don't live them, your feet of clay will soon be diagnosed by others, other doctors particularly. I think it's important that you live what you say and you do what you say.

I talk about pointing actions. We believe what people do, not what they say. Pointing action is very important, and role modeling is incredibly powerful. But I think you also have to do one thing...You've got to give away success and then you can't lose it. That's an old Chinese proverb and it's never been so true. Then you build camaraderie and loyalty because you're fair to people. If you're not willing to do that and you just want to be the leader, you probably won't be successful. You want to be a leader in a leaderful organization.

A downside in hospital administration work is lack of job security. There is frequent turnover in this field and medical directors can easily run afoul of the board, the administration, or the medical staff as they try to balance competing interests. A physician CEO of a large hospital advises:

Example 3.70: A potential downside of medical administration positions
It's not always a rosy picture being a hospital administrator, particularly in a
public hospital. Four years ago I had a seven-person board. Three wanted to
keep me, three wanted to fire me, one wanted to get off the board who liked me.
And that was because I was pushing a bond program, over a billion dollars
again. We're doing it now, but back then it was not politically correct.

I've always said you have to be willing to lose your job to do your job. If you
have to hold onto your job, then it's bad. That's one reason I kept my medical
skills for a long time. There were times in the past when it was very bad. There
were times when I had butted heads with politicians, including the governor of
the state, when I was chairman of the [State] Board of Health, that I would say
you didn't know day-to-day what was really going to happen.

In closing, please consider what one medical administrator liked and
disliked about her position:

Example 3.71: A lot of job satisfaction, but lots of politics too
I found very satisfying feeling like I was contributing to a larger cause and I
loved the relationships that I was forging with physicians, and I loved the fact
that we were goal-oriented and we were attempting to achieve programs and
things—specific things within the role. What I did not love was the bureaucratic
in-fighting, the politics—we had a lot of town and gown politics. Our hospital
was a community hospital that had been acquired by an academic medical
center, so there was a lot of what we called town and gown politics—the
university snobbery, the community doctors saying these folks in the university
don't know the first thing about how to really deliver clinical practice, good
clinical care to patients. There was that sort of rivalry and a lot of politics. A lot
of political jostling.

MEDIA

Many physicians have become successful journalists. Sanjay Gupta, Tim
Johnson, and Bob Arnot are probably the most recognizable three names
that come to mind. Journalism can be a great way to use your medical
degree to continue to make a large difference in many people's lives.
Here's what two of our physician TV journalist faculty members have to
say about a career in TV journalism:

Example 3.72: Opportunities for physicians in the media
I think there are a ton of opportunities in the media for physicians. There are
lots of opportunities in television, from being a medical reporter, to a reality
star, to a host of a show, to the expert on a show, to syndication, kids' health. I
think there's a lot in print; lots of non-fiction and fiction opportunities,

newspapers, magazines, lots of things geared towards health and also with radio.

The pay is just like in any business. There are some people who do okay, some people who do good, some people who do great, and there are some people who need to take a second job. It just depends. It can vary in markets. It can vary within markets. A lot of times it's hard to know because sometimes people start out in one area and then for some reason they catapult really high and they end up making exorbitant amounts of money. Some people just make a good living. I think it's just like any industry. You can make a good living, though, and you can make a living.

Example 3.73: Hours and training

The hours for a medical reporter are generally good hours when you consider that some people on TV have to get up at three in the morning. Usually a medical reporter is during the day, Monday through Friday, sort of a 9-5 or 10-6 kind of a lifestyle.

What goes on behind the scenes is, a lot of times, a lot of chaos in the newsroom, but it's an orderly chaos, depending on if there's breaking news, breaking health news going on. I think the newsroom is a lot like an emergency room. It can just be steady and nothing too chaotic, then something major can break and the machine starts. But, everyone knows what their job is and it runs orderly just like an emergency room would. Out in the field, we show up somewhere. We conduct the interview. We get any necessary B roll or video that we need for our story and then go back to the station and put it all together.

[When I started to explore getting into this field] I contacted news directors, I wrote to people who covered television as their beat in reporting, just to get some insight and advice.

Most of them ignored me, but one news director did call me back and said, "If you want to do this, you have to go back to school." And I think he was just kind of trying to get rid of me. I mean, you tell a doctor she has to go back to school, she's probably not going to do it. But then in fact, I showed him. I did go back to school, and I got my Masters degree in journalism and mass communications.

As part of that, I did an internship at [the station where I now work] and things worked out that I ended up staying on as the medical reporter there.

For salary information for television media jobs, please visit www.rtnda.org.

OCCUPATIONAL HEALTH

Employers have a legal and financial incentive to maintain a healthy and productive workforce. As such, there are numerous non-clinical opportunities for physicians as corporate medical directors of large organizations and the occupational health companies that service them. These positions exist in all parts of the country. Note that many of these positions, especially at the more entry-level positions, may require a mix of clinical and non-clinical work. As such, this can be a good career path for someone who is looking to ease into non-clinical work and see how they enjoy non-clinical functions.

Employers may be looking for board certification in occupational medicine (note that "mini-residencies" and other short training programs are available in many parts of the country). However, many will accept different experience for the right candidate. For example, one of our faculty members who is a senior corporate medical director for an automaker once hired a *70-year-old obstetrician* who had gained relevant experience by going back to school to obtain an MPH and volunteering in an occupational health setting.

As with any career, there are advantages and disadvantages with becoming a corporate medical director. The advantages include regular hours, a steady paycheck, potential for stock awards and bonuses, no weekends, no nights, no holidays, paid sick time, paid vacation, paid CME and license, no overhead, and no malpractice insurance. The disadvantages with a career as a corporate medical director include not being your own boss, company rules that must be complied with, corporate politics, low appreciation factor, decreased professional peer respect, and the potential for forced relocation.

A good resource for those interested in corporate medical director positions is the American College of Occupational and Environmental Medicine (www.acoem.org). ACOEM's Web site contains a great overview of career opportunities in occupational medicine. ACOEM also maintains a well-stocked job posting area on its Web site. Here are two sample postings in occupational medicine that give a good idea of the types of job functions that may be required:

Example 3.74: Sample occupational health job posting
Staff Physician
Los Alamos National Laboratory
Los Alamos, New Mexico

JOB DETAILS
Los Alamos National Laboratory has the following exciting opportunity available. Join us at the forefront of scientific frontiers, and help to drive our continued excellence.

TITLE: Staff Physician
LOCATION: Los Alamos, New Mexico
FULL-TIME/PART-TIME: Full-Time

DESCRIPTION:
Reporting to LANL's Site Occupational Medicine Director, the Staff Physician will oversee/implement medical surveillance and certification programs, provide direct patient diagnosis and treatment, maintain safety and security training and compliance, and perform pre-placement, occupational surveillance/certification, termination and fitness-for-duty physical exams.

Requires 5-8 years clinical experience/graduate degree in a relevant medical field; NM Board of Medical Examiners licensure, as well as current NM Pharmacy and DEA licensure; and board certification and proficiency in occupational medicine OR a clinically relevant medical field.

Preferred areas of expertise include: public health, epidemiology, industrial hygiene, or family, emergency, internal or sports medicine. BLS and ACLS are required, as are working knowledge of occupational health-related laws and regulations, patient advocacy, and complications/treatments relating to radiological, chemical and biological hazards and diseases, superior written/verbal communication and interpersonal skills.

Applicants must have the ability to obtain a Q clearance, which usually requires U.S. citizenship.

Besides enjoying a competitive salary and outstanding benefits, you'll find Los Alamos' temperate climate in Northern New Mexico is perfect to enjoy year-round recreation.

Example 3.75: Sample corporate medical director job posting
Associate Medical Director

Job Description:
Responsibilities

- Supervises all occupational health clinical care (on site and dispersed).
- Assures compliance with US OSHA regulations other national regulations federal and state statutes, [company] scorecard requirements and policies.
- Supports return to work and disability management.
- Works collaboratively with Environmental Health and Safety and Human Resources.
- Supports emergency response teams at sites and locations including disaster planning and responding to pandemic and terrorism threats.
- Serves as content area expert in Occupational Health for the business.
- Provides Occupational Health consultative advice to the Services and Sales organizations as they take on work in emerging markets.
- Shares responsibility with team MDs for travel medicine fitness for duty evaluations and ISOS emergency response on 24x7 rotation basis.
- Provides administrative oversight for outsourced clinical and ancillary medical services.
- Promotes the use of electronic medical record systems and digitization efforts.
- Assesses the ongoing health risks in [company]'s work places from established and new technologies, responds appropriately.
- Works in close cooperation with Health Promotion and Wellness Teams striving to keep our workforce healthy.
- Participates in Cardiovascular and Diabetes screenings as a one-to-one counselor to employees and spouses at conferences and onsite locations as required.
- Assures that quality care is being provided and that it is continuously improving.
- Develops and maintains clinic programs in health advocacy and active consumerism.
- Provide periodic reports of trends, costs and illness patterns to [company] leadership and the corporation.

Qualifications
- Medical Doctor with a current license to practice in one of several states.
- Ten year's experience in Occupational Health.
- Board Certification in a medical specialty (preferably Occupational Medicine).
- Deep understanding of population health and evidence-based medicine.

Eligibility Requirements
- No pending malpractice litigation
- Ability and willingness to travel often

Desired
- Global experience in Occupational health
- Ten years' experience with a large US based corporation
- Masters degree in Public Health
- Masters degree in Business
- Board certification in a primary care discipline and Occupational health
- Facility in statistics and data analysis, pc and the use of the internet
- Personal commitment to fitness and wellness
- Willingness to travel 25% of the time-domestic and international
- High level of business savvy
- Keen sense of organizational dynamics
- Proven, persuasive leader with excellent written and verbal skills
- Compassionate, clear thinking, high energy, self starter
- Personable and possessing a sense of humor
- Possess passion for improving the health of the workforce

General
Reports to the Director for Health Services and Medical Operations. [Company] is an equal opportunity employer, offering a great work environment, challenging career opportunities, professional training and competitive compensation.

The United States has regulations that govern the hiring of current or former US Government employees. If you currently work for (or have in the past) the US Government (in any capacity), you may have certain responsibilities under these regulations and certain restrictions may apply to your potential employment with [company]. Therefore, if you are contacted by [company] regarding a position of employment, and you have worked for the US Government at any time, please immediately inform the [company] representative of this fact.

MEDICAL-LEGAL

There are tremendous and lucrative opportunities available to physicians in the medical-legal area. Expert medical testimony is used or required in almost every contested personal injury, workers' compensation, or medical malpractice claim. According to SEAK's *National Guide to Expert Fees and Billing Procedures,* physicians earn on average more than

$500 an hour for their time in court. Many physicians earn in the range of $750–$1,000 an hour. One internist we trained has more than *doubled* his annual income by dedicating just one day a week to expert witness work. This has had a dramatic positive impact on his lifestyle.

Not for Everyone: Medical-legal work is not for everyone. If you are thin-skinned, it is not for you. As an expert witness your credibility will be a legitimate issue in every case. You can and will be pointedly attacked during cross-examination on your credentials, credibility, honesty, competence, and opinions. If you testify against another physician in a malpractice case you may be subjected to a professional and personal backlash. If you are a poor communicator or fear public speaking or confrontation, the courtroom or a deposition is not the place for you. In addition, what you do in the medical-legal field generally becomes public record and is open to public scrutiny. Therefore, if you are sensitive about your privacy, this is not a good field for you.

Need for Active Clinical Practice: Another important point to remember about medical-legal work is that it is highly preferable, and sometimes required by law, that you maintain an active clinical practice. Expert witnessing is all about credibility and it is difficult to appear credible in front of a jury if you haven't actually treated a patient in many years. An active clinical practice in some cases may also be a direct source of case referrals because the treating doctor of someone who has been injured is usually asked to testify on the patient's behalf as an expert witness. Physicians can sometimes satisfy the active clinical practice requirement by teaching or even volunteering at a clinic or hospital.

Three Types of Medical-Legal Work: There are three main types of medical-legal consulting work available for physicians.

1. Workers' compensation—personal injury
    Serving as an expert witness in workers' compensation and personal injury cases is the best fit for physicians in specialties that treat mental and physical injuries (such as PM & R, orthopedics, neurology, neurosurgery, and psychiatry). A big advantage of this type of work is that since the defendant is not a doctor in a

malpractice claim, it is not controversial in the medical profession. As such, you will generally not encounter any type of a backlash for your activities. The doctors best positioned to do this work maintain an active clinical practice and do not shy away from treating persons who have fallen, been in auto accidents, or were hurt at work.

2. Medical malpractice
   Serving as an expert witness in medical malpractice cases is possible for physicians in all specialties and can be extremely lucrative. For credible doctors with good communication skills, there are large amounts of mostly work-from-home opportunities available. There are some caveats about this work, however. First, you need to be prepared to stand in open court, under oath, and state that another doctor in your specialty was negligent and breached the standard of care. If you are not prepared to do so, this is not the field for you. A doctor who is only willing to testify for defendants can expect serious credibility issues. Second, you need to be prepared to travel out of state. Most plaintiffs' experts in medical malpractice cases are from out of state. Finally, you will need to maintain some sort of clinical practice if you want to remain a viable and credible expert witness.

   For training on how to become and excel as an expert witness, SEAK, Inc. is the best resource available (www.seak.com). We would suggest you start by reading SEAK's text *The A–Z Guide to Expert Witnessing* and then attend an interactive training workshop.

3. Independent medical evaluations
   In personal injury and workers' compensation litigation the defendant usually has the right to have the plaintiff/claimant examined by a physician of the defendant's choosing. This is an independent medical evaluation (IME). The IME physician typically examines the claimant and issues a written report. The IME physician may also be called upon to testify for the defendant.

   Physicians in specialties that treat mental and physical injuries (such as PM & R, orthopedics, neurology, neurosurgery, and psychiatry) are most in demand as expert witnesses. IMEs are generally ultimately paid for by insurance companies who oftentimes pursue the lowest bidder. As such, this is generally the lowest-paying type of medical-legal work that a physician can perform. Because you are working for the defense and the cases are generally not medical malpractice, physicians who perform this work typically suffer little or no backlash.

Of all three areas of medical-legal work, IMEs are most conducive to physicians who do not wish to maintain any type of a clinical practice—although it is always ideal to maintain a clinical practice. There are many successful independent medical examiners whose sole professional work is performing IMEs. These include doctors who have retired from clinical practice and now only do IMEs, doctors who have become disabled and now only perform IMEs, and some physicians who just choose a medical-legal practice specializing in evaluations.

Board certification in performing independent medical examinations is provided by the American Board of Independent Medical Examiners (www.abime.org). Training in performing IMEs is provided by ABIME, the American Academy of Disability Evaluating Physicians (www.aadep.org), and SEAK, Inc. (www.seak.com). A good way to spread the word about your availability to perform IMEs is to list yourself in the *National Directory of Independent Medical Examiners* (www.imenet.com).

There are also IME companies and brokers that will refer doctors cases in return for a fee of some sort. Placing yourself on one their panels is another good way to get started in this field. Examples of these companies include:

Abeton
www.abetongroup.com
(888) 822-3866

Benchmark Medical Consultants
www.benchmarkadmin.com
(800) 458-1261

MES Group
www.messolutions.com
(800) 942-5637

MLS National Medical Evaluation Services, Inc.
www.mls-ime.com
(248) 945-9001

National Claim Evaluations, Inc.
www.natclaim.com
(516) 433-1801

If you are interested in becoming an independent medical examiner, a helpful resource is the SEAK white paper *What All Physicians Considering Starting an IME Practice Should Know,* available at www.seak.com.

TRADITIONAL NON-CLINICAL JOB TITLES FOR PHYSICIANS
It is a good idea to familiarize yourself with the common job titles for "traditional" non-clinical jobs for physicians. Having an understanding of these job titles will facilitate electronic job searches and will make you sound more knowledgeable when networking and interviewing. The most common job titles for physicians in traditional non-clinical fields include:

- Assistant Director
- Assistant Vice-President of Clinical Affairs
- Assistant Medical Director
- Associate Chief of Staff for Education
- Associate Clinical Development Director
- Associate Clinical Director
- Associate Clinical Research Director
- Associate Director
- Associate Director of Medical Science Liaison Training
- Associate Drug Safety Director
- Associate Medical Affairs Director
- Associate Medical Director
- Associate Medical Research Director

- Chief Executive Officer
- Chief Medical Information Officer
- Chief Medical Officer
- Chief Operating Officer
- Chief Scientific Officer
- Clinical Affairs Specialist
- Clinical Development Physician
- Clinical Development Project Physician
- Clinical Director
- Clinical Informatics Director
- Clinical Pharmacology Director
- Clinical Research Director
- Clinical Research Manager
- Clinical Research Physician
- Community Health Program Manager
- Corporate Medical Director
- District Health Director
- District Health Officer
- Director
- Director of Medical Informatics
- Drug Safety Director
- Drug Safety Scientist
- Executive Medical Director
- Global Safety Director
- Hospital Medical Director
- Independent Reviewer
- Initiated Trial Programs Director
- Lead Medical Director
- Marketing Director
- Medical Affairs and Drug Safety Director
- Medical Affairs Director
- Medical Associate Director of Clinical Research
- Medical Communications Director

- Medical Communications Manager
- Medical Consultant
- Medical Curriculum Director
- Medical Director
- Medical Editor
- Medical Education Director
- Medical Information Manager
- Medical Information Scientist
- Medical Research Director
- Medical Liaison
- Medical Officer
- Medical Safety Director
- Medical Science Liaison
- Medical Sciences Field Director
- Medical Consultant
- Medical Writer
- National Medical Director
- Physician
- Physician Advisor
- Physician Reviewer
- Physician Specialist
- Project Physician
- Public Health Physician
- Regional Medical Director
- Senior Clinical Affairs Director
- Senior Clinical Research Director
- Senior Medical Director
- Scientific Affairs Director
- Scientific Director
- Scientist
- State Epidemiologist
- State Health Officer
- Supervisory Medical Officer
- Vice President

- Vice President Medical Director
- Vice President of Medical Affairs

3.4 You Can Do Anything: Non-Traditional Non-Clinical Careers for Physicians

You should not in any way feel constrained by the traditional fields described above. The sky is the limit in terms of what you can do with all your intelligence, drive, and talent. Your colleagues have been successful and have followed their passions into a number of non-traditional careers for physicians. Here are a few inspirational examples to keep in mind. Don't be constrained by these few examples. The possibilities are endless.

SPORTSCASTER

Dr. Jerry Punch was an emergency room physician prior to joining ESPN in 1984 as a pit reporter in NASCAR races. Turn on ESPN on a weekend and you may see Dr. Punch covering auto racing or college football. Dr. Punch didn't waste his medical training, either. He has been the first responder to more than one serious accident while covering auto racing.

POLITICAL PUNDIT AND COMMENTATOR

Dr. Charles Krauthammer is a psychiatrist who is now a syndicated columnist and commentator. His weekly column appears in *The Washington Post* and is syndicated in more than 200 newspapers and media outlets. He is a contributing editor to the *Weekly Standard* and *The New Republic*. Krauthammer appears regularly as a commentator on Fox News and as a weekly panelist on "Inside Washington."

POLITICIAN

Dr. Bill Frist (a thoracic surgeon), is a former U.S. Senator from Tennessee and was Senate Majority Leader. Tom Coburn, MD, (an obstetrician) serves as a U.S. Senator from Oklahoma and David Weldon, MD, was a U.S. Congressman from Florida.

NOVELIST

Tess Gerritsen, MD, Michael Palmer, MD, Michael Crichton, MD, and Robin Cook, MD, are all *New York Times* best-selling physician-authors.

Many of their works leverage their medical training by taking up medical topics.

TEACHER

Is teaching your passion? Do you not need to make a lot of money? Go for it. Take the example of a podiatrist who gave up a successful practice to become a high school biology teacher and athletic director. The financial trade offs were huge, but so is his new job satisfaction of teaching kids what makes them healthy and happy. He leveraged his medical training by teaching biology.

PARK RANGER

Want to give up your medical practice and follow your dream of being a park ranger? You wouldn't be alone. We know of a physician who did just that. His income went from $340,000/year to $24,000/year. He was got his finances in order first to make this work. When asked if he would do it again, his reply was "absolutely."

FINANCIAL ADVISOR

One of our faculty members was a practicing pediatrician for twelve years and became a successful Beverly Hills financial advisor and enjoys his work very much. Prior to becoming a financial advisor, he served as a financial analyst covering the pharmaceutical industry for a large Wall Street investment bank.

WALL STREET EXECUTIVE

Take the example of Dr. Robert H. Glassman who was featured in the November 27, 2006 *New York Times* article "Lure of Great Wealth Affects Career Choices." Dr. Glassman left clinical medicine after 4 years, responding to an ad in *The New England Journal of Medicine* from a business consulting firm hiring doctors. The firm was increasingly working with pharma and biomed companies and was in need of additional physician consultants. After 4 years of consulting (with heavy travel), Dr. Glassman moved to Merrill Lynch, where he worked first in private equity and then investment banking—in the process becoming a multimillionaire.

VENTURE CAPITALIST

Take the example of Drew Senyei, MD. Dr. Senyei left clinical practice and started Enterprise Partners Venture Capital, which has helped build 155 companies and has over $750 million in capital under management.

PATENT ATTORNEY

One of our faculty members went back to law school 19 years after obtaining her medical degree. After graduating, she rapidly rose to the level of partner in one of the largest and most prestigious law firms in Boston. She leveraged her medical degree by specializing in life sciences patent law.

HIGH-TECH EXECUTIVE AND PHILANTHROPIST

Consider Dr. Larry Brilliant, former chief executive of Cometa Networks. Dr. Brilliant was placed in charge of the Google.org philanthropic organization and was tasked with spending 1% of Google's annual profit and 1% of its stock.

FORENSIC HANDWRITING EXAMINER

Richard Fraser, MD, was laid-off from clinical practice. He became a very successful work-from-home forensic handwriting examiner.

PROFESSIONAL COACH

Philippa Kennealy, MD, runs her own business coaching MD executives, MD entrepreneurs, and other executives.

3.5 Big Company or Small Company?

Another thing to consider besides the industry you would like to be employed in is the size company you think would be the best fit for you. There are usually significant differences affecting employees that you need to take into account.

Jobs in big companies tend to be much more specialized. Employees for smaller companies may need to perform multiple job functions. Big companies usually have many other employees available for teaching and mentoring. In a smaller company you may basically be on your own. Big companies have much more support. For example, they have an entire IT department, facilities department, etc. In a small company, support may be harder to obtain. Small companies may pay more up front. Smaller organizations may also have a far greater potential upside if their product(s) take off. Small companies may also offer significantly less valuable fringe benefits. Jobs at small companies may be riskier than jobs at large companies. Smaller companies may be less structured, less bureaucratic, and more entrepreneurial. Large companies may require endless meetings and teleconferences to get decisions made.

Chapter 4   Online and Traditional Networking Techniques That Work

4.1 Executive Summary

- Networking is the number one way to research, find, and land a job.
- Start your networking by creating a list of networking contacts. You will be surprised at how big of a list you can come up with.
- Networking can be fun and personally and professionally rewarding.
- Joining professional organizations and attending conferences can facilitate networking.
- Online networking is an important component of successful networking.

4.2 Networking Works

Networking is reported to result in up to 70 to 80 percent of new employment obtained by job seekers.[1] These percentages may be even higher for professionals like physicians moving to non-clinical positions. These startling statistics make sense because up to 80% of these positions are not advertised. A noted expert on networking has the following to say about the effectiveness of networking in a job search:

> **Example 4.1: Networking is the number one way that people land jobs**
> It's the number one way that people land jobs. Depending on which survey you look at, consistently, networking is the number one way that people land jobs. If you are looking at the Execunet survey, if you are looking at Netshare, if you are looking at BH Careers, all these organizations including Manpower and so on, and Manpower is a recruiting agency, still say, and even the Bureau of Statistics, still says that networking is the number one way that people land careers. Number one.

Given the effectiveness of networking, it is crucial that physicians moving to non-clinical careers become effective networkers. Physicians who understand the importance of networking and actively and

---

[1] *Hire Me Inc.*, Blitzer, Entrepreneurialpress.com, p. 84 (2006).

successfully practice it will be best positioned to locate and obtain non-clinical positions. For examples of physicians landing non-clinical positions as a direct result of networking, please see Section 9.9.

Networking can also be crucially important in gathering information such as industry trends and what particular employers or industries are looking for from their employees. Please consider the advice of a noted personal branding expert:

> **Example 4.2: Networking will produce invaluable information**
> It's also important [to do] research, talk to lots of people, networking. Not networking to get jobs, but to get information. That's your currency. That's what's going to get you where you need to go. You want to talk to people about what it's like working where they work. What are the things people need to be successful in those kinds of places? Think about what you have that you can translate to that. The more information you can get, especially even on trends: what industries are going up? What are going down? Right now manufacturing is suffering. If you are going to go for a manufacturing job, you have to realize there are going to be a lot of people with a lot of experience ahead of you. Why do they want to hire you with very little experience? You may have a great value proposition, but so what? Somebody else does too and they have 20 years of experience in manufacturing. You want to look at what the upcoming industries are and the ones that are sliding. Make some hard choices about where you want to start looking. Get information and be as educated as you can and then start seeing how you think your experience fits that.

4.3 When to Network

Effective networkers are *always* looking for opportunities to meet new people and re-connect with old friends and colleagues. These networkers set aside a portion of their day and incorporate networking into their daily routine. In addition, they practice effective networking throughout their professional day.

4.4 Goals of Networking

The six main goals of effective networking are:

- Gather information,
- Help others with their problems/issues,
- Make new acquaintances,
- Build trust and working relationships,

- Maintain acquaintances and relationships, and
- Be thought of as a helpful expert and go-to person who can get things done.

Note that of the six goals mentioned above, three involve helping others by reaching out to them. This is one of the most underappreciated aspects of effective networking: helping others will result in them helping you, many times without you even having to ask. How do you develop meaningful working relationships? By reaching out and helping others, especially when you have not been asked to do so.

4.5 Networking Techniques

Your Networking List

Keep a list (computer, hard copy, or both) of people you meet and their names, addresses, phone, e-mail, where you met them, and little facts about them to jog your memory of who they are, and do favors for your network. Consider the advice of one networking expert:

> **Example 4.3: Career coach offers advice on compiling a networking list**
> What [physicians] really should do is, the number one thing to do is, just start by simply making a list of all your contacts. That means family, friends, relatives, 3rd cousin[s] twice removed. But also think bigger, outside the box. Who are your service providers? Who's your dentist? Who's your massage therapist? The more people that you list [the better]. Who's in your professional organization? Who are people that you still maintain contact with? Who are alumni? This is a great place to start because these are people who will be less likely to walk away from you and more likely to want to help you.

Most physicians meet numerous other professionals during their business day, on the phone, at meetings and conferences, during telephone calls, etc. The sophisticated networker obtains their business cards/contact information and notes where and how they met, friends or colleagues they have in common, and a few personal details about the person (for example, you grew up in the same city). This list, which should be maintained and expanded, will later become crucial when it becomes time to reach out to your contacts. You should not be shy about handing out your business card when appropriate. Do not forget to include people you know on the following list:

- Family
- Friends
- Colleagues in professional associations and at professional meetings/conferences
- Alumni (high school, college, med school, post-graduate)
- Past and present co-workers
- Vendors and pharma reps
- Your lawyer, accountant, vet, etc.
- Church/synagogue members
- PTA members
- Neighbors
- Fellow travelers and vacationers
- Professors and instructors
- Mentors or people you have mentored
- Co-presenters at meetings, etc.

You might initially be reluctant to list people you don't know well. However, once you accept the fact that you will not be bombarding them for requests for help, the list formation becomes much more palatable. In fact, as you will be doing some favors for your network, it is to their advantage to be on your list.

GATHERING INFORMATION

As in almost any endeavor, information is key in making a non-clinical career transition. One of the best ways to gather information is through networking. The types of valuable information you can gather through networking (and sometimes *only* through networking) include:

- The types of non-clinical positions open to physicians,
- What types of organizations hire physicians,
- What employers hiring physicians are looking for in a candidate in terms of education, skills, and experience,
- What a job at an organization would involve on a day-to-day basis so you can get a sense of whether it would be a good fit for you,

- Who the decision maker is at an employer regarding hiring so you can avoid HR and get your name in front of the key person,
- What makes the decision maker tick (see Section 8.3 on the interviewer's X factor),
- What specific employers might be looking for someone with your skills,
- Job openings that have not been advertised, and
- Compensation for entry-level and experienced persons in a particular field.

DOING FAVORS FOR YOUR NETWORK

The rule of three applies to your networking: do at least three favors for each one you might ask of the people on your list. The kind of favors you can consider doing include:

- Send them articles,
- Make referrals to them,
- Support their work,
- Meet with them when you are in town,
- Send them small, meaningful gifts,
- Help their careers,
- Ask their advice for difficult problems,
- Recommend them to the press or media,
- Invite or recommend them to speak at conferences,
- Join the relevant professional organizations and attend their meetings,
- Connect one colleague with another,
- Occasionally call people just to say hello,
- Get known as an information clearinghouse, and
- Act as a mentor.

Send Articles: An effective networking technique is to periodically send a person on your networking list articles that you come across that:

- May help them and
- They probably do not have access to.

These can be sent by snail mail or by scanning the article and e-mailing it to them. When done correctly, the recipient will almost always reply with a thank you e-mail.

Make Referrals: When you are offered potential work or assignments that you cannot or do not want to accept, refer it to one of the people on your networking list. They will be very appreciative.

Meet When You Are in Town: When you are traveling and in the same city as one of the people on your list, get together for lunch, dinner, or just to catch up.

Send Small, Meaningful Gifts: A small, thoughtful gift, book, or CD sends the message you:

- Are thinking of them and
- Are thoughtful enough to have selected a meaningful gift.

Help Their Careers: When you can put in a good word, give them a heads-up, or a lead, do so. It may take you only 5 minutes, but it may be very important to the recipient.

Ask Advice for Difficult Problems: By asking for advice, you are sending a clear message:

- You respect their knowledge and judgment and
- You consider them a friend.

Recommendations to Press or Media: When given the opportunity, give the names of people on your list to the press or media who are looking for an article, expert, quote, TV, or radio appearance.

Invitations or Recommendations to Speak at Conferences: By inviting or recommending your contacts, you can substantially increase their visibility and assist their careers.

Connect Colleagues: A simple e-mail or call putting one colleague in touch with another can be of substantial assistance to both of them.

Occasionally Call to Just Say Hello: Many people make the mistake of only calling colleagues when they need something. This is likely to be resented and not appreciated by the person you are calling.

Join the Relevant Professional Organizations and Attend Their Meetings: A good way to facilitate networking is to join relevant professional organizations. Membership in these organizations will allow you to meet others working in the field you are targeting. As an example, a neurologist client of ours was looking to set up his own full-time consulting practice to consult with the insurance industry. He joined the American Academy of Insurance Medicine and the contacts he made through the Academy yielded a large amount of consulting work.

THE EXPERTS OFFER EXCELLENT ADVICE ON HOW TO BEST NETWORK AT CONFERENCES[2]

1. **Have the tools to network with you at all times.** These include an informative name badge, business cards, brochure about your business, and a pocket sized business card file containing cards of other professionals to whom you can refer new business.
2. **Set a goal for the number of people you'll meet.** Identify a reachable goal based on the attendance and the type of group. If you feel inspired, set a goal to meet 15 to 20 people, and make sure you get all their cards. If you don't feel so hot, shoot for less. In either case, don't leave until you have met your goal.
3. **Act like a host, not a guest.** A host is expected to do things for others, while a guest sits back and relaxes. Volunteer to help greet people. If you see visitors sitting, introduce yourself and ask if they would like to meet others. Act as a conduit.
4. **Listen and ask questions.** Remember that a good networker has two ears and one mouth and uses them proportionately. After you've learned what another person does, tell them what you do. Be specific, but brief. Don't assume they know your business.
5. **Don't try to close a deal.** These events are not meant to be a vehicle to hit on businesspeople to buy your products or services.

---

[2] *The 10 Commandments of Networking,* Ivan Misner, 9/2/2002.

Networking is about developing relationships with other professionals. Meeting people at events should be the beginning of that process, not the end of it.

6. **Give referrals whenever possible.** The best networkers believe in the "givers gain" philosophy (what goes around comes around). If I help you, you'll help me and we'll both do better as a result of it.

7. **Exchange business cards.** Ask each person you meet for two cards–one to pass on to someone else and one to keep. This sets the stage for networking to happen.

8. **Manage your time efficiently.** Spend 10 minutes or less with each person you meet, and don't linger with friends or associates. If your goal is to meet a given number of people, be careful not to spend too much time with any one person. When you meet someone interesting with whom you'd like to speak further, set up an appointment for a later date.

9. **Write notes on the backs of the business cards you collect.** Record anything you think may be useful in remembering each person more clearly. This will come in handy when you follow up on each contact.

10. **Follow up!** You can obey the previous nine commandments religiously, but if you don't follow up effectively, you will have wasted your time. Drop a note or give a call to each person you've met. Be sure to fulfill any promises you've made.

Get Known As an Information Clearinghouse: The more people who know that you can provide valuable information, the more you become a valuable resource for others. When they think of one or more of your areas of specialty, they will naturally think of you.

Act As a Mentor: Acting as a mentor is seen as a selfless act and often it is. The more people you mentor, the wider your list of contacts. Once these people get established in their professions and positions, they are likely to want to help you any way they can.

WHAT NOT TO DO WHEN NETWORKING

- Never ask for a "quid pro quo."
- Do not even mention your favor.
- Do not be overbearing.
- Do not keep score.

Never Ask for a Quid Pro Quo: People who ask for a quid pro quo are resented, looked on with suspicion, and are always suspected of ulterior motives.

Do Not Mention Your Favor: Not only should you not ask for a quid pro quo, you should never mention a previous favor done for someone on your networking list or anyone else for that matter. If the favor was significant, you can be confident they will remember it.

Do Not Be Overbearing: Any of the above recommendations can be overdone. Making a pest of yourself is not appreciated by the person on the receiving end nor is it ultimately to your advantage. Don't overdo it.

Do Not Keep Score: Remember the rule of three. Don't be concerned or even keep track of how many favors you have done. Keeping score is not important. What is important is developing solid working relationships built on trust and respect.

ASKING FOR HELP
There will come a time in your search for a non-clinical position that you will want to ask your network for help or information. How you go about asking for help is just as important as what you ask for.

Be Brief and Specific: If you send out an e-mail, be specific about what you are looking for. For example, state, "Do you know anyone in pharma I could contact to start my search for a non-clinical position?"

Be Polite: Asking briefly about them, their family, etc. is always a good idea.

Follow Up with a Thank You: Always follow up with a thank you note, even when they did not really help you.

Do Not Abuse the Relationship: Do not contact the person too frequently. Try to not ask for something that will:

- Embarrass the person,
- Require a lot of work on their part, or
- Potentially backfire and ruin their reputation or relationship with their contact.

Ask Before Using Their Name: Request permission before using their name in an e-mail, note, or phone call.

Make an Appointment to Talk to Them: If you are going to call a contact, request a time convenient for them. Tell them it will only take 5 or 10 minutes. You should make the call. End the call on time or even early, if possible.

Those physicians who truly enjoy helping and mentoring others are usually excellent networkers.

4.6 Six Action Steps to Getting Your Network Up and Running

Ready to build and cultivate your own connections? These six action steps will help you get your six-degree network up and running:

1. Make a list of the 250 people most important to you. Keith Ferrazzi, CEO of Ferrazzi Greenlight, a marketing and sales consulting and training firm in Los Angeles, suggests you consider business leaders, community leaders, friends and family—basically anyone who can help you and to whom you might have something to offer. Start cultivating those relationships.
2. Become a master at relationships. It's not just about picking up the phone; it's about creating long-term connections and developing a real rapport. Ferrazzi says to remember things like your contacts' birthdays and favorite hobbies.
3. Join business and social groups. Start attending meetings, luncheons, mixers, whatever—anything that will build your

contact list. "As you grow [your] business, your circle—your network—should grow as well," says Zoe Alexander, networking expert and founder of Divas Who Dine, LLC, a women's business networking group in New York City.

4. Assess your attributes. Clearly define what you can bring to the table for all your new contacts. The more you bring to the party, the more willing people will be to help you, Alexander points out.

5. Engage in conversations. No matter where you are, start talking with your seatmate or line buddy. Ask questions about their business or industry and talk a bit about yours, Levine suggests. You'll get ideas, inspiration, and, if you're lucky, a really good six-degree contact.

6. Bone up on current events. "Leaders are readers," says Steve Harper, author of *The Ripple Effect: Maximizing the Power of Relationships for Your Life and Business*. To be relevant to your desired contact, you're going to stay abreast of news, happenings and the like. Doing so will also give you good conversation-starters for any networking situation.[3]

4.7 Online Networking

Many physicians will want to start or augment their traditional networking efforts with online networking. The reasons given for using online networking include:

- It is more efficient
- I can multitask
- I can do it all hours from all time zones
- I can network with more people at once
- I don't have to travel
- I'm more gutsy online[4]

There has been an explosion of sites dedicated to or useful for networking. While the number and nature of these sites is rapidly developing, some of the more useful ones for physicians include:

---

[3] *It's Who You Know,* Torres, N, Entrepreneur, p. 13, 12/2005.
[4] Downtownwomensclub.com, 2006 online networking survey.

- LinkedIn
- Twitter
- Ryze
- Doostang
- 85 Broads
- Jobster
- MyWorkster
- Facebook
- MySpace
- Alumni Networking
- Alumni.NET
- Bright Star
- FastCompany
- Friendster
- MeetUp.com Work and Careers
- Classmates.com
- Monster Networking

In addition to these networking/social networking sites, a new series of online sites is developing. These next generation job sites seek to replace executive-search firms with cash incentives and matching algorithms. These sites include:

- NotchUp.com
- Jobfox.com
- BlueChipexpert.com
- H3.com

The power of these sites can be dramatic. For example, LinkedIn.com has over 130,000 medical professionals, mostly physicians, registered. These medical professionals have at their disposal many groups. A few of the groups include:

- Medical Device Network
- Physicians Alternative Career Network (PACnet)
- Healthcare Physicians Practice Network

- Bio/Pharma Professionals
- Health Informatics Technology (HIT) Group

As with traditional networking, using the proper accepted etiquette and netiquette is crucial. An excellent reference tool to navigating the online networking world is *The Savvy Gal's Guide to Online Networking* by Diane K. Danielson and Lindsey Pollak.[5] According to them, some of the mistakes online networkers make include:

- Not delivering what you promise,
- Failure to mind your manners,
- Not knowing your audience,
- Skipping over a polite introduction,
- Failing to thank them,
- Not speaking in specifics,
- Failing to choose your subject line carefully,
- Failing to include contact information on your signature line,
- Using people's names without permission,
- Blasting out e-mails to everyone, and
- Making spelling and grammatical mistakes.

POTENTIAL ONLINE NETWORKING PROBLEMS

The potential problem with these online sites is that the more popular they become, the more e-mails you and others will receive from them, resulting in networking overload and failure. It will not be too long before recipients may fail to open or respond to these online sites. Danielson and Pollak sum up the issue well:

> Online networking is not—in no way, nada, not in a million years—a substitute for in-person, eyeball-to-eyeball relationship building. Online networking complements in-person networking and is most effective when done in combination with live networking. This is why we advocate a "clicks and mix" strategy. In today's increasingly wired society, you can—and should—combine both. For those of you who can't get enough of online networking, don't forget that you need to balance your Web interactions with

---

[5] Published by booklocker.com (2007).

live connections to reap the best results. And, all the face-to-face advocates should consider online networking a tool to help manage and maintain contacts between meetings.[6]

4.8 Conclusion

Physicians who enjoy helping and mentoring others even when there is nothing in it for them tend to be the best and most effective networkers. On the rare occasion when these physicians do ask for help, their colleagues will rush to bend over backward to help them.

Remember as well the little secret of networking. Even if you don't land your dream job, getting in touch with people, meeting new people, doing favors, and gathering information can be and usually are fun and rewarding.

---

[6] Danielson and Pollak, p. 3.

Chapter 5 Where Non-Clinical Jobs Are Listed/Posted

5.1 Executive Summary

- Online and print job postings are an effective way to see what industries look for and to locate job opportunities.
- Most companies post jobs internally. There are so many companies that employ physicians that you will want to target those of most interest by geography, industry, etc.
- Non-clinical jobs are posted on medical society sites, recruiter sites, generic job search sites, and sites specifically focusing on non-clinical careers, such as medzilla.com.
- For jobs with the federal government, visit usajobs.com.
- For state and local government jobs, visit the Web site of the entity you would like to work for (such as the state health department).

5.2 Introduction

Most jobs are not found through job postings. Recruiters and, above all, networking are responsible for most physicians finding their first non-clinical positions. That said, many physicians do identify their first job opportunities through job postings.

Searching job postings can be valuable in a different way as well. Job postings show what employers are ideally looking for, what types of companies hire physicians, where these companies are located, and sometimes give an idea as to the compensation the position pays. This chapter concisely covers the types of places non-clinical opportunities for physicians may be posted.

5.3 Individual Companies

Almost all large employers post job openings on their own Web sites. There are so many potentially relevant sites that checking them all would be a full-time job in and of itself. The authors instead recommend that you target the industries and employers of most interest to you, bookmark their job search pages, and then get into the routine of checking their job listings. You can also set up many of these sites to automatically notify you when a desired job becomes available.

Example 5.1: Targeting companies most likely to desire someone in your specialty
You have determined that you want to work for industry. You are flexible in terms of being able to move. You research which companies are researching and marketing products in your area of therapeutic expertise and then check for positions available regularly on the applicable company Web sites.

Example 5.2: Targeting companies in the desired field in your geographic industry
You have determined that you would like to work in the insurance field. You are not willing to relocate. You identify each insurer with a major office within commuting distance of your current home and regularly check for job postings.

5.4 Medical Journals

Medical journals often have online and print classified ads offering jobs to physicians. The most important such journals of general circulation are *The New England Journal of Medicine* and *The Journal of the American Medical Association*. You should also check to see if the applicable journals in your specialty offer job postings.

5.5 Medical Societies

State and specialty medical societies will often post job listings on their Web sites. Note that there may be specialty societies serving a particular field of non-clinical medicine. If you are targeting a particular industry, it can be a good idea to identify and check for job postings on the Web site of the society that serves non-clinical physicians in that particular field. State specialty societies can be good if you want or need to target jobs in that particular state.

Example 5.3: Specialty medical societies serving non-clinical areas
You are interested in a career in insurance. You identify the American Academy of Insurance Medicine as the specialty society serving non-clinical physicians in that field. You regularly check the AAIM site for job postings.

5.6 Generic Job Search Sites

Non-clinical positions for physicians can be found on generic job search sites such as monster.com or careerbuilder.com. Please also consider Indeed.com, which features a Google-like search function and allows you to easily restrict your search to a geographic area. A better fit for physicians may be sites that focus on high-paying jobs. An example of this is www.theladders.com.

5.7 Job Search/Posting Sites Specific to Medical Professionals in Non-Clinical Careers

A better search tool for physicians is often a site designed to be used by healthcare professionals. The biggest of these is probably www.medzilla.com, which focuses on pharma, medical devices, and biotechnology. Please also consider www.hirelifescience.com, www.centerwatch.com and www.mdjobsite.com. The American College of Physician Executives (www.acpe.org) also maintains an excellent job posting site.

5.8 Government Jobs

If you are interested in working for state government, most states post positions available for physicians on the Web site of the state department of health or department of health and human services. You might also want to check the Web site of your state's medical licensing board. For positions in the federal government, the most important resource is www.usajobs.com.

5.9 Recruiters

Recruiters will often post job offerings on their Web sites. For examples of this, you can visit www.cejkasearch.com, www.bornbicknell.com, and www.hcrintl.com.

Chapter 6 Pros, Cons, and Utility of Advanced Degrees Such as an MBA, MMM, MHA, or MPH

6.1 Executive Summary

- You do *not* need an advanced degree to be hired and advance in numerous non-clinical careers. There are many things employers look for that can be more important than an advanced degree (such as, clinical expertise, a passion for the field, communication skills, leadership ability, and business sense).
- The information and skills you learn while pursuing your advanced degree can be helpful in your new career.
- Getting an advanced degree is extremely expensive and time consuming. Tuition alone at top schools can be $40,000–$50,000 per year. There is a large opportunity cost in lost income and lost time with your family. To get the best return on your investment, the sooner you go back to school, the better.
- An advanced degree from a prestigious program can open many doors. The quality of a degree can also provide a physician with the pedigree to be positioned to rise to the highest levels of the corporate world.
- Any advanced degree will demonstrate your commitment to your new non-clinical career. This will help in your job search and may lead directly to your first non-clinical job. Taking the time to get an advanced degree is very strong evidence that you are serious about a non-clinical career and will usually reflect well on your job candidacy.
- An advanced degree is no guarantee of a successful career transition. If the field does not value the degree, if you don't interview well, if you look too unfocused or present with other problems, you are not guaranteed a successful non-clinical career.
- A benefit of an advanced degree that many people overlook is the networking possibilities the degree opens up. You will meet many people in graduate school who will go on to careers for many different employers. You will also become part of a new alumni network that offers powerful possibilities in terms of networking and career services.

- Some people just really enjoy learning. This includes many physicians. If you want to go back to school because you would find it intellectually stimulating and fun, go for it.
- Different people are likely to give you different advice on this topic.

6.2 Career Value of an Advanced Degree

The career value of an advanced degree depends a lot on the non-clinical career path you choose. If you want to become a lawyer, a law degree is going to be a requirement. In other pursuits, it may or may not be worth the time and money. A SEAK faculty member who coaches physician entrepreneurs has this to say about whether you should pursue an advanced degree:

Example 6.1: The value of an advanced degree depends greatly on the field you are targeting
It really depends on what your aspirations are for once you leave medicine. If you're seeking a senior management role in a fairly substantial company—business, organization, hospital chain, insurance company no matter what—I personally think that the discipline of some kind of management oriented training, be it an MBA, be it a Masters in Public Health, be it a Masters in Health Administration, be it the—I think that that probably would become a requirement these days. It's looking more and more like it's going to be that those extra credentials, I think, are helpful.

But if you're looking to go start a business that you've been stewing and brewing over for a period of time, and you're looking at putting anywhere from $75,000.00 to $120,000.00 into your business versus into an MBA—I don't necessarily feel that it's necessary to have that degree because quite honestly, I have interviewed a lot. I do a series of podcasts called Conversations with Trailblazers, and I interview successful physician entrepreneurs and I think out of the 30 or so that I've interviewed, only two have gone back to school and gotten their MBA. The rest of them have all just figured it out.

My degree was very helpful in that it gave me a little bit of a sense of business. But it did not teach me anything about entrepreneurship and starting a business.

An MBA or other advanced degree might not help you land your first non-clinical job. Consider the narrative from a SEAK faculty member who moved into pharma. It did not assist him because of the type of skills the employer was looking for:

Example 6.2: MBA did not help physician land job in pharma but it helped him enjoy industry

I did the MBA when I was in clinical practice doing clinical trials, and I became very interested in the business side of medicine, did my MBA, people asked me did it help me getting a job in the industry—it did not. But it has helped me enjoy industry much more. And I think that that's really important because I can tell you, when I hire physicians, what I look for are physicians who are going to be happy in the job. The MBA has made me very happy doing what I do because I can understand at a different level what's going on and I can articulate what I need to do to my business colleagues in a better way because I understand how they think.

But as far as getting that first job, it was my therapeutic expertise and my scientific knowledge.

Example 6.3: Chief medical officer for health insurer—"Nice to have [MBA], but it's really not required"

My personal belief is an MBA or an MPH or a second degree is nice to have, but it's really not required. I do not look for that right off the bat. I'm much more interested in who the person is, what they've done, how they've done it and what they can do for me. Those are kind of the four things. The questions that go through my mind in an interview are again who is this person that's sitting in front of me? Who actually—what values do they have? What do they think? What are they interested in? And then what they've done in the past, how they did it and what they can do for my company and my division going forward. Those are the things that run in my mind when I do an interview. Only about 15–20% of physicians today in the managed care health insurance world have a second degree, probably the younger you are, the higher the expectation is that you'll have a second degree but in my opinion it is not required.

Here is what a physician hospital CEO who does not hold any advanced degrees has to say:

Example 6.4: Advanced degree helpful if you have time and money, but what you really need is to be conversant—self-study and on-the-job training can substitute

I think it would have helped me to have an MBA, if I'd have had the time. If I had a degree I'd probably get a Masters in Public Health, because I'm so interested in community medicine and preventative medicine. I wish I had the epidemiology skills, the statistics and that sort of thing, but I'd rather do on the job training and do a lot of reading. And it's risky, because people might not give you, I guess, the benefit of the doubt. Because you're a physician, they don't think you're a very good business person.

I found that not to be true in many cases, but in general a lot of times it's something that doctors get in trouble with, because they have the vision, they have the idea, they have the service ethic, they have the curiosity and intellect, but they may or may not have the jargon. You've got to be able to stand toe-to-toe with the CFO. You don't need to be a surrogate CFO. You don't have to have an MBA, but you've got to be conversant. You can't let people intimidate you with knowledge.

Here's the opinion of a neurologist who went back part-time to obtain a journalism degree and then became a TV medical reporter:

Example 6.5: Advanced degree helpful but not required and cannot teach the same things as real world
I went part-time in my practice and went to school part-time to get my degree, and I should say not everybody needs that. You don't need to go back to school to be a journalist. That's all part of it, but yes, I went back part-time. And I'm glad I went back because I think one, it gave more seriousness to me changing careers. I mean, people looked at this—yes, she really wants to do this. She's going to go back to school and get this additional training.

Also, you learn things in journalism school that you aren't going to learn on the job and vice versa. You learn about how to write the right way. You learn about ethics. You learn about history, things that you were never going to learn in a newsroom. But again, there's nothing like a news room to teach you the time pressures of putting together a piece on deadline.

So, I'm glad I went. I thought it was a useful experience. Plus, it gives me an avenue for teaching this to others now.

The story of a pediatrician who moved into the financial industry is instructive:

Example 6.6: Physician in process of getting MBA stops program once he breaks into industry—"Once you got the job, what do you need an MBA for?"
I started an MBA program on the East Coast at a big institution. I also started a CFA program, which is a sort of a chartered financial analyst program and also started networking and talking to lots and lots of my friends and people who were involved in the business world. And I was trying to find that intersection

of where my expertise in health care, or pediatrician, whatever could somehow segue into something that was a job that was business related.

And as I was talking with people, it became more clear to me that what I really wanted to do was to try to become a drug analyst on Wall Street for a variety of reasons. And then it doesn't happen overnight and I had to talk with a lot of people—a lot of networking and many interviews and so on and so forth. And finally, thank God, I landed the job at a major Wall Street firm as an associate analyst. But that was after probably—for me it was probably a good year and a half after I really had already made the efforts to really land that plum job.

And this is a really difficult job to do that because there were probably a few hundred people vying for this position. So I was very excited to get that. And then people always ask me at that point, "Did you finish your MBA?" The answer is no. I ask people at that point, "Do you finish your MBA?" They said no, the reason for getting the MBA is to get the job. Once you got the job, what do you need the MBA for? So I never went back and finished it and I never found that it was necessary that I have that. I mean, I'm glad I started it and so on and so forth. If I needed it for something then I would go back and finish it.

Consider the story of one SEAK faculty member who suddenly found himself without a job practicing clinical medicine:

Example 6.7: MBA from Ivy League school leads directly to job offer

In 1996, on February 14th, what we affectionately call the Valentine's Day Massacre, five of us who worked at a VA at [a particular location] were told that because of a budget crisis we no longer had a job. I was a five-eighths employee, a part-time employee there, and I also worked as an associate professor at Dartmouth. Basically, that set in motion a whole journey that I really never had any idea exactly how it was going to work out, but it has exceeded my wildest expectations.

Well part of the reason I'm doing what I'm doing is after two weeks of—within two weeks I had offers to go take jobs doing work as a full-time academic surgeon with a promotion to professor. One was in New Jersey and one was in New Mexico. My wife, who is a New England girl, said that she wasn't ready to leave and that we needed to look at something else. So that led to a quick application to the Dartmouth MBA program, so that we didn't need to move, and I fortunately found out that I was accepted there in May.

And for the first semester in business school I thought I was Tuck's dirty little secret. I mean I was one of about 10 percent who hadn't had a recent business major or an accounting major or economics major. So it was a struggle, but by the end I was asked to be class commencement speaker, and I think that was because I had 20 years of helpfulness training over the rest of my colleagues in the class.

[My MBA led directly to my first job at a consulting firm.] In fact, the partner who hired me was a Tuck graduate from about ten years before. So he was familiar with the education and how they train people to work in teams. That was something that was a big difference from medical school, because in business school 30 to 50 percent of my grade in every course I took came from team projects. And in medical school I've talked to over 2,000 physicians and I've asked them, "What part of your grade came from team projects?" and they tell me, "Zero, mean, median, mode, standard deviation."

Our advice is to talk to as many people as possible in the field you are targeting and then make your own decision as to whether pursuing an advanced degree is in your best interest given the time and cost involved. There is no one-size-fits-all answer to this question.

6.3 Where and How to Pursue an Advanced Degree

If you are serious about a career change, can get into a top-flight program, and have the time and money to invest, going for it full-time is a viable career option. The median starting salary for a 2007 Harvard Business School graduate is $120,000 for those going into consulting (a perfect role for physicians). Five-year median salaries for top-school graduates are greater than $250,000. The long-term economic benefits of a degree like this are usually quite positive if you can then prove yourself in business. On the negative side of things, 2009 tuition at Harvard Business School was $41,900. Because of the time, money, and lost income involved, going full-time to a prestigious school is probably the best option for someone relatively young who is certain about going into management and business. With tuition costs, opportunity costs, and the blood, sweat, and tears involved, earning back your investment in an MBA will take a long, long time.

Here's how a SEAK faculty member described her decision to go to a lesser-rated business school over a more prestigious one because of the flexibility the lesser-rated school allowed:

Example 6.8: Balancing practice and school nearly impossible at a top-ten business school
[The ability to practice and go to school at the same time] was a really strong factor in the program I chose. I applied to a lot of very top-level schools. I got into a lot of schools, but I ended up choosing my alma mater for where I went to medical school because they have extreme flexibility, courses throughout the

year and into the summer. It enabled me to work and go to school over the course of a period of about two and a half years.

I wasn't only in school and not working at any given time. I was quasi working, quasi in school. Financially I approached it with a hybrid model. And that was really important for me, because I didn't want to completely leave the workforce. I didn't want to stop practicing medicine. I didn't want to take that hiatus.

I think that that decision is a very personal one for some folks. If you go to Harvard Business School, if you go to a top-ten business school, it's very unlikely you're going to have the time to really effectively practice medicine in a meaningful way while you're getting trained and make a reasonable income. Generally, you're going to have to take a hiatus.

And things probably have maybe evolved a little bit, but I think that's still pretty much the case. If you have a family and children at home, to try to do all three, work, go to school, and take care of a family that's a really tall order, but it's not that it can't be done. I think there's a lot of where there's a will there's a way.

A common route to obtain an advanced degree is to do so part-time while continuing to practice. This can be done live, online, or as a mixture of the two. Many institutions offer Executive MBAs specifically designed for physicians. These include the University of Hartford, Auburn, and the University of Tennessee. Descriptions of their programs can be found on their Web sites.

Example 6.9: Description of University of Tennessee Executive MBA for physicians program
The Physician Executive MBA program is an advanced educational degree offered by The University of Tennessee College of Business Administration exclusively for physicians seeking high quality leadership, management, and business operation skills.

The program is conveniently available nationwide, requiring only four one-week on-site residence periods during the 12 month program. All other course hours are available at your computer desktop via the Internet. Classes start in early January. Graduation is in December of each year.

UT's Physician Executive MBA incorporates these unique features:

Short residency periods and distance education technology allow you to
    continue your career
Fast completion—only one year long
No business prerequisites required

Classes are composed of physicians only
Continuing Medical Education credits available
Personalized leadership assessment and development program
Extensive computer skills development
Active Physician Leader Alumni Network[1]

Balancing practicing medicine and going back to school can obviously be a challenge. It can be done, however. Many of your colleagues have successfully completed advanced degrees while practicing medicine.

Another technique is to take an entry-level job as a non-clinical physician and then pursue your MBA or other advanced degree at that time. There are two advantages to this strategy. First, you may have a lot more time to pursue the advanced degree when you are no longer practicing medicine. Second, your employer may reimburse you for all or part of the cost of your tuition, which is obviously a major benefit. The drawback to this strategy is that you will not have the advanced degree to help you land your first non-clinical position. You will, however, have the benefit of the advanced degree to assist your long-term career goals.

One SEAK faculty member describes his experience and thoughts on getting an MBA:

Example 6.10: Employer advertising agency pays for Executive MBA for physician employee

After seven years in medical advertising I went back and got my MBA, because what that does for you, it immediately establishes credibility, because even there I was very creative.

...We used to do a Christmas party there and I was in charge of the Christmas party, but you had to prove that you're creative, 'cause you're the doctor. How could you be creative? So what the MBA did for me was, "Oh, he must know business. He has an MBA."

But I also want to say you don't get an MBA just to get an MBA. It's an amazing, amazing two years of content that you learn that really does mean something. You learn about marketing. You learn finance, accounting, just great courses, human resources. And it means something after you've been in business or after you've worked for a while. I'm sort of against the MD/MBA combo program, because the MBA doesn't mean anything unless you've really experienced the workforce for a while.

I did the executive MBA program, which I thought was terrific. It was alternating Fridays and Saturdays, 36 weeks a year for two years. Tuition was

---

[1] http://pemba.utk.edu/

pretty hefty in those days. This was in '88. It was like $25,000, but if you happen to be with a company already it's good, because they pay. They have tuition reimbursement and that's not bad. But [my employer] paid only 75 percent for an A and 50 percent for a B. You're motivated to get good grades because it means big bucks.

The American College of Physician Executives (www.acpe.org) offers many online and live leadership and management courses for physicians. It also offers board certification in medical management (please visit www.ccmm.org). ACPE courses are generally available for CME credit. ACPE has partnered with four universities (Carnegie Mellon, Tulane, UMass Amherst, University of Southern California) and also offers MMM (Masters in Medical Management) and MBA degrees. The programs are designed for practicing physicians who require flexibility in pursuing their advanced degrees.

6.4 More on the MBA Degree in Particular

The decision about whether a physician moving to non-clinical work should seek an MBA is uniquely personal. It depends upon many factors, including: your age, the type of non-clinical position you are seeking, the time, money, and effort you are willing to expend, and whether you have identified a career path.

AGE

Generally speaking, the younger the physician, the more time there will be for the physician to make the MBA pay off. Having said this, because many physicians and other professionals are working into their 70s, 80s, and beyond, it is probably never too late to seek an MBA.

NON-CLINICAL POSITION SOUGHT

The type of non-clinical position sought may be a deciding factor in whether an MBA is worthwhile. Talk to physicians who moved over to similar non-clinical positions. How many have MBAs? What do they say about the utility of getting an MBA?

TIME, MONEY, AND EFFORT

Getting an MBA may take two years or more and cost $100,000 or more in tuition. When you factor in the time spent and the opportunity cost (lost income while you could have been working elsewhere) the cost is much higher. Physicians will want to examine their reasons for seeking an MBA. If the reason is to postpone the move to non-clinical medicine, this may not be the wisest course of action. If, on the other hand, it is part of a well-thought-out career plan, the choice may make more sense.

LEAVING OPTIONS OPEN

For those physicians moving to non-clinical medicine who have not yet identified a clear career path, getting the MBA may be a way to leave their options open. The MBA is likely to give them the broadest career options when the time comes to make a choice.

EMPIRICAL RESEARCH

There is very little empirical research on the utility of physicians getting an MBA. In the study "An MBA: The Utility and Effect on Physicians' Careers," the authors found that the average age of the respondents was 41.4 years. The major motivations for going back to school included learning the business aspects of the healthcare system (fifty-three respondents; 67%) and obtaining a more interesting job (forty-one respondents; 52%). The time that the respondents allocated for healthcare-related activities before and after obtaining the degree was 58.3% and 31.8%, respectively, for patient care ($p < 0.001$); 8.5% and 3.68% for teaching ($p < 0.001$); 4.57% and 1.46% for basic-science research ($p = 0.11$); 4.23% and 4.55% for clinical research ($p = 0.90$); and 11.8% and 33.5% for administrative responsibilities ($p < 0.001$). The physicians stated that the most pertinent skills they had acquired were those related to evaluating systems operations and implementing improvements (thirty-nine respondents; 49%), learning how to be an effective leader (thirty-five; 44%), comprehending financial principles (thirty-three; 42%), working within a team (twenty-seven; 34%), and negotiating effectively (twenty-five; 32%). Sixty-four physicians (81%) believed that their business degree had been very useful or essential in the advancement of their careers.

Many physicians decide to acquire a Master of Business Administration degree to understand the business of medicine. After they complete the degree program, their practice patterns substantially change, which is reflected particularly by an increase in time spent on administrative responsibilities. In order for physicians to overcome the multifaceted challenges of the evolving health-care system, it is essential to continue educating a proportion of physicians in both medicine and business.[2]

The above study was based on only 79 completed surveys and was not intended to measure the need or utility of getting an MBA for physicians switching to non-clinical medicine.

ADVANTAGES AND DISADVANTAGES OF GETTING AN MBA
When the authors conducted research on the specific question of advantages and disadvantages of physicians who are moving to non-clinical medicine getting an MBA, we received the following responses:

Advantages

I think there are huge advantages to the MBA:

- It sends the message that the doc is really interested in broadening his/her skills set.
- Once the MBA is completed, one makes the assumption that s/he has a firm grasp of commercial principles and can read a balance sheet.
- The finance and strategy components of the MBA are critical for someone whose career goal in industry is outside clinical research, i.e., medical affairs, business development, "C" level positions.
- While MDs do run companies, without the MBA, they are at a disadvantage, i.e., people see them as physicians sans a business mindset.

Learning the language and principles of business is critical when joining industry. Can someone run a business without an MBA? Certainly.

---

[2] *Journal of Bone and Joint Surgery (American), 2007; 89:442–447.*

- Greater understanding of business and therefore acceptance and utility in pursuing a career as an administrator.
- Enhanced quantitative skills for social decision making (policy making), societal risk benefit analysis.
- More opportunities outside of clinical medicine should one decide to change careers, investment analysis, etc.
- Make your mother happy.
- Greater chance of finding a life partner/spouse who can support you and the family.

- Credibility with non-physician executives; presumes an Executive MBA, ideally, branded (Kellogg, Tuck, Wharton, etc.).
- Substantive finance and operational perspective (e.g., a money-losing test may contribute to a highly profitable service line; business decision making around costs).
- Organizational management theory and practice.
- Social network that needs to come with that MBA (may be a local things versus the brand above).
- Peer-to-peer relationship with other physician executives.

- Acquire skills in the management sciences, such as organization, marketing, finance, personnel and facility operations.
- Acquire ability to manage financial aspects of healthcare.
- Acquire ability to manage the emerging area of medical informatics (electronic medical data).
- Develop a complete skill set to be able to provide healthcare, as well as manage the delivery of healthcare.
- Expand your career opportunities to include healthcare management.

The advantages to obtaining an MBA for a physician moving to administration from clinical medicine would include:

- Greater insight into the mechanics of the business world, including the topics of finance, economics, accounting, marketing, human resources, managerial and leadership skills, information technology, and health and workplace law.
- Improved ability to use the above skills to manage the business aspects of a medical practice (small group, large group, hospital).
- Improved marketability—competitive edge in the job market compared with non-degreed applicants with the same background and experience.
- Wider range of job choices.
- Ability to command a higher premium for services rendered (higher salary).

- Develop proficiency in the language of business.
- Gain perspectives into the size of the world economy and where individual industries, individuals and other inputs fit.
- Develop an ability to define value and act upon misallocation of resources (whether money or talent).
- Get a paper credential and plug into the career services (more important for a Harvard or Wharton than a Fairleigh Dickinson).
- Develop a network of your classmates.

Two big ones:

- Vocabulary (knowing EBITDA from BCR/ABL at board meetings and cocktail parties).
- Contacts (helps to hire people, to get hired, to keep current, etc.).

For physicians in particular:

- Pedigree—Very important for credibility with managers, who trust physicians only as much as physicians typically trust managers....

- Team building and team work—Medicine is hierarchical and trains individuals, not necessarily team players (need to understand a team to be able to build and lead one).
- Structured thinking around management, not medicine—How to write a coherent business plan or proposal (not a grant or paper).
- Presentation skills needed to persuade non-scientific audiences— Leading with the answer, not building to disprove the null hypothesis.
- Differentiating between medical leadership and professional management—Physicians learn to lead (vision, define end state, etc.), but not to manage (execute against and measure progress).

Here are some ideas for why a physician considering a move out of clinical medicine would consider an MBA:

- Advancement of career
  –Earn more
  –Potential employers would view positively a mid-career physician with an MBA
  –Improve likelihood of becoming a member of an advisory board
- Healthcare management
  Combining knowledge of healthcare industry with business management will lead to better decision making, including:
  –Finance
  –Policies
  –Project management
  –Computer systems
- Team leadership
  –Ensure physicians are effectively performing their clinical duties
  –Patient care quality
  –Departments budgets
- Communication skills
  –Learn business language
  –Delegate responsibilities
  –Organize meetings
  –Employee relations

- Practice improvement
  –Accounting
  –Marketing

- An MD provides credibility as a physician, of course, but it also plays to stereotypes (e.g., that you are not a good collaborator or have poor listening skills). An MBA can help counteract this stereotype (and can make you aware of these pitfalls if they describe you).
- Much of the subject matter and skills required to succeed in the non-clinical world are not learned in medical school or practice. Examples include strategy, finance, marketing, accounting, negotiation, etc.
- As more physicians move to non-clinical careers and their numbers become less scarce, an MBA is frequently noted as "desired" in job postings, and its presence or absence is increasingly determining who gets the job.
- The process of obtaining an MBA [provides] access to a business network that can prove valuable as one advances in one's career.
- While "traditional" medical director roles may still be had without an MBA, many other types of non-clinical jobs—such as those in the areas of investment management, strategic planning, mergers and acquisitions, etc.—are effectively closed off to those without the degree.

If they are staying in clinical medicine, the advantages are:

- Ability to understand their own financials.
- Ability to evaluate the drivers of their business and how to influence them.
- Ability to communicate effectively with bankers, etc.
- Networking opportunities with other students and professors.
- Credibility during negotiations, etc.

Leaving clinical medicine:

- A degree which will broaden their opportunities and open up a new sector.

169

- Networking opportunities.
- Credibility with potential employers (i.e., health plans, PE groups, etc.).
- Understanding a new language and developing a new skill set.
- Ability to start and manager their own business.

Disadvantages
The disadvantages for getting an MBA for physicians are well known. They include:

- Cost,
- Opportunity cost/lost time,
- Delays career transition, and
- It can be an escape mechanism.

The SEAK Non-Clinical Career Faculty had this to say about the disadvantages of seeking an MBA:

For most MDs an MBA is a waste of time. You can get most of what you need by stringing together a few week-long executive courses.

The disadvantages would be the investments in both time and money, and the delay in proceeding with the next job while undergoing the coursework.

- 2 years of lost earning potential.
- 2 years taken away from family and personal time if MBA pursued while still working.
- I think the MBAs are going to be devalued as a consequence of the current economic crisis.
- One must weigh the decision to pursue an MBA against the pay back on two years spent studying in a clinical fellowship that may result in greater job satisfaction and/or economic benefits.

My personal belief is an MBA or an MPH or a second degree is nice to have, but it's really not required. I do not look for that right off the bat. I'm much more interested in who the person is, what they've done, how they've done it and what they can do for me. Those are kind of the four things. The questions that go through my mind in an interview are again, who is this person that's sitting in front of me? Who actually—what values do they have? What do they think? What are they interested in? And then what they've done in the past, how they did it and what they can do for my company and my division going forward. Those are the things that run in my mind when I do an interview.

TYPES OF PHYSICIANS EMPLOYED IN NON-CLINICAL POSITIONS WHO HAVE OBTAINED MBAS
- Vice president of medical affairs: At a start-up cardiovascular medical device company.
- Chief medical officer: At a start-up biopharmaceutical company.
- Chief operating officer and general manager: At Medpole. Providing tailored strategic advice and implementation support to medical device companies or technologies at the early stages to facilitate approvals and maximize the commercial impact of a new product.
- Venture capital: Emergency room doctor (still spends 1 night/week on an 8-hour shift) who specializes in medical device and biotech venture capital.
- Venture capital: Non-practicing oncologist who specializes in pharma venture capital.
- Clinical consultant: Provides expertise to pharma and biotech industry on managing clinical trials.
- Biodesign fellow: Stanford University Graduate Program for next generation of physician entrepreneurs of medical devices.
- Government: Senior manager at FDA (Drugs).

HOW PHYSICIANS USE THEIR MBAS IN THEIR NON-CLINICAL POSITIONS
A senior manager at the FDA (Drugs) explains:

I am a neurologist with 8 years of federal government regulatory experience. My primary duty is to write or otherwise develop through working groups, guidance, and policy regulatory documents related to Good Review Practices. I employ my MBA skills to enhance the process of drug regulation at all levels of the organization. I formulate and run working groups that address mission critical projects. I aid in updating review management tools, provide input resulting in decisions for IT systems and projects. Through my work, I enhance communication between FDA and its stakeholders.

6.5 Conclusion

- You do not need an advanced degree in order to be hired and advance in numerous non-clinical careers.
- The information you learn while pursuing your advanced degree can be helpful in your new career.
- Getting an advanced degree is extremely expensive and time consuming.
- An advanced degree from a prestigious program can open many doors.
- Any advanced degree will demonstrate your commitment to your new non-clinical career, which will help your job search.

Chapter 7 Drafting a Powerful Non-Clinical Resume

7.1 Executive Summary

- A CV is not a resume. For most non-clinical positions you will need a resume and not a CV.
- Your resume is a sales document. You are selling yourself.
- The key to effective resume writing is listing your major tangible accomplishments that would be of most interest to employers in the particular field you are targeting.
- A functional, as opposed to a chronological, format is usually best for those searching for their first non-clinical position.

7.2 A CV Is Not a Resume

Physicians transitioning to non-clinical positions will need to create their non-clinical resume. While there is no shortage of resume-building books, services, and advice, one thing all the experts agree on is that a curriculum vitae (CV) is not a resume. Consider what a noted resume expert has to say about the difference between a CV and resume:

Example 7.1: CV is background-oriented, a resume is oriented toward the future
The distinction between a CV and a resume is that a CV is typically much longer. It can be short; but typically much longer. There's a vast difference about the content. A CV is typically, what we call, task oriented, skills oriented, and background oriented. A resume, at least a resume done right, should be much more oriented towards the future. Using what you've done in the past to predict your ability to do that type of thing in the future. Always, again, around the bottom line: what's it going to mean for the employer; translating your physician skills into real-world corporate skills. The biggest part of a resume is to show chemistry and fit by showing your brand and your value proposition.

Your value proposition being the biggest thing that you bring to the table. The contents of the resume support that value proposition. There is also a confusion because, in Europe and other parts of the world, resumes are CVs. Here in the United States, a CV is typically something that a doctor or a physician would use and a resume is something that you are going to have to have for that transition. A CV is just not going to get you in the door.

The CVs that many clinicians have include lengthy recitations of their:

- Personal information
- Education
- Honors
- Board certifications
- Memberships in professional societies
- Committee activities
- Articles written
- Presentations given
- Research conducted
- Continuing education courses taken, etc.

7.3 Drafting Your Non-Clinical Resume

START FROM SCRATCH

Physicians drafting a non-clinical resume are best served by starting their resume from scratch. Your non-clinical resume is a business document drafted specifically with the purpose of obtaining one or more specific positions. As such, you need to carefully consider the type(s) of jobs you will be seeking before you draft your resume. A resume for someone looking to become a medical reporter should read much differently than a physician looking to work in clinical affairs in the pharmaceutical industry. The key is thorough networking and research to find out as much as possible about what the particular employer/industry is looking for and then highlighting your accomplishments in these areas.

SALES OR MARKETING DOCUMENT

A resume is essentially a sales or marketing document. Depending upon the position you are applying for, the purpose may not be to impress the reader with your medical knowledge, success, or accomplishments. Note that many non-clinical employers are looking for excellent clinicians because this clinical knowledge is crucial to the non-clinical job function. For example, if you want to become a high-net-worth personal financial advisor, how many articles you have published in a certain area of medicine will be neither important nor relevant. If, on the other hand, you are going to work in medical affairs for a pharma company developing a drug in your niche area of medicine, your clinical knowledge and experience might be critically important to your employer. The key is to gather in advance as much information as possible about the job and industry you are targeting. Once this is done, you can tweak your resume, highlighting what you have to offer (medical and/or non-medical) that industry or employer. For more information on what skills and experience are sought in which industries, please see Chapter 3.

The goal of the resume should be to address several questions:

- What can you do for the employer?
- What have you accomplished?
- What are the skills, abilities, and competencies you bring to the table?
- Is there a good fit between the employer, its corporate culture, you, and the position you seek to fill?

Your goal should be to distill in one to three pages (preferably one page) the unique abilities, experience, judgment, and accomplishments you bring to the employer.

The keys to getting your resume noticed include:

- The resume is not the time to be humble. Think of your list of accomplishments.
- Review your performance at past positions and answer the following questions:
  o What was your impact on your organization/group/company/ division?
  o What would not have happened if you hadn't been there?
  o What are you proudest of during your time with the company?
- If you have favorable past job evaluations, utilize the material in your resume.
- Measure results. Think about your performance, and apply numbers where possible, using percentages, dollar signs, and quantifiers (i.e., saved $100 million).
- Cite recognitions. If you were recognized with an award, cite it on your resume if it was for significant accomplishments.[1]

---

[1] "Standing Out in a Sea of CVs: Results a Key to Getting Resume Noticed," *The Wall Street Journal,* 1/16/2007, B8, Mattioli.

- Points made on a resume are usually more powerful if they quantify something as opposed to being vague. For example, "I have given over 150 lectures and trained over 2,500 of my colleagues in the field on oncology" is much more powerful than "I am an excellent communicator."
- Your accomplishments listed should be major ones (triples and home runs).
- Make sure the one or two pages you write are full. Don't leave a half page blank—it will look like you are lacking in accomplishments.
- Absolutely ensure that there are no typos or other mistakes.
- Write in concise phrases, not sentences.

7.4 Formatting Your Resume

Many resumes use a chronological format, organized by date. Other resumes use a functional format, organized by what you did for your employers.

The problem with a chronological format is that it is effective for obtaining the same type of positions the physician previously held, namely clinical positions. Functional formats are preferred over chronological formats for physicians looking to leave clinical medicine for a new type of position. The authors have studied the resumes of physicians who have successfully transitioned from clinical to non-clinical positions. These resumes are functional and emphasize accomplishments, core competencies, results, and performance. When possible, they are specific.

CONTACT INFORMATION
Page one of the functional resume includes the person's name, degrees, address, telephone, cell phone, and personal e-mail address.

Example 7.2: Resume contact information

Steven Cohen, MD, MBA
176 Shore Rd.
Pasadena, CA 91103

Phone: (555) 555-1234   Cell: (555) 555-5678   E-mail: StevenC@yahoo.com

SUMMARY/PROFILE

This first full paragraph of your resume should address your core competencies, what you bring to the table, and what you have already accomplished. Physicians seeking non-clinical employment will want to tweeze out their business, management, and leadership accomplishments to fit the needs of their prospective employers. Clinical physicians without full-time non-clinical experience may have to thoroughly examine their duties, responsibilities, training, and accomplishments. Positioning yourself for career change through obtaining resume-building experience can greatly assist with this. For more on resume-building strategies, please see Section 9.20.

In the example below, note how the physician emphasizes what she thinks the employer would most want to see in a physician employee:

Example 7.3: Summary of physician looking for first non-clinical job with a managed care company
Well-respected board certified internist with 15 years clinical experience. Recognized physician leader, former class president, and head of numerous committees and task forces. Accomplished innovator and change agent. Superb communications skills. Noted expert in evidence-based medicine.

Note how the summary paragraph in the following example specifically targets an ad agency. Had the physician been looking for a position in a different industry, different skills, experience, and accomplishments would be highlighted:

Example 7.4: Summary of physician looking for first non-clinical job with a medical advertising agency serving pharma
Medical doctor with ability to combine clinical knowledge with communication skills. Prolific author with a strong track record of pushing projects through to their conclusions and working on large interdisciplinary teams. Implemented

print and online marketing campaign for my group practice, which resulted in a 22% boost in revenues and 32% increase in profits in one year.

Example 7.5: Sample #1—Summary from an experienced physician executive
Physician-executive, medical director, and clinician with 20 years experience in management of health programs, in development of health-education projects, and in preventative medicine (Board Certified). Development and implementation of large programs as Operations VP at Core and as a chief medical officer. Outstanding skills in creating quality assurance programs, strategies, and implementation plans, and in training of medical professionals. Proven ability in developing and selling care management strategies, wellness programs, utilization review and working with employee groups, HR, adjusters, managers, unions, and others to define, describe, and develop cost-effective medical programs with measureable quality and outcomes. An enthusiastic leader experienced in the motivation of professionals in teams. Internationally recognized author in preventative medicine. Excellent presentation, analytic, and computer skills.

Example 7.6: Sample #2—Summary from an experienced physician executive

SUMMARY
Healthcare executive with 15 years of clinical experience and an additional decade in healthcare management. Specific expertise in healthcare services, information technology, biotechnology, and consumer-driven healthcare. Demonstrated success in the following areas:

- Development and implementation of clinical strategy in aggressive commercial organizations
- Building relationships with clinical thought leaders and professional societies
- Creating and growing high performance teams in both start-ups and large company environments
- General management including P and L ownership
- Business development – including network development and optimization

Example 7.7: Sample #3—Summary from an experienced physician executive

SUMMARY

An accomplished healthcare executive with over 25 years of business and clinical experience as a healthcare consultant and board-certified internist. In-depth industry knowledge across key stakeholders—payors, providers, patients, employers, and specialty companies. Areas of expertise include disease management, wellness, healthcare analytics, and telemedicine.

Known for the ability to identify key clinical and business issues, design population care management solutions, and create the methodology and metrics to determine the impact of clinical programs and the performance of provider networks.

Recognized as a teacher and mentor. Fluent in Spanish.

EXPERIENCE

In this section, the physician will want to start with her most current employer. For each employer, the physician will want to list her title, duties, scope of the position, responsibilities, and accomplishments that would be most relevant to the position and industry the physician is targeting.

Example 7.8: Stressing accomplishments and responsibilities most relevant to employer

1998–Present General Hospital—Emergency Room Physician. Active clinician with significant leadership and management experience. Served on quality control committee which implemented changes resulting in a 23% decrease in adverse events. Top physician in charge of transition to electronic health records resulting in a savings of $2.3 million over 3 years. Elected chief of emergency medicine by my peers.

Example 7.9: Describing experience for a non-clinical employer for an entry-level position

2001–Present WeCare, Inc. Physician and managing partner. Time spent 75% as practicing clinician and 25% as managing partner. Accomplished negotiator and leader. Negotiated numerous provider agreements resulting in a 7.5% average annual increase in reimbursements. Decreased fix costs by instituting top to bottom atomization and cost control. Negotiated more favorable insurance policies. Saved $300,000 annually from vendors by renegotiating terms. Reduced staff turnover to less than 3% annually by implementing new and innovative work policies.

Example 7.10: Experienced physician executive describes his experience 2006 to the present as medical director, physician strategies at a major disability insurance company
Head of Corporate Physician Strategies Group charged with developing clinical programs and initiatives to influence physician behavior and thereby drive improvements in quality, cost, and satisfaction. Also managed team of 50 Market Medical Officers in commercial markets throughout US, with accountability for clinical sales support, customer analytics and reporting, identification and mitigation of drivers of medical cost trend, and provider relations.

We suggest including an introductory paragraph to your experience. Under the experience introductory paragraph, highlight your specific accomplishments. The keys are: 1) finding out what employers in the field you are targeting are looking for, 2) building your resume if necessary with talking points you can point to, and 3) expressing in the best light your accomplishments that potential employers in the targeted industry would find most helpful.

Example 7.11: Sample experience introductory paragraph for physician seeking entry-level position in medical informatics

ACCOMPLISHMENTS
- Led 50-physician practice group in transition to electronic health records.
- Successfully negotiated with electronic health records vendor.
- Supervised training of 300 employees on new EHR system.

Example 7.12: Sample experience introductory paragraph for physician seeking entry-level position at management consulting firm

ACCOMPLISHMENTS
- Led task force to evaluate, address, and lessen practice group risk.
- Conducted top to bottom 360 review of practice's operations resulting in increased net income of 14%.
- Managed a team of 15 professionals and led team toward results and resolution.

Example 7.13: Experience introductory paragraphs from experienced physician-executives

ACCOMPLISHMENTS

- Managed a team of engineering and medical reviewers. Reviewed, edited, and signed-off on team's work.
- Negotiated clinical trial design and FDA-approved requirements with device manufacturers.
- Developed approach to regulating combination products.

ACCOMPLISHMENTS

- Reduced business unit costs by $1.5 million over 2 years via implementation and direction of integrated disability management program which used payroll data to document cost of absences.
- Initiated community wellness fairs, featuring traditional and alternative vendors and preventative programs.
- Achieved 85% smoking cessation for one month.
- Achieved 70% smoking cessation for 6 months.

ACCOMPLISHMENTS

- Led the development of advanced clinical solutions to address safety, quality, and value.
- Created the vision, product roadmap, and specific strategies for market entry.
- Grew base from zero in 2006 to 23 clients sold, contributing 20 million dollars to top line.
- Defined a partnership with Microsoft Corp.
- Led clinical acquisitions of national pharmacy chain.
- Presented at multiple national industry conferences.
- Built and developed a team of physicians and nurses for sales and product development.

Some of the business buzz words traditionally used to start sentences describing a physician's accomplishments include:

- Acquired
- Analyzed
- Assisted
- Assumed
- Chaired
- Completed
- Conducted
- Coordinated
- Decided
- Designed
- Developed

- Directed
- Evaluated
- Facilitated
- Grew
- Headed
- Implemented
- Instituted
- Introduced
- Led
- Managed
- Negotiated

- Optimized
- Oversaw
- Presented
- Provided
- Recommended
- Reengineered
- Represented
- Strengthened
- Supported
- Taught

Many experts recommend that you use action verbs where possible to describe your experience. In the words of one noted resume expert:

Example 7.14: Importance of using action words

Putting "responsible for" on a resume is a big no-no in my book. You want to change that to action verbs rather than "responsible for:" directed, managed, oversaw, etc. Using those kinds of terms, cutting down the lists that typically go with "responsible for" and replacing them with concrete accomplishments that...actually mean something to the reader who's hopefully the decision maker, who's going to decide if they're going to hire you or not are the things that I would say are typical mistakes that go in resumes. Not putting those things on. Make sure you do put those things on.

EDUCATION

Here you should briefly describe your education with your most current degree appearing first. For example:

MD	**Yale University School of Medicine**
	School of Medicine/MSTP, 5/05
MBA	**Boston College Graduate School of Management**
	Marketing and Strategic Management, 5/94
BA	**College of the Holy Cross**
	Economics, 5/92

182

ADDITIONAL INFORMATION

Physicians with many years of experience will be sorely tempted to list:

- Journal articles,
- Boards they serve on,
- Awards, and
- Presentations, etc.

The authors advise that less is more. List only those additional items that:

- Are relevant to the position you are seeking and
- That specifically make you a more attractive hire.

7.5 Branding Yourself Through Your Resume

Deb Dib, one of the few resume/branding experts who has studied physicians transitioning to non-clinical careers makes the following recommendations:

Branded Resumes 101
For Physician Transitions to Non-Clinical Careers
CV to Resume Quick Tips

1. **Use a resume format rather than a traditional CV for most transitions**. Use a resume when you are shifting your professional focus from direct healthcare to business performance such as consulting, CEO/President or another management position. A CV would be appropriate if applying for a position as Chief of Medicine at a hospital, in medical research or to teach at a university.
2. **Determine your career target(s) before you begin writing your resume.** To craft a powerful and effective document, know what your professional interests are. Focus your resume on a particular objective.
3. **Identify skills relevant to your new career objective/industry target.** Do not focus on your direct clinical tasks. Instead, paint a picture in words of how you want to be perceived. Tailor your resume to specifically emphasize information about your

background that relates to your target career. Omit information about clinical skills that have no meaning to the target position.

4. **Create a document that communicates and promotes the value of what you are offering an employer.** Know what differentiates you (your personal brand) from other candidates. Include quantifiable results or the outcomes of your contributions. If you increased revenues, state the percentage. If you improved productivity, state the percentage. If you created a new program, state the end result of that effort.

5. **Research and compile key words for your career target(s) and industry.** You want to convey a specific message so that employers and recruiters will find your resume when conducting an electronic search. Find key words by reviewing advertised positions and analyzing the qualifications, soft skills, experience, and other requirements they are seeking.

6. **Focus on major management achievements.** Include new program development, cost savings, technology advances, efficiency and productivity improvement, special projects, new products, consulting, training, human resources, and other leadership initiatives. Avoid detailing responsibilities. A few stats on revenue created, budgets managed, and profits grown will tell more than a paragraph of "responsible for...."

7. **Organize your resume into consistently formatted sections for impact.** Use highly visible headings in a larger point size and place employment dates at the right side of the page. Be consistent with format structure such as placement of employer names, titles, and dates.

8. **Use the function you are transitioning to as your title to demonstrate level/role.** For example, if you are a primary care physician in private practice and also the Partner/Manager or President, list your title as President if that is the role you are seeking next.[1]

---

[1] *SEAK Non-Clinical Careers Handbook,* Dib, p. 33, 2007.

7.6 Conclusion

A physician making the transition to a non-clinical career will want to draft an error-free, powerful resume that highlights her accomplishments, success, experience, core competencies, skills, abilities, and judgment. Those physicians who are not comfortable drafting the resume on their own should seek assistance from experienced resume experts.

Chapter 8 Selling Yourself and Excelling at Your Interview

8.1 Executive Summary

- Your interview is your opportunity to allay your potential employer's fears and sell yourself.
- Show a positive attitude and demonstrate attributes and key competencies the employer is looking for.
- Thoroughly research the industry, the employer, and the interviewer to prepare answers to common interview questions.
- The employer will also research you. Prior to interviewing, Google yourself and look for any damaging or embarrassing information.

8.2 Using the Interview to Allay the Fears of Your Potential Employer

When employers hire an employee they are looking for many things. These include the ability to do the job well, an apparent understanding of the position and industry, a sense that the candidate will fit in and be happy with the job, and that the candidate will not leave after a short amount of time. Your interview is your opportunity to identify the potential concerns of the interviewer and address them head on.

One way to allay these concerns is to learn how to speak "corporate." You can learn the language of the industry you are targeting by reading trade publications and job descriptions, joining relevant professional organizations, attending conferences and continuing education courses, going back to school, and—most importantly—through networking and being mentored. Being able to speak a prospective employer's language will make you a far more attractive potential employee because this will show your interest and familiarity with the field and indicate that the employer will not need to spend as much time getting you up to speed.

Consider the advice from a chief medical officer for a large health insurer who has interviewed and hired numerous physicians for non-clinical positions:

Example 8.1: What the CMO at a large health insurer looks for in physicians he hires

There are several attributes that I would say I look for. The first and foremost is clinical credibility. You have to be what I would call a great clinician. You have to be a solid physician. You have to be up to date on your clinical skills. You have to know what is going on in your particular field. You don't have to know everything in every field, obviously, but you have to be aware of the latest advances, the drugs, the things going on in your field.

First and foremost is being a good clinician. Integrity is critical. We absolutely do not sacrifice anything relative to ethics or integrity or honesty. We look for people that can be team players. One of the differences between medicine and business is you have to be a team player in business, so we look for people who will be good team players. We look for people who will be humble. We look for people who can communicate very effectively to a wide variety of audiences, people who are good problem solvers, who can think critically, who can think on their feet and finally, who can listen.

Physicians like to talk and think that they can dominate everything. We want people who will step back and listen to what other people are saying.

After you've interviewed for many years, as I have, you kind of get a sense of is this person kind of someone that's going to fit in the business, [are they] going to fit within your medical team? I've interviewed people that within five minutes, I've known they're very arrogant and they're not going to be a good fit. I've interviewed people that I think will be good fits.

You never—the expression I use—you never can tell how someone's going to work out until you're either married to them or you work for them. And quite honestly, I've hired people that I've had to let go because they didn't work out...on the other hand, people that have come on board that we liked and did a great job—it wasn't for them. And they've had to leave because it didn't meet their expectations. So it works both ways.

POSITIVE ATTITUDE

Physicians changing from clinical to non-clinical positions should carefully guard against negative comments about clinical medicine, their prior employers, overburdening paperwork/government regulations, long hours, unfair compensation, etc. Physicians who come off as "burned out," disgruntled, or trying to "retire" to the corporate world stand little chance of success at their interview.

Looking to new challenges and being able to use the knowledge and skills developed in clinical practice appear more positive and are more attractive to employers.

ATTRIBUTES FOR SUCCESS EMPLOYERS LOOK FOR
When you interview, consider the attributes for success SEAK faculty members suggest that employers look for. This will vary, of course, depending upon the precise position sought. For example, clinical credibility is not an issue if you want to become a stock broker, but it might be critical if you work for a health insurer.

Clinical Credibility: Position yourself with board certification and clinical experience. Be prepared to talk medicine at your interview. One of the reasons you may be hired is because as a doctor you will have inherent credibility with practitioners, the public, and others. You need to demonstrate at your interview that you have that credibility.

Personality: Likeable, interesting, extroverted people are far more likely to get hired. In the words of a physician who has hired dozens of doctors for work in industry:

> **Example 8.2: The importance of personality**
> You have to have a personality. It's that simple. You have to be likeable. You have to be interesting enough that somebody wants to sit with you. And how I judge that when I interview people, if I have to look at my watch and I can't wait for the interview to end, then I know. Why would a chairman of Mass General internal medicine want to sit there and look at you and talk to you, if you're just boring, you're boring or you're dreary or miserable, or you're just not interesting to be with? You have to have the interpersonal skills.

Teamwork: Being a team player is a must. Be prepared to cite examples of working successfully as a team leader and a team member to solve problems. Examples could be serving on task forces and committees. Employers look for people who won't step on toes and can navigate office politics.

Unassailable Integrity: You may be asked questions that subtly try to get a sense for your integrity level.

Humility: Don't be full of yourself in the interview. Be proud of your accomplishments without being a braggart. For example, if the interviewer comments: "I see you graduated *summa cum laude*. Will you be comfortable working for and with a lot of people who aren't nearly as smart as you?" A good answer might be, "I wouldn't assume that I'm smarter. A big reason I was able to graduate summa is my work ethic. I am a very hard worker." Here the doctor demonstrates humility while at the same time communicating a very desirable trait, that he is a hard worker.

Communication Skills: Communication skills are critical in many jobs. Demonstrate your communication skills in your interview. Position yourself to be a better communicator as part of your transition plan. Take every opportunity to teach, lecture, and serve as an expert. Consider joining Toastmasters.

Listen Carefully: Respond to the questions you have been asked and demonstrate that you are a good listener.

Change Agent: Be prepared to cite examples in your career where you were able to bring about positive change despite facing resistance and difficulties.

Translator: Speak colloquially when discussing medical terms (for example, say "collarbone" instead of "clavicle").

Critical Thinking: You may be put on the spot to analyze a problem or situation. The idea is to see how you would think something through. For example, you may be asked, "How would you market a product that did X?" Be prepared for this.

Thoroughness: Make sure your CV or resume is mistake-free. Do your homework on the company and people interviewing you and seize opportunities to demonstrate this during your interview. For example, by asking questions such as, "I see that your company just came out with X product. Do you think I would have an opportunity to work on that?"

A "Self-Starter": Cite publications, presentations, chairing meetings and committees, and examples of your ability to work without direct supervision.

Stability: If you have changed jobs frequently, be prepared to explain why this was for advancement and not ambivalence.

Ability to Travel: Be prepared to mention how you enjoy a reasonable amount of travel.

Computer Literate: In many positions, knowledge of Excel would be a good talking point demonstrating business and quantitative skills. In any event, basic computer skills such as e-mail and word processing will almost always be required.

8.3 Interviewing Techniques

It is critical to research the company and the position as much as possible. This will demonstrate interest and a good work ethic. You will also then be prepared to best articulate what you can do for the company and why you are interested in the opportunity. It is the kiss of death in an interview to focus on your wanting to leave your current position and not how excited you are to help the new organization in a new role. Consider the following:

> **Example 8.3: Physician chief scientific officer gives interviewing advice**
> I think that for any interview you have to know as much as you can about the place where you are interviewing, and the position that you are interviewing for. When I did my interviews I made sure that I went on to the websites of the companies, I made sure I talked to some people, trying to find out about the company atmosphere, the type of position I would be stepping into, and I made sure it was something I wanted to do. When I went in to the interview, I was knowledgeable, I showed them and really demonstrated that I knew about the company, that I had at least a general sense of what the position was about, and I was very interested in it. I think that if you are sincere about what you want to do and show that, I think that especially for physicians who are making a career transition, if you are showing that you are excited about moving towards something instead of running away from something, I think that's very important. I'm now in a position where I interview, even more than interview, I speak to physicians all the time who are considering changing careers and what I hear a little bit too often is doctors who know they don't want to do what they're doing and they're considering making a jump that they don't really know enough about. I feel that they generally haven't researched it enough. You can tell when somebody comes across and talks to you about why they want to do the career that you are talking about. They come across as being excited about

191

it, you get excited about it, and you want to work together. I think that's very important.

PREPARATION

Learn as much as possible about the prospective employer and the person(s) interviewing you.

Prospective Employer: The more you know, the better able you will be to:

- Answer and ask intelligent questions,
- Determine the values, skills, company culture, and talents the employer is looking for,
- Appear to be motivated,
- Align your competencies and transferable skills to the employer's mission statement, and
- Impress the interviewer with your research abilities, preparedness, and tenacity.

Research: Research the company by first going to their corporate Web site and studying it. When practicable, it is a good idea to print their entire site.

You will want to learn as much information as possible about the company. For example, if you were going to interview at a publicly traded pharmaceutical company, the Web site would likely include:

- company history,
- leadership,
- locations,
- treatments,
- products,
- R & D,
- products in the pipeline,
- news and press releases,
- careers,
- corporate culture,
- benefits,

- job searches,
- codes of conduct,
- earnings,
- stock information,
- corporate governance,
- shareholder information,
- compliance, and much more.

The better prepared you are for your interview, the more likely you will be:

- relaxed,
- informed, and
- successful.

Highly motivated physicians will continue their due diligence on their prospective non-clinical position, their business, products, and future prospects.

Physicians who talk with past and current employees will likely find out information that is not generally publicly available. This insider's insight can be invaluable in evaluating a company and impressing the interviewer.

Additional information can be obtained about prospective employers by searching:

- Dun and Bradstreet reports
- SEC filings if a public company (EDGAR Database: visit www.Sec.gov)
- Better Business Bureaus
- RipOffReport.com
- Google (try typing in the company's name in quotes and adding words like "lawsuit," "bankruptcy," "layoffs," "restructuring," and "default")

Prospective Interviewer: Learn as much as possible about the person who will conduct the interview. The more you know about the person, the better you will be able to:

- make a good first impression,
- connect personally,
- avoid alienating the interviewer, and
- demonstrate the personal style and professional skills sought and anticipate, prepare for, and excel at the questions you will be asked.

If possible, obtain and study the interviewer's resume or curriculum vitae. This document is often very revealing. You will also want to learn about the company's hiring process. For example:

- initial phone interview,
- personal interview, and
- group interview, etc.

Your interest and competence can be demonstrated through preparation. It is good advice to prepare as much as possible for your interviews. The time spent preparing can yield a huge return on investment. Consider the case of the neurologist who brought along a binder of his past IMEs when interviewing for a medical director position at an insurance company:

Example 8.4: Preparation for interview pays off for physician
The interview went pretty well. One thing I did that I thought would be helpful is, because I had the medical legal experience, I actually came in with a ring binder with cases that I had done in the past to have them reviewed to see my work product, basically. From what I heard later on, they were really impressed by it.

INTERVIEWER WILL RESEARCH YOU
Before your interview (before your job search begins too) it is a good idea to Google yourself. Any reasonable employer or recruiter will do the same. If you have listings on social networking sites or if you have a blog, you will want to make sure there is no content in these areas that is potentially embarrassing. In addition, if there is damaging content about

you that you cannot control (for example, a news article) you want to at least be prepared to put these articles in their best light.

Your presence on the Internet can also, of course, be a benefit. If your name produces numerous hits of articles published, positions of importance, and other favorable material, this will reinforce your stature as a physician leader.

TAP THE INTERVIEWER'S X FACTOR

It is a good idea to get as much intelligence and do as much research as possible on the person interviewing you. The most common ways to get such information is to look at the bios on the company's Web site, check out social networking sites, do Internet searches on the person, and talk to your network to gather information. Once you have this information, you want to look for things that make the interviewer tick or that you have in common with the interviewer. The idea is to get the interviewer to like you and hit it off with you. Consider the following case examples:

Example 8.5: Showing a common interest
You discover through Googling the interviewer's name that the person interviewing you is active in veteran's affairs and the USO. Your father served in the Marine Corps. You want to bond with this person and for this person to like you. When he asks how you think you would get along in a hierarchical organization, you reply, "I don't think I'd have any problem with this. My father was a Marine Corps officer, so from a young age I became accustomed to following orders."

Example 8.6: Tapping the X Factor
You learn through your interviewer's social networking site that he has 5 children. When asked your three greatest accomplishments you state raising three well-adjusted children.

Example 8.7: Stroking the ego
You discover from online searching of old newspaper articles that the interviewer had won an industry award many years back. You congratulate the interviewer and tell her how impressed you were with this and how excited you would be to work with such a talented team. This shows your diligence and strokes the interviewer's ego.

For many physicians, interviewing for a non-clinical position will be a completely new and somewhat foreign experience. These physicians may not have been interviewed for many years. For most physicians, this will be their first non-clinical interview since becoming a physician. Those who are prepared for their interviews are best positioned to excel.

NAILING YOUR INTERVIEW

Physicians who excel at their non-clinical interview are the ones who are able to articulate in a succinct fashion:

- What they bring to the table,
- How they can help the company, and
- Why they should be hired.

You should be able to expound upon each talking point you make with a specific example:

Example 8.8: Talking point—Good with deadlines
I am extremely good and diligent about deadlines. For example, at my hospital I wrote a 20-page monthly newsletter for 10 years, was never late with one issue, and won several awards for the quality of the newsletter.

Example 8.9: Talking point—Excellent communication skills
I pride myself on my excellent communication skills. For example, I have conducted numerous one- and two-day training sessions and, in fact, developed a "train the trainer" program for young physicians in my hospital.

ARTICULATING KEY COMPETENCIES

Prospective employers judge what *key competencies* the interviewee brings to the table. The three questions employers seek to answer at the interview are:

1. Can the prospective employee do the job?
2. Do I/we like him and connect with him?
3. Can we afford him?

The interviewer will look for which core competencies the prospective employee brings to the interview:

Competency: Accountability
Definition: Takes personal responsibility for outcomes.
Talking Point: "You know, I take responsibility for the health and even the life of my patients on a daily basis. It is something I am very accustomed to."

Competency: Adapting to Change
Definition: Is very flexible and adaptable; copes well with changes.
Talking Point: "When we moved to electronic records, I led the physicians' committee to help accomplish this."

Competency: Business Mindedness
Definition: Understands the nature of the company's business and how his role affects the bottom line.
Talking Point: "I appreciate the fact that pharma has a responsibility to its stockholders and the general public."

Competency: Communication
Definition: Express oneself well verbally.
Talking Point: "When people have trouble understanding what I am trying to express, I feel that the failure is on my end and will express myself in a clearer fashion."

Competency: Conflict Management
Definition: Finds common ground to resolve issues.
Talking Point: "The issue is not who is right or wrong, but how we can reach a mutually satisfactory resolution."

Competency: Cooperation and Collaboration
Definition: Works well with others to achieve business and team goals.
Talking Point: "Getting the best out of each employee and making the team stronger are two of my strengths."

Competency: Creating and Communicating Vision
Definition: Makes real to everyone inspiring a vision.
Talking Point: "Explaining what we are trying to accomplish, getting people to buy-in, and leading by example has worked well for me in the past."

Competency: Critical Thinking
Definition: Develops solutions to business problems.
Talking Point: "Coming up with simple, elegant solutions is one of my strengths."

Competency: Customer Focus
Definition: Concentrates on customers' best interests.
Talking Point: "Teaching and educating customers as to what serves them best are the keys to customer focus."

Competency: Dealing with Ambiguity
Definition: Embraces change and can comfortably handle risk and uncertainty.
Talking Point: "The ability to accept the ambiguity inherent in complex problems so you can move on the solutions is crucial for success."

Competency: Detail-Oriented
Definition: Is meticulous and precise in approach; quality-conscious and thorough.
Talking Point: "I will take the time to make sure that my work product is accurate, mistake-free, and of the highest quality."

Competency: Development
Definition: Improves oneself or others professionally.
Talking Point: "Making the others on the team you work with better employees, by mentoring them and sharing the credit is crucial to employee and team development."

Competency: Drive for Results
Definition: Consistently meets/exceeds goals; is action-oriented and passionate about the work; seizes opportunities.
Talking Point: "When I work on a project I follow the advice of Gene Kranz of mission control for Apollo 13: 'Failure is not an option.'"

Competency: Functional Knowledge
Definition: Well-developed knowledge of own functional area of expertise.
Talking Point: "I am thought of as one of the 4-5 'go-to' experts in the field."

Competency: Influencing Others
Definition: Negotiates "win-win" outcomes in tough situations.
Talking Point: "The ability to negotiate solutions that satisfy all parties is a key to my past success."

Competency: Initiative
Definition: Demonstrates self-motivation through action.
Talking Point: "I do not need or depend on others for motivation. That comes from within—the desire to succeed."

Competency: Innovation
Definition: Generates creative new ideas.
Talking Point: "The ability to look at what everyone else looks at and see something different is what makes me creative."

Competency: Integrity/Ethical Behavior
Definition: Is trustworthy and demonstrates strong personal and professional values.
Talking Point: "My word is my bond. That is the way I was brought up and continue to live my life."

Competency: Interpersonal Skills
Definition: Relates well to all kinds of people at all levels within and outside the organization.
Talking Point: "I truly enjoy getting input, perspectives, and ideas from others, and this shows."

Competency: Leadership Potential
Definition: Motivates and inspires others.
Talking Point: "I motivate by example. I do not ask others to do what I would not, will not, could not, or have not done myself."

Competency: Learning Attitude
Definition: Pursues learning with drive and vigor.
Talking Point: "Understanding that there is always more to learn is crucial to professional growth."

Competency: Maintaining Composure/Flexibility
Definition: Is tolerant of people and processes, and can deal well with change and new information.
Talking Point: "Maturity is the ability to successfully deal with processes, people, and new information."

Competency: Management Skills
Definition: Sets employee goals; coaches and monitors performance.
Talking Point: "I look at myself as the player/coach. My goal is to make the overall team stronger so we can work to achieve our goals."

Competency: Managerial Courage
Definition: Doesn't hold back; makes tough decisions even when those decisions are unpopular.
Talking Point: "In business, you often have to put the company and the project first and make tough calls that are not always popular."

Competency: Motivating Others
Definition: Empowers others to succeed.
Talking Point: "Sharing credit graciously helps others succeed and they appreciate working with you."

Competency: Planning and Organizing
Definition: Uses time and resources efficiently to accomplish work objectives.
Talking Point: "Understanding the realities of the workplace, i.e., not always having the time or resources you would like, makes one a realist and forces you to work with what you do have."

Competency: Priority and Goal Setting
Definition: Quickly discovers the source of problems and generates thoughtful, effective solutions.
Talking Point: "Spending sufficient time and thought to identify the problem is often crucial. Getting the right answer to the wrong questions is often the result of haste."

Competency: Problem Solving
Definition: Takes control of challenging projects with foresight and implementation focus.
Talking Point: "To succeed you need to identify the problems, analyze the solutions, and implement the efficient solutions."

Competency: Project Planning
Definition: Focuses effort on most important goals and objectives.
Talking Point: "Culling out secondary goals and concentrating time and resources to achieve core goals leads to success."

Competency: Risk-Taking
Definition: Takes well-calculated business risks, learning from mistakes and false starts.
Talking Point: "The refusal to take calculated, well-thought-out risk results in inaction. Oftentimes the riskiest thing to do is nothing."

Competency: Service Orientation
Definition: Committed to meeting and exceeding customer expectations.
Talking Point: "For 30 years I have strived to exceed the expectations of patients and I will continue to do so in the industry."

Competency: Strategic Ability
Definition: Is visionary; anticipates future consequences and trends.
Talking Point: "The ability to spot trends, learn from other industries, and translate that experience to your situation is crucial to success."

Competency: Teamwork
Definition: Works well with others to achieve shared goals.
Talking Point: "Building a strong team that enjoys working together to achieve one goal is one of my strengths."

Competency: Technical Knowledge and Proficiency
Definition: Accurately and consistently applies technical principles and practice to situations on the job.
Talking Point: "Continuing professional development is crucial to continue to be considered one of the 'go-to' persons in this industry."

Competency: Time Management
Definition: Uses time effectively and efficiently, concentrating efforts on the most important priorities.
Talking Point: "I always tackle the most difficult job first each day. After that, all other projects are easy by comparison."

Competency: Works Independently
Definition: High degree of comfort operating autonomously.[1]
Talking Point: "Once asked to accomplish a task, you can consider it done, professionally, on-time or early, with the highest quality."

8.4 Interview Questions

Physicians interviewing for their first non-clinical position should be prepared to actively listen to the questions they are asked. Active listening involves listening carefully to the question that is being asked and also listening for what is implied in the question. Practice active listening skills so that you can hear what is being said and also what is not being said.

---

[1] *501 Great Interview Questions for Employers and the Best Answers for Prospective Employees,* Pudmoroff, Atlantic Publishing Group, Pp. 275–280 (2005).

Example 8.10: Figuring out what the interviewer really wants to know

Q. Do you think you have too much experience for this position?

Active Listening: The interviewer may be getting at one or more things:

1. Too old for the position,
2. May require too high a salary, and/or
3. May be bored with the position.

Artful Reply:
A. I don't think you can have too much positive experience. I look at this position as challenging and a step forward. I am willing to do what it takes to obtain and excel at this position.

<u>*Interview Questions to Prepare For:*</u> Physicians moving to non-clinical positions should be able to articulately answer the following questions. To excel at interviewing, practice these questions with a tape recorder or video camera. Work hard to remove unflattering verbal mannerisms, such as "umm." Listening to yourself or, even better, watching yourself, can be very revealing. It is one thing to say that you are articulate and a good communicator. It is quite another thing to prove it with your answers to an interviewer's questions. One good technique is to listen to the question and see it as if it was written on a white board.

Answering questions in a bulletpoint fashion with short, succinct, grammatically correct sentences will demonstrate your:

*   Intellect,
*   Ability to think on your feet,
*   Knowledge of the subject, and
*   Ability to communicate.

Example 8.11: Being well-prepared to answer an interview question

Q. What do you read to keep up with the information in the business world?

A. I have three main sources:

1. *The Wall Street Journal*, cover to cover,
2. Business magazines like *Forbes, CEO, The Economist,* and the *Harvard Business Review,* and
3. Online business sites such as Bloomberg, BNET, CNN Money, and Business Week.

Some of the specific questions physicians need to be prepared to answer are listed below, along with potential answers. Keep in mind that the best answer for you depends upon your particular situation and the position you are applying for. A helpful technique is to produce a one- or two-page sheet of talking points prior to the interview and study them very closely. These talking points could include many points from your resume and other facts and accomplishments you can cite to allay the concerns of your prospective employer.

Example 8.12: Sample question and answer #1
Q. Why should we hire a doctor for this non-medical position?
A. I have the skills and drive you are looking for and I will make you a lot of money.

Discussion: This simple, direct reply is particularly appropriate to a position in the financial industry looking for a self-starter.

Example 8.13: Sample question and answer #2
Q. Why did you decide to give up medicine as a career?
A. After 20 years of practice, I find that I am more and more interested in the management side of things. It gives me the opportunity to be more creative and to have a greater impact. I want to work in a field where I have unlimited growth potential if and when I prove myself.

Discussion: Here the physician emphasizes what he is moving toward as opposed to what he is leaving.

Example 8.14: Sample question and answer #3
Q. How will your medical training help you in this position?
A. A large part of the position, as I understand it, is reviewing marketing materials for medical accuracy. My medical training will be invaluable.

Discussion: The physician demonstrates an understanding of the position and is easily able to demonstrate how his medical training and expertise will help the company.

Example 8.15: Sample question and answer #4
Q. What transferable skills do you have that will help you in this position?
A. Almost too many to list. Phenomenal work ethic. I routinely put in 70–80 hour work weeks now. Problem solver. Diagnose, treat, and don't make things worse. Calm under fire. I'm dealing with life and death on a daily basis and I don't lose my head. Communications. Every day I need to communicate with colleagues, management, patients, and many other players. Passion. I don't go half-in on anything. You don't get to become a doctor if you do.

Discussion: The physician indicates that he is a driven Type "A" personality used to dealing with difficult challenges. He is not a clock-watcher, but is a person who gets the job done.

Example 8.16: Sample question and answer #5
Q. Do you expect to make as much money in this position as you did in your previous position?
A. I expect to be paid largely on my performance and I expect to perform superbly.

Discussion: Here the physician is not shy about wanting to be paid well. He successfully ties in his financial desires to performance.

Example 8.17: Sample question and answer #6
Q. Will you be giving up your medical license?
A. No. There is no reason to do so and it could diminish my value to you as I may have less credibility with clients and key opinion leaders.

Discussion: The physician points out why it is to the employer's advantage for her to maintain her license.

Example 8.18: Sample question and answer #7
Q. How much money are you looking for?
A. I'd be happy to discuss that if and when you offer me a position and I know the details of the position.

Discussion: The physician will discuss money if he is offered the job and the job requirements are established and agreed upon.

Example 8.19: Sample question and answer #8
Q. If there was a medical emergency in the office, what would you do?
A. Everything I can to help out. The specifics would obviously depend on what exactly the medical emergency was.

Discussion: The physician does not shy away from being helpful. The answer demonstrated common sense.

Example 8.20: Sample question and answer #9
Q. Tell me something about yourself not on your resume.
A. My proudest accomplishment is my family. I have a lovely wife and two small children. I will work extremely hard to see them taken care of.

Discussion: Here the physician talks about his family and the need to support them well. He ties his future hard work to his family's well-being, all but assuring he will work very hard.

Answering Open-Ended Questions: You need to be able to answer open-ended questions as well. Through the use of such questions, the interviewer is testing you to see:

- How articulate you are,
- If you can organize your thoughts and express them in a coherent manner,
- How selective you are and if you can answer in both a concise and complete fashion, and
- If you can answer with a beginning, a middle, and a conclusion while weaving in a crucial theme.

Example 8.21: Sample open-ended question #1
Q. Why don't you tell me about yourself?
A. I was born and raised in Brooklyn and was the first one in my family to go to college. I worked my way through college and medical school.

My wife Nancy and I met at medical school and we will have been married 24 years on November 1st of this year. Our two girls, Kathy and Staci, are doing very well at Wheaton College outside of Boston.

I practiced family medicine for 16 years and built up the practice to 10 physicians and 7,000 active patients. Over the last 4 years I moved over to administering and growing the practice full-time. I found that I loved the administrative duties. I obtained my MBA at night and sold the practice to my partners. I am very excited about your opportunity in administrative medicine at this hospital.

With my years of clinical practice and my administrative experience, I know I can make a real difference at this hospital.

Discussion: The physician emphasizes his roots, achievements, solid family credentials, clinical experience, administrative experience, additional business training, and his passion for business.

Example 8.22: Sample open-ended question #2
Q. Why should I hire you?
A. These are six main reasons:

1. My credentials, clinical experience and business training all are an excellent fit for this position and the company.
2. I am a quick study and get along well with team members I work with. I have met the team here and I enjoyed talking with them and I know I would fit in.
3. I am an excellent public speaker and make powerful, memorable presentations.
4. My negotiation skills are superior and I can help this company immediately with the ongoing negotiations.
5. I have studied the job description and the company and I am excited about the opportunity to excel and grow.
6. I am available to travel and I actually enjoy it. The bottom line is I would do an excellent job for you.

Discussion: The physician here emphasizes his skills, experience, and core competencies. He reveals his abilities and passion and can hit the ground running.

Example 8.23: Sample open-ended question #3
Q. What are your major strengths?
A. Four areas I feel that are my major strengths are:

- Integrity—I have been told by many people I am the most honest person they have ever met.
- Reliability—Once I am given a project or assignment, I will see that it is completed on time, within budget, and in a high-quality fashion.
- Persistence—I do not like to fail and do not give up until the assignment is complete.
- Passion—I believe once you take on an assignment you excel when you really believe in it and love what you are doing.

Discussion: The physician hits some of the hot-button issues the interviewer is probably looking for.

Example 8.24: Sample open-ended question #4
Q. What are your major weaknesses?
A. I am obsessive and drive myself pretty hard. My wife Sally is working on me to loosen up a bit.

I expect others around me to work at my same pace and with the same degree of dedication. I am gradually learning to temper my enthusiasm a bit and to be more understanding with my co-workers.

In the past I did not take much vacation time but again, with the help of Sally, I am seeing it is important to take time off and recharge.

Discussion: Here the physician frankly suggests a weakness that he hopes his prospective employer will actually see as a strength.

Example 8.25: Sample open-ended question #5
Q. What sort of pay do you expect to receive?
A. I expect to be paid competitively for this position based upon my experience and training. I would be happy with the higher end of your salary range. I understand about the benefits, bonus, and options and that also makes this position attractive to me and my family.

Discussion: The physician does not box herself into a salary demand. She sends the message that she expects to be well paid. The fact that her family is already on board is a plus as well.

Example 8.26: Sample open-ended question #6
Q. How does your previous experience relate to the jobs we have here?
A. Numerous ways. You're looking for someone who can bring people together and push through change. I've done that my whole career. Specifically...

Discussion: The physician is prepared to cite specific instances of how her experience will help the employer.

Example 8.27: Sample open-ended question #7
Q. What are your plans for the future?
A. To obtain this position and excel at it growing with the company. My husband was born 12 miles from corporate headquarters and he can't wait to move back home. I am prepared to make a long-term commitment to this company.

Discussion: The physician sends the strong message that she is in this for the long haul. The fact that her husband is strongly supportive drives the point home.

Selling Yourself and Excelling at Your Interview

Example 8.28: Sample open-ended question #8
Q. What will your former employers say about you?
A. If they weren't afraid of lawsuits, they'd say very positive things I am quite sure. As you know, because of the liability issues involved, most employers will only verify dates of employment. That said, I can certainly provide you with numerous colleagues as references.

Discussion: The interviewee demonstrates a sophisticated knowledge of risk management and business practices.

Example 8.29: Sample open-ended question #9
Q. Why are you looking for this sort of position and why here?
A. As you know, I practiced gastroenterology for 12 years. I have gotten to know and understand the importance of drug safety and have been on the speakers' bureau for Novartis and Schering Plough. I am also a bit of a software geek and programmer. The more I worked with the pharmaceutical industry, the more I enjoyed it and realized the impact I could have in patient safety. I am here because of my keen interest in drug safety software development, in which you are one of the international leaders. This is where it is happening for drug safety software and this is where I want to be.

Discussion: The physician lays out his reasons for career transition, his clinical and relevant experience, and his unique combination of talents that are a good fit for the employer.

Example 8.30: Sample open-ended question #10
Q. Why don't you tell me about your personal situation?[2]
A. I am married with a 5-year-old son and 2-year-old daughter. I have family roots here in Maine and would love to move back here.

Discussion: The physician simply and directly answers the question without getting into the propriety of the question. He does not ramble on and intentionally keeps his reply brief.

Example 8.31: Additional questions to be prepared to answer
Note: There are many effective answers to these questions. The most effective answers depend on your personal experiences, style, and the position you are applying for.

Q. What is your greatest accomplishment?
A. Two of them actually. My son Jimmy, aged 5, and my daughter Katie, aged 3.

---

[2] *Next-Day Job Interview: Prepare Tonight and Get the Job Tomorrow*, Farr, Jist Publishing, 2005, p. v (questions only).

209

Q. Tell me more about your choice to change your career.
A. I think we've already covered that. I have developed arthritis and can no longer practice surgery, but I would like to continue to use my medical skills and knowledge. I have zero interest in retiring.

Q. What is the most important element you require in a job?
A. I don't know if there is any one thing that is most important. Some things that come to mind are that the job is challenging, collegiality of team members, and believing in the product.

Q. What has given you the most satisfaction at work?
A. Making dramatic positive differences in patients' lives.

Q. How would you describe your leadership style?
A. Lead by example. If you want people to work harder, be the first one in and the last one out. Also, don't take yourself too seriously and be a great listener.

Q. Tell me about an important written document you have completed.
A. I've published 3 books. I know how to write and how to stick through a project to completion.

Q. What is the best written proposal you have created?
A. That's hard to say. One that comes to mind is a recent proposal on cost reductions at our group. 7 of 8 recommendations were accepted and implemented and we saved 5% total on all our fixed expenses, which is really an extraordinary number.

Q. Describe a situation where you failed at work.
A. I attempted to get my partners to agree to hire an additional physician for the practice to reduce call for the younger physician. I failed the first 2 times I brought it up, but they eventually came around.

Q. How do you prepare to give a presentation?
A. Preparation is the key to a successful presentation. I determine what the audience is interested in and work hard to deliver meaningful content.

Q. What was the most successful presentation you gave?
A. One that comes to mind is the presentation to my partners on my proposed cost-cutting measures. I coherently and concisely made the pitch and was ready with answers to most of the concerns that were raised.

Q. Describe a time in which you had a complex assignment at work and generated a solution.
A. I was tasked with finding an EHR solution for our office. I had to communicate with all the stakeholders, do complex analysis, make a recommendation, and then sell that recommendation to everyone involved. No easy task, but it was a great experience.

Q. Describe a time when you anticipated potential problems and developed preventative methods.
A. I anticipated the housing bubble and was able to push through a sale and lease back of our medical building in 2007.

Q. Give me an example of a time you had to make a difficult decision and what you did.
A. This happens all the time. At one point we had two long-term employees who were at each other's throats and poisoning the entire staff. I made the decision that one had to go and I fired him. Not pleasant, but absolutely necessary.

Q. Tell me about a time you overcame great obstacles to achieve something significant.
A. I was planning on running the Boston Marathon to celebrate turning 40. When I was 38 I broke my leg and was laid up for 6 months. I still came back and finished in less than four hours.

Q. Give me an example of your working well under stress.
A. I was serving in Iraq in 2003 when they brought in a critical soldier with a live rocket-propelled grenade stuck in his abdomen and I had to remove it. I did and he survived.

Q. Tell me about a creative solution you had to a work problem.
A. I do expert witness consulting work and wanted to generate a higher volume of work. I decided to raise my prices, which would seem counterintuitive. Because the higher price has generated a higher perceived value, the volume of my work has increased markedly because lawyers think, "Hey, he charges a lot, he must be really good." You need to be prepared to think out of the box.

8.5 Asking Questions at Your Interview

Physicians should be prepared to ask intelligent probing questions which demonstrate knowledge, insight, and preparation. Many of these should be prepared in advance of the interview. At least one or two should be inspired by the interview itself.

EXAMPLES OF QUESTIONS TO ASK AT AN INTERVIEW

Q. What do you like best and least about working here?

Q. What is your turnover rate for physicians?

Q. What are your plans to increase profitability?

Q. Do you have any concerns about me that we haven't addressed?

Q. Do you know what management's long-term plans are in terms of independence or merger?

Q. Who would I be reporting to?

Q. How many direct reports would I have and what level would they be?

Q. How would you best describe the culture here?

8.6 Concluding the Interview and Sending a Thank You Note

When making your closing comments, consider covering three main points:

1. I can do this job and do it well.
2. I will excel at this position.
3. I will fit into the corporate culture and I will like it here.

Example 8.32: Sample parting words
Thank you so much. I think I'm exactly what you are looking for and would love to be part of your great team here.

Example 8.33: Sample parting words
I could make a big contribution for you right away. The types of things you need are exactly what I've done at...

Example 8.34: Sample parting words
I really like your management philosophy. It mirrors my own. I would fit in very well and welcome the opportunity to do so.

Sending follow-up thank you e-mails to your interviewers is also a very good idea. Such an e-mail can also serve as an opportunity to address any issues that you feel may need clarification:

Example 8.35: Thank you e-mail
Charlie:

Thank you so much for having me in. I was very impressed with your organization. I feel strongly that I would do a superb job for you. I would be very excited at the opportunity.

Also, one thing I did want to mention is that I had chaired for 5 years the finance committee and building committee at my local synagogue. I forgot to mention that when you asked about management experience not on my resume.

Thank you again,
Steve

8.7 Conclusion

The physician who is well-prepared, comfortable with her experience, abilities, and competencies and makes a favorable impression will excel at her non-clinical interview.

Chapter 9 Transition Strategies and Tactics That Work

9.1 Executive Summary

- To achieve your career goal, narrow the fields you are interested in so you know where you are trying to get to.
- Career transition is best accomplished through persistence and dedicating adequate time to the process.
- Successful transition techniques include:
  - Reading *The Wall Street Journal.*
  - Getting out before you complete your medical training.
  - Seizing unexpected opportunities for career change when they present themselves.
  - Not obsessing about a job description. This is often a wish list that decision makers will bend for the right candidate.
  - Build your resume while you transition by gaining part-time experience.
  - Network your way to an interview.
  - Improve your communication skills because they are highly sought after by potential employers.
  - Find and use a mentor or mentors to help you learn about particular industries and guide you through your transition.
  - Contact and utilize as many legitimate recruiters as you can.
  - Go back to school and earn (or at least start) an advanced degree.
  - Keep up-to-date on relevant job postings.
  - Blitz a targeted industry with your resume.
  - Create your own job by starting or buying a business.
  - Save your money to allow a financial cushion to assist your career transition.

9.2 The First Step: Figure Out What You Want to Do

The first and probably most important step in your career transition is to figure out what you would like to do in a non-clinical career. This is crucial. You do *not* under any circumstances want to end up in a new non-clinical career that you like less than your current clinical one.

Once you know what you want to do, it is a lot easier to develop a plan to get there. See Chapter 12 for a sample career transition roadmap. Once you know you want to work in a particular industry you will be able to:

- Develop a plan to build your resume with qualifications and experience that the industry you are targeting values,
- Get up to speed on industry issues and jargon,
- Join applicable professional societies,
- Target that industry for networking, and
- Look for and apply for openings in that field.

A great way to figure out what you might like to do is to attend SEAK, Inc.'s annual Non-Clinical Careers for Physicians Conference (www.seak.com). This conference features numerous speakers, mentors, and recruiters from many traditional and non-traditional industries. Networking and talking to as many people as possible to learn what is out there and what it involves is important. Reading job postings can also be helpful as it gives you a partial sense as to what is out there, what employers in a field are looking for, and what job responsibilities are. That is one of the reasons why we have included several sample job postings in this book.

9.3 Persistence and Time Commitment

Two keys to a successful career transition are persistence and time commitment. After our conference we regularly follow-up with our attendees via e-mail to see how they are progressing on their career transitions. One typical type of response is as follows, "Haven't made any progress. Too busy with work. Loved the course though!" The authors shudder when we read responses like this.

We routinely deal with physicians who, for varying reasons (see Chapter 1) are deeply dissatisfied with their clinical careers and are basically unhappy. If you find yourself in this situation and are serious about a career change, you simply need to set aside time every week to devote to your career transition. This time commitment needs to be kept until you have successfully transitioned. For example, on a weekly basis you should dedicate time to:

- Make at least one networking call, meeting, or e-mail,
- Search job listings and submit resumes to openings that appeal to you,
- Read trade or business journals and newspapers,
- Polish your resume,
- Talk with your mentor, and
- Build your brand by working on writing, speaking, blogging, etc.

9.4 Read *The Wall Street Journal* and Appropriate Trade Journals

Non-clinical positions are generally going to be in a for-profit business. An excellent way to keep up-to-date on what is happening in the business world is to subscribe to and read *The Wall Street Journal* every day. This can make you much more conversant in what moves business people, how they communicate, and the jargon they use.

If you have settled on a particular industry that you would like to pursue, it is a good idea to subscribe to the major journals in that field. This will keep you current on what is happening and serve as training. Many of these journals also have job listings in your targeted field. Joining professional societies that focus on the field you would like to get into is another good idea.

Two great books to read are Dale Carnegie's *How to Win Friends and Influence People* and Stephen Covey's *7 Habits of Highly Effective People.*

9.5 Get Out Before Your Training Is Complete

Depending upon the field you would like to get into, one of the best times to leave clinical medicine is prior to completing your training. We have interviewed dozens of physicians who have had very successful non-clinical careers who have told us their only regret is that they should have got out much sooner.

Leaving clinical medicine before your training is complete has two obvious advantages. First, a pay cut is not an issue in the first job because physicians still in training are so poorly paid. Second, you won't have to suffer through the punishing work and call hours typical of physician training.

The downside of not seeing your training through to board certification is obvious. Without completed training, you would need to go back and finish your training to go back to practicing clinical medicine.

There is another arguable downside, as well. Board certification can make you to varying degrees more valuable to a non-clinical employer. Being board certified implies deep knowledge in your boarded specialty. It also brings with it inherent credibility if you have to deal with other physicians in your new non-clinical career. The question really is, is the financial, physical, and emotional cost of completing your many years of training worth the added credibility? Could your time have been better spent gaining experience in your new career or getting an advanced degree in business?

Another problem is that for many physicians, they are too late in making the decision to switch to a non-clinical career. If you are still in your training, sticking things out can often be a mistake. The story below from one of our physician faculty members is fairly typical of the ones we hear:

Example 9.1: Physician in successful non-clinical career as medical journalist regrets sticking through training that made her miserable

Chronic Discontentment with Medicine
I had a chronic discontentment with medicine, even from the very beginning—I think it was just bad decision making when I was 20. To understand how I got into this field, you have to understand how I became a doctor in the first place. I made the decision to go to medical school when I was 20. And it was mostly because…college graduation was approaching. I was a biology and a chemistry major and I had to figure out what I was going to do with my life. At the time, I saw my only options as industry or med school.

Little Life Experience
Of course, you have no life experience at 20 to make big decisions like this, so you kind of rely on your surrogates. My teachers are saying, "Oh, you have good grades. You're a smart girl, why don't you go to med school?" My parents—my dad's a doctor. He'd be exceedingly proud if his daughter became a doctor, too, so you have that pressure. And then all my friends—they're applying to med

school, they're getting interviews, they're getting in—and me being the super-achiever that I am, I wanted to play the game, too.

Going Along
So of course, I go along and I make a decision like a 20 year old and apply to med school. And of course I get in. So here I am. I'm not terribly happy with what we're studying and just being in med school in general. So I meet with the school counselor and I think I'm really doing the wrong thing with my life. But of course, her job is to keep you in the system.

Sticking with It
She says, "Well, maybe you don't like it now because you're just studying for tests all the time. Wait 'til you get to your clerkships," or "Wait 'til you get to residency. It'll get better." So you stick with it, again, relying on somebody's advice who you think knows better. It doesn't get better, it just gets different. But there I was going through med school, through residency. I even did a fellowship after residency. Because once you're in the medical education system, there ain't no getting out. So then I was in private practice, 'cause that's the only thing to do. And I was doing the same thing over and over again every fifteen minutes and I thought, "This is going to kill me if I have to do this for the next 20 or 30 years."

BENEFITS OF EARLY TRANSITION
Leaving clinical medicine before your training is complete is a proven transition technique. One of our faculty members left his surgical residency to work for an international non-profit. Fourteen years and several positions later (he's now in his early forties), he is the chief medical officer (top physician position) at an international biotech company. His success reaching such a level of high responsibility and remuneration was based upon his performance and was not held back by his missing a piece of paper from an ABMS Board. Another SEAK faculty member left clinical medicine during his surgical residency and is now a very successful management consultant.

One of our clients successfully started his career in industry before even finishing his internship. A recruiter landed him an entry-level job running clinical trials and assessing safety for a cardiovascular product. He didn't have to take a pay cut (he was an intern) and the company was willing to train him. In his own words, "I cut my hours probably 66 percent and increased my salary probably three times."

Another faculty member of ours left for industry in the middle of his ENT residency. Here's his story in his own words:

Example 9.2: Physician recognizes his discontent with medicine and has courage to leave before his training was completed

Creative Bent
I did general surgery first, then went into ENT, but I had decided all along that I was always more interested in the creative part. I was editor-in-chief of my yearbook in medical school, and I used to write and direct the class shows. I've always had that creative spirit.

Medicine Very Rote
I thought to myself, "Medicine becomes very, very rote, no matter what you're doing." If you're a cardiac surgeon or a dermatologist, it can become the same thing everyday. I tell people the reason why I left medicine is because I didn't want a job that I could tell you what I'd be doing 30 years from now on a Tuesday afternoon. Now that's what I thought medicine was like.

Interested in Creative Writing
So I always had this—I was into creative writing. I'm not a writer, but I was just into that kind of thing. So...in 1982 I wrote 30 letters to the CEOs of advertising agencies in New York. I can still remember, "Perhaps my interests are germane to your needs." I can still remember that sentence. And luckily enough I had lots of responses.

Getting the Interview
I remember in '82 it was pretty taboo for a doctor to jump into advertising or even industry. One agency, which was part of Saatchi & Saatchi, Klentner, sent me a letter. The chairman was nice enough to send the letter down, sent me a letter and said, "Would you like to come interview?" And you know what? Didn't even go, 'cause I did this as a whim.

Then as I got more and more depressed, it was Christmastime at the Pittsburgh VA. I called and I said, "Is that job still open?" They said, "Yes," and (I lied) I said, "I'm gonna be in town tomorrow for a reunion, a family reunion."

I flew to New York, interviewed, and two weeks later I got the job. I didn't even know what a medical director does at a medical advertising agency. I had no clue. I didn't even know what the job was.

No Explanations Needed
I remember the first thing people would say is, "How could you leave after all that training, not seeing patients?" Now the number one question I get is, "Here's my card. How do I get into something like this?" I mean you have to

remember in '82 that really was nobody left. Nobody would leave medicine to do this.

9.6 Seize Unexpected Opportunities When They Present Themselves

Many career transitions are completely unplanned. We have interviewed numerous physicians who are currently working in successful non-clinical careers. An oft-repeated story is that they were not actively looking for a non-clinical position when the opportunity for such a position first presented itself. Consider what one of our faculty members, a self-employed consultant has to say:

> **Example 9.3: "A lot of life is not according to plan"**
> You know, a lot of life is not according to plan. So the key is how quick on your feet are you when you get strange little career things that happen to all of us? Sometimes we are instrumental and sometimes the forces are external to us, but either way you have to adapt, and that's what I think makes a successful business person, especially a successful client, a successful consultant.

If you are presented with a non-clinical opportunity, be prepared to go for it. This is true even if you have in your mind a longer timeframe for transition (say 3 to 5 years). It is good practice to have a general contingency plan for jumping on an opportunity that presents itself sooner. Things to consider in your contingency plan could include:

- A financial bridge if this first job results in a pay cut,
- Winding down your current clinical job (tails, patient coverage, etc.), and
- Having general buy-in from your spouse or significant other, discussing the possibility that something may present itself.

SEIZE AN UNEXPECTED OPPORTUNITY
Consider the example of one of our faculty members who was a practicing internist and seized an opportunity to go to work for an insurance company. He was flexible enough to seize the opportunity when it presented itself, knowing that a similar opportunity might not reappear for a long time—if at all.

Example 9.4: Physician seizes opportunity when contacted by a recruiter about a non-clinical position
I fell into the administrative role totally by accident. I was contacted by a recruiter out of the clear blue. I wasn't looking. Apparently somebody had given a recruiter my name as someone who was a good doctor, and asked me if I was interested in doing a medical director-type role.

It sounded intriguing. I had been practicing for ten years. I wasn't looking for a change, but I wasn't opposed to getting involved in something new and so I thought I would try it. And so actually, I went on a leave of absence from my clinical role to try this medical director role.

9.7 Don't Obsess about the Job Description

When employers write job descriptions, they are in effect making a wish list. Unfortunately, they may not be able to get any candidates who meet all their criteria. Many employers will hire a bright, hard-working person who fits in over someone with the paper qualifications they were looking for. Bottom line, if you think you'd love the job, apply anyhow. The best way to do this is to use your network to have your resume submitted to the person in charge of hiring. If at all possible, you want to avoid the human resources filter that may ding your resume for it not meeting certain requirements. Take as an example the neurologist below who applied for a job at an insurance company. They were not looking for his specialty, but he got the job anyhow:

Example 9.5: Physician gets non-clinical job despite not fitting job description
When I saw an ad in *The New England Journal of Medicine* for [a local insurance company], I had an idea of what they were looking for and I applied knowing that my medical legal experience would be helpful in that kind of setting. They were advertising for numerous doctors and various specialties, such as cardiology, psychiatry, orthopedics, oncology, physiatry. The one specialty they weren't advertising for was neurology, but I sent in my application with a cover letter explaining to them why they needed a neurologist but they just didn't realize it...I didn't hear from them for a couple of months. Then I was at the naval air station having a reserves physical when I met the doctor who was working there. We starting chatting and I found out that he worked at [the insurance company]. After we talked for a while, he told me that he would be getting in touch with the medical director and I would be hearing from them in a couple of days. A few days later they called me for an interview and shortly after that they offered me a position.

9.8 Easing into Work While Building Your Resume

It is often a good idea to ease yourself into the non-clinical field by first getting some part-time experience in the field you are interested in. There are two huge advantages of doing this. First, you are able to test how much you might like working in the new field. There is nothing worse than leaving clinical medicine and going into a field you like even less. The second advantage of this strategy is that it allows you to build your resume and talking points. Doing some part-time work in a targeted field will get you experience and knowledge and demonstrate to prospective employers your interest in a field. Classic ways to do this include serving on committees and task forces in areas such as utilization review, quality assurance, strategic planning, credentialing, or privileging for their hospital, group, or independent practice association. Volunteering and consulting are also good ways to build a resume and test the waters. There are also many positions that offer a split between administrative and clinical work. Writing articles, speaking, and being an active leader (board member or officer) in professional organizations can also help build a resume.

> **Example 9.6: Family physician becomes hospital medical director and then CEO**
>
> I originally started out as a hospital medical director and then became that hospital's CEO, Santa Monica UCLA Medical Center. I did what most doctors do, I sort of ran back to school and got myself a Masters in Public Health in a new program that had just started at UCLA which was very business-oriented. And in the midst of that—it was a two year program—at the end of the first year was when the position came open as the medical director. So I applied for it and got it. I'd been pretty active on my medical stuff, so people knew me at the time.
>
> I'd volunteered on a lot of committees. I was on the executive medical board. People knew me and I was at that point indicating—signaling that I was ready to change careers. It was originally going to be a part-time position, but in a month it was obvious that that would never happen. I actually, at that point, decided to leave—I was going to try to do family practice part-time and this medical director position part-time but it didn't work. Within a month I left practice, basically and became a full-time medical director. Went into the role where it was fairly ill-defined because I don't think the hospital knew what they really wanted from a medical director. I looked around and saw that there was a lot more that I was capable of doing and so I offered to take on things and I expanded my role and that put me in the position of being part of the UCLA executive team and once I was part of the UCLA executive team when the CEO of

our hospital was leaving I knew the folks well enough that they turned around and said, "Well, would you consider being the CEO?" And so that's how I became the CEO.

Example 9.7: Podiatrist becomes TV reporter
A podiatrist wanted to become a medical TV reporter. She eased herself in by doing a corporate video for a large corporation and by granting interviews and appearing as a medical expert on TV. This part-time experience was instrumental in her landing her first job as a TV reporter.

Many physicians maintain a reduced clinical practice when starting their non-clinical careers. This hedges the physician's bets, serves as an opportunity to maintain clinical credibility, and can be personally and professionally rewarding to continue helping patients.

9.9 Go Around Human Resources by Networking
One of the main advantages of networking is to circumvent the dreaded human resources department. HR executives generally don't make hiring decisions. What they will do is screen resumes and exclude ones that do not fit the rigid job descriptions that they have drafted (computers often assist in this). Another problem with HR employees is that they generally will not have the medical and technical expertise to recognize why you may be a good fit for the company. The more you can get around human resources and get your candidacy in front of the decision maker(s) you would be working for, the better off you will be because you will be one important step further along in the process. The way to get around human resources is by networking.

Please reconsider Example 9.5 above in Section 9.7. Going through human resources, the neurologist applicant went absolutely nowhere in his pursuit of his position at an insurance company. Neurology was not a specialty in the job description and HR was dinging his application. Once the applicant was able to get his resume, through networking, in front of the decision maker—thus circumventing HR—he had an interview almost immediately and a job offer shortly thereafter.

9.10 Improve Your Communication Skills

Perhaps the most common item in job descriptions for non-clinical work is excellent communication skills. For more on communication skills, please see Section 2.5. The better your communication skills, the more valuable you will be as an applicant and employee. Doctors with good communication skills also tend to have the easiest time transitioning because they interview well and have a skill that is high in demand.

There are many ways physicians can improve their communication skills. These include:

TEACHING

Seize opportunities to teach. Teach as much as you can. The more you teach, the more you will be comfortable in front of people and the better the communicator you will become.

DITCH THE POWERPOINT

We recently ran a national occupational medicine conference and had a very high-powered Ivy League physician presenter. There was a problem with the LCD system and we were having trouble getting the physician's slides going. Now his slides were just words (not photos or video showing a procedure or anything) and they were reprinted in the conference handbook that the speaker and all attendees had in front of them. We asked the speaker if he could proceed without the slides and his answer was "no." This was a shocking response to us and demonstrated a gross lack of communication skills. If you are wed to PowerPoint, try to wean yourself off it as much as possible. You will become a much better communicator and a much more valuable candidate.

SERVE AS AN EXPERT WITNESS

The function of an expert witness is basically to teach the jury about medicine. Serving as an expert witness can help to improve a physician's communication skills. The tough questioning you are subjected to can also be of great help in building your ability to think on your feet as you prepare for the business world.

WRITE
Communication skills include written communication. Try to write and publish as much as you can. This will serve as great practice and will demonstrate your communication skills.

SERVE ON COMMITTEES
Serving on committees and in other areas where you need to give presentations and answer pointed questions is yet another way to gather valuable experience and improve your communication skills.

SEEK HONEST FEEDBACK
After making presentations always ask to see the written evaluations. In addition, have someone you trust to give you an honest answer sit in on your presentation and give you suggestions for improvement. If you are not satisfied with your improvement, hire a coach to help you polish your communication skills.

Consider the following example of a physician greatly improving her marketability by becoming a better communicator through practicing her skills:

> **Example 9.8: As communication skills improved, physician became more and more in demand**
> I think that I seized upon every opportunity to hone my writing skills and the effectiveness of my ability to articulate why I thought clinical systems and clinical guidelines and the intersection of those things were really important to the landscape of care in confronting a really cost-focused model for how we manage care. I think that writing and the willingness to speak, seeking opportunities to speak and accepting them when they just landed on my doorstep, over the course of two years my life evolved from one where I was seeking to one where I was being sought.

9.11 Use a Mentor

It can be very helpful to have a knowledgeable mentor or mentors guide you through your career transition. Mentors can greatly assist in speeding your career transition by helping you find direction. They can also greatly help you network and avoid mistakes.

A surgeon who became a very successful medical communications executive discusses how important having a mentor was to him:

Example 9.9: "The main thing that helped me is that I had a mentor"
It took me a couple of years to really plan out what I really wanted to do. The main thing that helped me was I had a mentor. I had a family member who had left medicine in the past and had run a couple of businesses. He offered to meet with me every single week for dinner. So we met every Wednesday at a restaurant that was half-way between my house and his house. We very systematically started to approach how to change careers. At the time I really didn't know what opportunities were out there, I only knew about a fraction of the opportunities that are out there for clinicians. The only thing I really knew about was working with a pharmaceutical company and even that I didn't know very much about. What we did was, we sat down every week and in the beginning he just had me write down what my priorities were, write down what I liked about my job and what I didn't like about my job. Some things that sound pretty straightforward and fairly simple, but as you do that you really learn a lot about yourself and you learn a lot about what you actually don't like in your current career and what you are looking for in a future career. So we spent a couple of years doing this and as we went through it, every week he would give me an assignment at the end of the discussion. I would have to come back the next week and say ok, I called doctor A and doctor B and I got in touch with these other people and I looked on a certain website for job opportunities and this is what I found. Very systematically and progressively, I learned a lot about what I needed to do and what I was looking for. He really helped me and I think that's very important for someone looking for a change in careers. It's pretty complicated, so I think a mentor is very valuable.

A pediatric oncologist discusses how he used a mentor to help land himself a job in industry:

Example 9.10: Mentoring can be very helpful
[Once I decided I wanted to move into industry, I sought mentoring from someone in industry who could give me advice.] I had a very interesting situation occur, and that is I used to put on a range—a number of international bone marrow transplant meetings in pediatrics, and one of the speakers whom I had invited years before was a colleague of mine, so to speak—a professional colleague, and I went looking for her one day. It must have been maybe three years before I actually made the switch to the pharmaceutical industry. I wanted to ask her a question and found out that she had quit her job at an academic institution and gone to work for a pharmaceutical company. And lo and behold, the pharmaceutical company for which she worked was located directly across the street from the hospital that I was working at.

227

So, we arranged to meet and I ended up hiring her to work part-time for me during—when I was at medical meetings or had to be away, because none of the other people with whom I was working were as senior as I was, and therefore did not have the experience and she did. I paid her a hefty sum every day and she would cover for me. And she loved doing it. She had let her medical license lapse, so we were able to get it back for her and get her privileges at the hospital and it was actually her influence that guided me into the pharmaceutical industry because she had already made that leap.

She had made the leap for other reasons, and that was that the academic institution that she was at was actually closing the program that she had headed, so she had no choice. I mean, she had to do something different and so she was forced to—she was at the edge of the cliff and she was forced to make that leap into something else and decided to quit academia. But the question, as you posed it a minute or two ago was such that it was very clear that most of my guidance came from talking to a colleague who was already in the pharmaceutical industry.

9.12 Finding a Mentor

In order to have a mentor you first need to find a mentor. If you know what industry you would like to get involved in, you can try to find a mentor through networking (see Chapter 4), a colleague in that industry that can help you with advice. People like to help other people. Physicians who have left clinical practice tend to be very giving of their time because they can easily remember back to when they were struggling with their own career transition. Don't abuse or waste their time and you may be able to find someone who will be very helpful to you.

The trickier situation is if you don't first know what industry you would like to be involved with. It is impossible to find someone who knows everything about all the opportunities out there for physicians. SEAK's Non-Clinical Careers for Physicians annual conference (www.seak.com) provides free mentoring for physicians through a panel of volunteer mentors. Another possibility is to try to find a mentor in every field in which you have an interest. This can be feasible as long as you limit the number of fields you would like to explore. Finally, the authors and others offer fee-based coaching/mentoring. The downside to this approach is obviously the cost involved.

9.13 Networking

Networking is probably the most important and effective technique you can use to find a non-clinical job. Networking works. Networking is indeed so important that we dedicated an entire chapter (Chapter 4) to how to be a better networker. A SEAK faculty member describes how he broke into pharma:

Example 9.11: Networking works to get physician a job in industry
[I was dissatisfied] with emergency medicine. I was talking to a colleague who had been in pharmaceutical medicine before. In his day, though, I think it was very much different than the experience I had subsequent to joining the pharmaceutical industry. He thought it was just window dressing and paper pushing. However, when he talked I saw the little light bulb in my head and said well, gee, I'd like to pursue this. I knew nothing at the time about pharmaceutical medicine and he said...he had a good friend who was still in one of the pharmaceutical companies and that he would be glad to tell this fellow about me. Lunch was arranged and I brought my CV. [The contact] was kind enough to take my CV and submit it to the research department of that particular pharmaceutical company, and I got hired.

A single mom who has not completed residency describes how she found her non-clinical position through networking:

Example 9.12: Networking leads to job
One of the first things that I did was that I drafted a letter, "Dear Family and Friends," and I essentially told them about my plans in the most positive way that I could, why I felt that this was a good track for me, and sort of in broad terms what I was looking for, and just that I wanted to let them know, and that if they had any thoughts, suggestions, recommendations, or leads for me to please let me know. And I included a little bit more information in that on how to get back to me.

I sent that letter to about 150 people and found some pretty interesting leads. The job that I ended up landing was through networking with a local friend, but I was very surprised at my aunt, who had an old neighbor who had a job in industry. You know, different connections that you wouldn't have suspected. It wasn't necessarily my admissions director at [my medical school] who was able to find me the connections. Sometimes the connections came from unlikely sources.

An academic surgeon who became a consultant landed a job through an informational interview:

Example 9.13: Informational interview (networking) directly results in job offer
At [my business school] there was the chief operating officer, who worked with a guy at Cambridge, when he was working at [a prestigious] clinic. There was a merger, and despite the fact that the merger had to be undone those two remained friends. And so the guy at [the clinic], who also was a Tuck graduate, said, "Why don't you contact Andy at [consulting company] and set up an informational interview?" I did a whole round of networking interviews [and that's how I got my job]. [My] job came from an informational interview. I didn't expect to be offered a job. The partner was impressed with me, and his last question was, "Well what can you sell?" And I said, "I can sell my time. I can sell my talent. I can sell my insight based on being a practicing physician."

A resident who became a management consultant also found a non-clinical position through networking:

Example 9.14: Networking during residency leads to non-clinical position at blue-chip consulting firm
I had some contacts in residency for some consulting work. There were some device companies in the area that had some physicians on their advisory boards, so actually it was kind of easy. And in a way it was deceptively easy, because getting consulting work and getting all those opportunities is not just handed to you on a plate.

So, in a way that was made available, so I did...some consulting projects for these device companies as I left the residency. And then at that time I also applied to the blue-chip or the big consultancy firms, and so I kind of did things in parallel.

9.14 Use a Recruiter (Headhunter or Executive Search Firm)

Most positions filled by recruiters require significant prior non-clinical experience. However, recruiters do place physicians without prior significant non-clinical experience. Each year, recruiters come to our Non-Clinical Careers for Physicians Conference (www.seak.com) in search of inexperienced physicians to place. One of our clients was actually placed by a recruiter in a pharma job before even completing his surgical internship. Using a recruiter is a viable strategy for career transition. Recruiters should not be ignored as a useful tool simply because much of the time the positions they place require significant non-clinical experience.

A pediatric oncologist who moved into pharma found his non-clinical position through a recruiter:

Example 9.15: First non-clinical job landed through a recruiter

[I found out about my first non-clinical position] through recruiters. There are a few pharmaceutical companies, both large and small, and biotech companies that will actually have websites in which they list potential openings. But the vast majority of them work through recruiters because they don't have the personnel to really go out and find the people out there who are sort of lurking in the shadows, who really want to make the jump but don't know how to do it and don't know how to approach anyone. And so it's not unusual that academicians get many phone calls from recruiters—are you interested? And of course, many of them really are, but they were afraid to make the leap, they were afraid to even make the phone call. They were afraid to inquire. So recruiters are out there banging the doors and looking under the carpets and in the closets to see who out there really wants to make the switch, who has the credentials and the background for which we're looking.

The key to successfully working with a recruiter is to correctly differentiate between recruiters who may actually have a job opportunity for you and recruiters who are just trying clever ways to sell you their services. Legitimate recruiters are generally paid exclusively by the companies they place candidates with, not by the candidate. The recruiter will receive on average 20% to 35% of the newly placed employee's first year salary. Avoid recruiters who want to charge you for membership and other fees.[1] One good way to differentiate between recruiters who have jobs and others who may just be trying to sell you their consulting and coaching services is to ask them how they are paid. Another good technique is to ask them for a job description. If they can't produce one, they probably don't have an actual job to fill.[2]

Legitimate recruiters are usually paid strictly on performance. They make money only by successfully placing candidates and having these candidates stay for a specific period of time (for example, one year). As

---

[1] Frank, W and Babitsky S, *Non-Clinical Careers for Physicians* (SEAK Seminar Handbook, 2006) at 337.
[2] Frank, W and Babitsky S, *Non-Clinical Careers for Physicians* (SEAK Seminar Handbook, 2006) at 337.

such, they don't want to send candidates who will make a poor impression on their clients.

When working with a recruiter you must first sell yourself to the recruiter. Be cooperative. Demonstrate good communication skills. Be reachable. Return phone calls promptly. Don't act like a know-it-all who knows more science than the recruiter—even though in many cases you will.

If you have done some due diligence on a recruiter and they suggest that you meet, agree to do so. Many recruiters won't submit the name of a candidate that they haven't met face to face. A face-to-face meeting will be critical so that the recruiter can kick your tires, so to speak, and make sure you don't have teeth coming out of your head.

Your personality and communications skills matter greatly. Here's what a successful recruiter has to say about that:

Example 9.16: Recruiter describes how important communication skills and personality are
We want to make sure they have a good personality, somewhat outgoing but also very professional. We want to make sure we can actually hold a conversation with them. It's easy to speak with them and we're getting ideas from them and they are a nice person overall.

It's a good idea to talk to as many reputable recruiters as you can. A good technique to finding the right recruiter for you is to look for recruiters who specialize in the industries and geography you are most interested in. This information can often be found online and in directories. The most famous of these is Kennedy Information's *Directory of Executive Recruiters* (www.kennedyinfo.com) (the big red book). Another resource to consider is the National Association of Physician Recruiters (www.napr.org). Of course, the best way to find the right recruiters for you is to network and talk to colleagues in industry. Examples of recruiters include:

- Cejka Search: www.cejkasearch.com
- Furst Group: www.furstgroup.com
- Tyler and Company: www.tylerandco.com
- Witt/Kiefer: www.wittkiefer.com

- Korn Ferry: www.kornferry.com
- Russell Reynolds: www.russellreynolds.com
- Spencer Stuart: www.spencerstuart.com
- Healthcare for Hire: http://healthcareforhire.com

It's often a good idea to talk to as many good-fitting recruiters as you can. Recruiters are not like real estate agents who have access to everything that is on the market. Recruiters only make money from the positions they are trying to fill. As such, talk to as many as you can so that you don't miss promising opportunities.

Some larger recruiters will allow you to submit your resume to them. Your resume will then be placed in the firm's internal database. If an opportunity arises that meshes with your qualifications, you might be contacted.

Because recruiters only get paid when you land a position, they have a vested interest in helping you succeed. One way this manifests itself is that they will generally help you to punch up and tweak your resume, mentor you, and discuss any job- or industry-related issue. These can be very valuable free services.

There are three things to look out for with recruiters. First, make sure the firm is reputable. You can do this by checking references. Politely ask the recruiter for past client physicians you can talk to. Second, verify that the recruiter will not send out your resume to an employer without your permission. Such a breach of confidentiality could be very problematic. Finally, verify that the position in question is permanent. Many recruiters are just trying to fill temporary or contract positions.

9.15 Go Back to School

Going back to school can range from being indispensable (say, if you want to become an attorney), to very helpful (for instance, you go to a top MBA program), to a very expensive learning experience that does not help you find a job or excel in your job. The pros and cons of going back to school along with many case examples are discussed in detail in Chapter 6.

9.16 Build a Brand by Finding a Niche

Anyone looking for a career change should keep in mind the law of supply and demand. The lower the supply, the greater the value of something in demand. Building expertise in a narrow niche area can be a powerful way to make yourself more valuable. Please consider the following examples:

Example 9.17: Pediatric oncologist moves to pharma
One SEAK faculty member was a leading pediatric oncologist with a niche interest and track record in a particular area. When pharma developed a drug in this area, he was very well positioned for the switch.

Example 9.18: Consulting in niche area
Another SEAK faculty member gained valuable experience while working for the military in dangers for exposures to certain chemicals. Very few people have similar expertise. Upon leaving the military he was quickly able to establish a successful consulting practice in this narrow niche field.

9.17 Read and Apply to Relevant Job Postings

Keeping up-to-date on job postings and applying to positions of interest can be successful career transition tools. Where non-clinical jobs are posted in print and online is discussed in detail in Chapter 5. For example, one of our faculty members obtained his first non-clinical job after applying to a job posting from an insurance company in *The New England Journal of Medicine*

9.18 Blitz a Targeted Industry

It's a long shot, but doing a mass unsolicited mailing to the key people in firms you would like to work for can and does work. The key is to target an industry you have interest in and to make a great pitch as to why you'd be able to help them. Remember that a long shot only hits if you take it. Be optimistic and try it out. Please consider the following two success stories:

Example 9.19: Surgeon blitzes communications industry with mass mailing of resumes and gets lucky
(Note that in this story the physician did get lucky—but that to a large extent he made his own luck by doing his homework, developing a plan, and being disciplined enough to do the hard work to follow-through with the plan.)

I looked at a way to combine my medical background with something else that I really loved and in this case it was writing. I ended up looking for something where I could combine my medical experience and my love for writing. I found out about medical communications and gradually learned about resources where I could find [a] list of companies that did medical communications. Once I did that, I ended up putting a letter together and just sent a letter to probably about 50 companies that were in about a 75 mile radius of my house that did this type of work. I added my CV and I said "You don't know me and I've never done this before, but I'm very interested in it and these are the reasons that I find this type of work interesting and why I think I would be great at it." I sent the letter out to all these places and one company got back to me. That was a company that at the time just picked up work on a product that was useful for plastic surgeons. It was an artificial skin essentially. So, they had this incredible need [for] someone with expertise in that particular area and I had the desire to do that type of work. It was the perfect fit. I think in a lot of ways I got lucky with that. I think that it's probably more likely that people will find jobs through direct networking and eventually meet somebody who has an opportunity for them. It just happened to work out for me that there was just a perfect fit and I've been happy ever since with that career.

Example 9.20: Intern blitzes advertising firms with resumes and gets job offer
I always...was into creative writing. I'm not a writer, but I was just into that kind of thing. In 1982 I wrote 30 letters to the CEOs of advertising agencies in New York. I can still remember, "Perhaps my interests are germane to your needs." I can still remember that sentence. And luckily enough I had lots of responses.

I remember in '82 it was pretty taboo for a doctor to jump into advertising or even industry. One agency sent me a letter. The chairman was nice enough to send the letter down, sent me a letter and said, "Would you like to come interview?" And you know what? Didn't even go, 'cause I did this as a whim.

Then as I got more and more depressed, it was Christmastime at the Pittsburgh VA. I called and I said, "Is that job still open?" They said, "Yes," and (I lied) I said, "I'm gonna be in town tomorrow for a reunion, a family reunion."

I flew to New York, interviewed, and two weeks later I got the job.

9.19 Create Your Own Job

A surefire way to get a non-clinical position is to hire yourself. As you can see in the prologue this is how author Steven Babitsky successfully transitioned out of a stressful law practice. Many physicians leave clinical work to run their own businesses or to become consultants. The most common way to do this is by starting and running the business part-time and then eventually ceasing or greatly reducing your clinical work in order to concentrate more and more on the non-clinical business or consulting. Businesses and franchises can also be purchased if you are financially positioned to do so. Please consider the following examples:

Example 9.21: Occupational medicine physician spends part-time running a specialty food producing business he started
The plan is to build the business to the point where he can devote his efforts full-time to the business.

Example 9.22: ER physician buys franchises
A successful ER physician positions himself for the future by buying a franchise of physician weight loss centers. He still practices medicine for now. The franchises allow him an obvious escape route, allow him to diversify his income streams, and create a valuable asset that can later be sold or passed down to family members.

More on consulting and on running your own business is contained in Section 3.3.

9.20 Build Your Resume

Once you know the industry you are going to target, it can be very helpful to immediately start doing what you can to build your resume and add accomplishments that will make you more attractive to a potential employer and give you a competitive advantage over other candidates. Please consider the following examples:

Example 9.23: Resume-building for the insurance industry
You are interested in working for a disability insurer. You start doing independent medical exams as part of your practice and you join the American Academy of Insurance Medicine and the American Academy of Disability Evaluating Physicians. You attend relevant continuing medical education.

Example 9.24: Resume-building for clinical affairs in pharma
You are interested in a clinical affairs position. You take a job at an academic institution and participate in clinical trials.

Example 9.25: Resume-building for government work
You would like to work in public health for the government. You go back to school part-time for an MPH.

Example 9.26: Resume-building for administration
You are interested in medical administration. You agree to serve on committees and complete a certification program through the American College of Physician Executives. You practice and improve your communications skills by teaching and lecturing.

9.21 Save Your Pennies

Career transition can be much easier if you have built up a financial cushion. A financial cushion will allow you maximum flexibility if you would like to go back to school and can allow you to take a temporary pay cut for an entry-level position. Having some liquid assets also opens up the possibility of buying a business or allowing you to start your own business. Living well within your means while practicing can greatly help your career transition.

Example 9.27: Saving up opens the possibility for a dream job
Successful surgeon saves aggressively and is then able to take dream job of buying and running a small business that gives fantasy fighter flights to laymen.

9.22 Earn and Maintain Your Board Certification

Some non-clinical jobs require board certification and a certain number of years of clinical practice. (As seen in Section 9.18 above, some certainly do not.) If you are interested in such a position, finishing your training and gaining clinical practice are a must. They key once again is to figure out what you want to do first and then come up with a plan to get there. Board certification is also quite valuable if you ever decide to go back to clinical medicine.

9.23 Continue Practicing Medicine Part-Time

Many physicians keep practicing medicine part-time while they start working in their non-clinical careers. There are many advantages to this approach. First, it provides a stream of income. Second, it helps to keep the physician's options open in case the physician decides to go back to clinical medicine. Third, and most importantly, it can help the physician maintain credibility and gain insight with what is happening in clinical care. These could be crucial advantages in some non-clinical careers.

As one SEAK faculty member put it:

Example 9.28: Part-time practice makes physician consultant more credible

One of the physicians said to me, he was a psychiatrist, he said, "No matter how difficult it is, you have to continue doing locum tenens work because there are plenty of retired docs out there and we don't listen to them."

So the people knew that I was there three weeks out of four at a consulting assignment, and that really gave me credibility as they said, "[He's] going to do his doctor thing." Then I could talk to some of the physicians about what I learned or something along that line or what we did. We could always tell stories. I remember one time I was with a guy in California. He's an oncologic surgeon. He said, "So what did you do this last weekend?" I said, "There was a guy who cut himself on his edge skiing, and as we brought him into the operating room you could see the trail of blood, and I sewed up probably 25 different blood vessels in his butt." And the oncologic surgeon, who does all sorts of major types of operations, he just looked at me and said, "Oh, I hate trauma."

Example 9.29: Half-time practicing physician, half-time in medical advertising

Consider the example of Dr. Jeff Gold featured in the February 5, 2008 article in *The Wall Street Journal* entitled "Doubling-Up on Careers Suits More Workers." Dr. Gold works part-time in a rehabilitation center in the Bronx in clinical medicine and part-time in Manhattan doing medical advertising. This allows Dr. Gold to have higher levels of job and financial security. In Dr. Gold's words, "If one industry suffers a downturn, I am still likely to be employed by the other."

Chapter 10 Negotiating Your Job Offer

10.1 Executive Summary

- Prior to negotiating, it is important to receive the job details and a job offer.
- In addition to salary, do not forget to negotiate bonuses, equity awards, fringe benefits, covenants not to compete, and termination provisions.
- Gain power in the negotiation by developing alternatives and being able to cite industry standards.

10.2 Preparing to Negotiate Your Job Offer

When you switch from a clinical to a non-clinical position, you will be faced with negotiating your job offer. The issues faced in negotiation of a non-clinical offer will be vastly different from any contract negotiation you have experienced.

Prior to negotiating a job offer, you should diligently prepare for the negotiation. Generally, you should know:

- What you want,
- What you are worth, and
- What your prospective employer is likely to pay.

When preparing to negotiate your job offer, you should:

- Gather all relevant information about the person you will be negotiating with: her interests, her goals, the company, and the company's programs or products. The more you know, the better your chances of success.
- Clarify the issues to be discussed and negotiated. Prepare a written agenda.
- Analyze the information you gathered. Give yourself time to think it through.
- Set your goals and targets and figure out what the other side is likely to argue or seek.
- Develop a decision tree so that you are prepared for all scenarios.

- Be flexible so that you can react and incorporate new information you learn during the negotiation.

10.3 Get the Job Details First

It may be tempting to start negotiating financial issues such as salary, bonuses, and benefits before the duties of the position are locked down. This is a tactical and strategic mistake for many reasons. These reasons include:

- The salary, bonuses, and benefits desired may be based in whole or in part on the specific job duties involved.
- Talking about the job, its demands, its requirements, and your responsibilities demonstrates to your prospective employer the importance you place on understanding and excelling at your future duties.
- It sends a message that the type of work you may be doing and how it is to be done are just as important as the financial considerations.

Start with a job description containing the proposed duties and responsibilities. You want to avoid any nasty surprises that may make the position more difficult and less attractive. Particular attention should be paid to:

- What you are to do on a daily basis,
- Where you will perform your duties,
- To whom you will report,
- Members of your team,
- Any support staff you will be provided,
- The type of travel and amount of travel, if any, that will be required (local, national, or international),
- Presentations you will make,
- Marketing/selling required,
- Hours,
- Private office/cubicle, and
- Administrative/clerical duties.

Do not assume that the job description you have been given is accurate or complete. There is often a disconnect between the HR people who develop the job description posted and the realities of the workplace.

It is crucial to determine the true needs of your prospective employer and whether you can and want to fully meet these needs. Once you feel comfortable with your proposed duties, you are ready to negotiate the terms of the offer.

10.4 Terms of the Offer

The four general categories you want to recognize and negotiate successfully are:

- Salary and increases,
- Bonuses,
- Fringe benefits, and
- Ancillary income.

SALARY

You want to obtain a salary that you are happy with. It makes little sense to accept a salary you are not satisfied with unless you have short- and long-term room for advancement. You will want to know beforehand (or should learn as quickly as possible):

- The general salary parameters for the position,
- What factors can push you to the higher end of the scale,
- How and why the scale is exceeded,
- The authority of the person you are negotiating with to set/exceed the scale, and
- The timeframe the employer is working with (the longer they have been looking, the tighter the timeframe and the more flexible they may be on the salary).

Winning over the person you are negotiating with can be crucial to obtaining a salary at the top edge or even above the salary range. Once won-over, this person can become your advocate. He can go back to the company and explain why it is in the company's best interest to pay you top dollar. If you are overeager to wrap up the financial negotiations, you run the risk of selling yourself short. You want to convey the impression that you are easy to deal with, but, at the same time, you expect to be paid what you are worth. You should also determine how you are to be paid: weekly, bi-weekly, monthly, etc.

It is important to determine how salary increases are handled in the company:

- What formula, if any, is used to determine salary increases?
- Are increases merit based or based on company performance?
- What are the general parameters for salary increases?
- What have the increases been for the past 5 years?
- Have there been any salary reductions in the past 5 years?

Do not bluff when asked about current and past earnings. Employers will often ask for pay stubs or W2s to document the past earnings you are claiming.

BONUSES

For many physicians, annual bonuses will play an important role at their non-clinical positions. In many of these non-clinical positions bonuses may be a significant part of the annual compensation. You need to obtain hard information (in writing if possible) concerning:

- How and when bonuses are paid,
- The formula the bonuses are based on,
- The typical bonuses paid, and
- The amount of the bonuses paid for the past 5 years.

STOCK OPTIONS

When negotiating with a publicly traded company, do not overlook the importance of seeking and obtaining stock options as part of your compensation package. These options can be very lucrative and give you the upside you did not have when practicing clinical medicine:

It is crucial that you get the options priced as of the day you sign up with a company not in the future after what you have worked on becomes a success. Getting stock and/or options from a company can be a "sweetener" for your package with a public or private company as well as providing potential *significant* upside. The upside will obviously be more if you receive the options before the value of the stock goes up significantly. For example, if you are given 50,000 options at a price of $5.00 and a company becomes "successful" and the stock goes to $25.00, you have just made $1,000,000 plus your cash compensation. Imagine how you would have felt if you waited to get options at a price of $25.00 knowing you could have gotten it when the price was $5.00.[1]

FRINGE BENEFITS

While the salary you will be paid is of primary importance, it is not uncommon for prospective physician employees to overlook the breadth of potential fringe benefits to be negotiated. Common benefits include:

- Tuition and CME reimbursement,
- Health insurance,
- Car allowance,
- Vacation leave,
- Sick leave,
- Maternity leave,
- Life insurance,
- Professional dues,
- Paid holidays,
- Journal subscriptions,
- Relocation expenses,
- Dental insurance,
- Profit sharing,
- Disability insurance,
- 401(k) and other retirement plans,
- Parking,
- Flex time, and
- Loans.[2]

---

[1] Jacobson, "The Biggest Mistakes You Can Make When Negotiating a Consulting Agreement with a Pharma/Biotech Company" handout at the SEAK Non-Clinical Careers for Physicians Conference, (2008) www.brjacobson.com.
[2] *The Biggest Mistakes Physicians Make and How to Avoid Them,* Babitsky, Mangraviti, SEAK, Inc., p. 159 (2005).

ADDITIONAL/ANCILLARY INCOME

You will want to determine the employer's policy regarding any additional/ancillary income you may earn in the future. The outside income to be discussed and, if possible, protected includes:

- Honoraria for lecturing,
- Royalties for writing treatises and articles,
- Consulting work,
- Testifying as an expert witness,
- Inventions,
- Patents,
- Copyrightable works,
- Discoveries, and
- Other intellectual property.

Income streams you are currently enjoying for past work performed will need to be protected in writing.

TERMINATION PROVISIONS

You will want to fully appreciate what happens to you financially if:

- Your contract runs out and is not renewed.
- You are terminated
  o for cause or
  o without cause.
- You are downsized.
- You are transferred to a new location or substantially different position.
- Your employer is purchased, sold, or taken over.

RESTRICTIVE COVENANTS NOT TO COMPETE

Pay particular attention to any provisions in a contract of employment with unduly restrictive covenants not to compete. You should be concerned with the following noncompetition provisions:

- Length of term (in years or months),
- Geographic limitation (e.g., a certain radius in miles or states), and

- Provisions for exceptions (e.g., teaching, working for an insurance company, or working as a medical director of a noncompeting company).

Unduly restrictive covenants not to compete can force you to relocate or force you out of a particular industry.

10.5 Negotiation Strategies, Techniques, and Tactics

Physicians negotiating their first non-clinical career contract will want to employ proven negotiation strategies, techniques, and tactics to achieve the best possible offer.

STRATEGIES
The key strategy to employ during an employment negotiation is to increase your power. Your power can be increased by:

- Gaining knowledge,
- Developing alternatives,
- Understanding industry standards, and
- Having unique abilities.

Gaining Knowledge: If you fully understand the industry and position you are interviewing for, you will gain power in the negotiations. To find out what the job really consists of, talk to people doing it. When the interviewer tells you there is little travel involved and you know for a fact that you will be on the road 25% of the time, this is knowledge that you should be able to use to increase your compensation. If you are offered a compensation package that is less than one being paid for a comparable position in a similar company, this is leverage you can use. Specific knowledge about past compensation, bonuses, layoffs, promotions, and stock options will help you have power in negotiations.

Developing Alternatives: The physician with no job alternatives is generally in a weak negotiating position. The experts suggest you develop a BATNA (Best Alternative to a Negotiating Agreement). The physician who has one or more job offers in hand is in a much stronger position to command the best compensation package. The physician who has no alternatives and is desperate to leave clinical medicine immediately will likely end up settling for less.

Understanding Industry Standards: The physician who comes into the interview with a good understanding of the general parameters for starting salary and compensation packages, bonuses, stock options, and advancement possibilities is best positioned to understand an offer and compare it to industry norms.

Unique Abilities: Those physicians who truly have unique, rare, or hard to find abilities, training, experience, and something to offer need to identify and articulate what makes them unique. These physicians may be able to use their uniqueness to push the employer to the limit in terms of duties, hours, compensation, and benefits.

TECHNIQUES
Some of the techniques you can employ to achieve a successful contract include:

- Relating to the person you are negotiating with,
- Active listening and watching,
- Asking questions, and
- Going off the record.

Relating to the Negotiator: The physician who relates well to the negotiator and wins him over can build an ally in the company. Once the person you are negotiating with likes and respects you, he may very well go to bat for you pushing the company to sweeten any offers.

Active Listening and Watching: Practice active listening skills. A verbal leak by the negotiator such as, "We can't do much better than that" means to the active listener who recognizes it that they can and will do better. Missing verbal leaks or subtle changes in body language, tone, and inflection, can be very costly.

Asking Questions: A well-phrased question at the right time can make a significant difference in the outcome of the negotiation. For example:

Q. What is your timeframe for filling this position?
Q. What is the most you ever paid to a physician filling this position?
Q. Is there anything else I should know about the position before I decide about taking the offer?

Going off the Record: If you find yourself at a negotiation impasse, asking to go "off the record" and then floating one or more trial balloons can be helpful. For example:

Q. If I were to ask to work one day a week from home, do you think the company would accommodate me?

TACTICS
Some of the more common tactics you are likely to encounter are:

- Split the difference,
- Selection from a limited menu,
- Limited authority, and
- You have got to do better than that.

Split the Difference: This tactic is simple, sounds fair, and costs people negotiating more money than any other tactic. For example:

Negotiator: You are at $180,000. I am at $150,000. Let's split the difference and call it $165,000, OK?

Defense: The physician anticipating this tactic should start with a higher initial demand when asked to "split the difference." A polite reply is "I can't afford to do so."

<u>*Selection from a Limited Menu:*</u> This gives the physician two choices. For example:

> *Negotiator:* So you can work 4 days a week at $120,000 a year or 5 days a week at $140,000. Which would you prefer?

> *Defense:* Just because you are presented with a limited menu does not mean you cannot go "off menu."

> *Physician:* I will need $150,000 for 5 days a week.

<u>*Limited Authority:*</u> In this tactic, the negotiator either has or professes to have a limited authority to negotiate. For example:

> *Negotiator:* Here is the confidential memo on how much I can pay. See paragraph #3. $175,000 is tops. What do you say?

> *Defense:* Get or suggest getting someone with greater authority.

> *Physician:* I appreciate your candor. Who do we need to call down from corporate to get greater authority to get this negotiation finalized?

<u>*You Have to Do Better than That:*</u> Here the negotiator tries to get the physician to bid against herself. For example:

> *Negotiator:* You asked for $200,000 base salary. Before we proceed, you really do need to do better than that if you really want this position.

> *Defense:* Refuse to bid or negotiate against yourself.

> *Physician:* You asked my salary requirements and I candidly gave them to you. What I need to hear is how close you can come to the $200,000.

If you are uncomfortable negotiating, there are professional consultants who will negotiate for you. Some employers are receptive to this, some are not. The advantage of this approach is avoiding any personal bad feelings being created as a result of the initial job negotiation.

10.6 Conclusion

Physicians negotiating a non-clinical job offer are best served by:

- Being prepared for the negotiation,
- Negotiating from a position of power (having other job alternatives),
- Knowing what the marketplace is willing to pay,
- Having an employment attorney assist them before they finalize the agreement,
- Talking to their spouse/significant other about the offer,
- Being prepared to walk away if they are not happy with the offer, and
- Sleeping on their final offer.

For additional information and an in-depth treatment of physician negotiation strategies, see *The Physician's Comprehensive Guide to Negotiating,* Babitsky, Mangraviti, SEAK, Inc. (2007).

Chapter 11 The Biggest Mistakes Physicians Make in Transitioning to a Non-Clinical Career and How to Avoid Them

11.1 Executive Summary

Physicians who avoid the following mistakes will have the easiest career transitions.

11.2 Asking the Wrong Question

Many physicians considering a transition to a non-clinical career ask themselves the following question, "How am I going to replace my current income?" This is the wrong question to ask. For the vast majority of physicians, the correct question to ask is, "How much money am I losing by staying in clinical medicine?" By almost any metric (training, hours, stress, talent, or value of service), most clinical physicians are *grossly* underpaid. Many experienced physicians also face the frustrating situation whereby their income is level and even declining.

Physicians in non-clinical careers commonly earn far more in the short- and long-term than those physicians who are in clinical medicine. Non-clinical positions have the benefit of salaries that are not in effect set or limited by the government or an insurance bureaucrat. In addition, it is much easier to leverage oneself in a non-clinical career than a clinical setting where your earnings are limited by how many procedures or patients can be crammed into a day. Finally, unlike clinical medicine, the sky is really the limit in terms of the earning potential of a non-clinical physician.

11.3 Waiting Too Long

We have interviewed dozens of physicians who have transitioned into non-clinical careers. These transitions typically result in better pay, less stress, and far more regular hours. When asked, the most common regret that these physicians state is that they should have left clinical medicine sooner because they are so much happier now. If you are unhappy as a practicing clinician it is usually a mistake to keep delaying action on a transition to a non-clinical career. (This is true even for interns and residents.) It is unlikely that things are going to change and you are going

251

to all of a sudden start to love practicing clinical medicine. The extra procedures you do or patients you see are not likely to better prepare you for a non-clinical career. Waiting even longer makes the conversation you need to have with your family even harder as your clinical career will be further along. Finally, waiting too long can make relocation more difficult if your children are getting more established in their school and community.

11.4 Not Asking for Help and Mentoring

Mentoring can be very helpful to a physician seeking a career transition. Most physicians who are in non-clinical careers can easily empathize with a colleague looking to make a similar transition. You will be surprised how giving and helpful your colleagues will be if you humbly ask for help and advice. A mentor who can point you in the right direction, facilitate networking, answer questions, and help you avoid common mistakes can be invaluable. Physicians seeking a non-clinical career should actively seek the help and mentoring of their colleagues.

11.5 Thinking That an MBA Is Required

One of the most common questions we face in counseling physicians on non-clinical career transitions is, "Do I need to go back to school?" The short answer to this question is "no." Getting an MBA can impart serious and helpful knowledge. It also looks great on a resume and can help open some entry-level doors for a physician. However, getting an advanced degree, even if done online, can be extremely time consuming and expensive. Once you get started in your non-clinical career your success and advancement will depend almost exclusively on your performance, not whether you have an MBA. The real question is whether you need the MBA to get your foot in the non-clinical career door. For many positions, the answer will be no. Look at the positions you are considering transitioning to and determine for yourself whether the time and expense of getting your MBA is warranted. Do not use getting an MBA as an excuse to delay your career transition. Bottom line: an MBA can be helpful, but it is very expensive and is not a requirement for many successful transitions.

11.6 Not Networking

Most non-clinical jobs are found through networking. Physicians should understand that done right, networking can actually be fun. You get to connect with a lot of people and they can help you learn a great deal about a career, industry, or organization. It is a best practice to set aside a certain amount of time each week for in-person, telephonic, or e-mail networking.

11.7 Being Discouraged by Rejection

Physicians are accustomed to success. They were typically at the top of their class in school and generally have been successful at most everything they have done. It can be quite a shock when a physician starts applying for non-clinical positions and is rejected over and over again. Persistence and a thick skin are key attributes. We have worked with numerous physicians who responded to ads and were rejected for many of the jobs they applied for. They kept at it and eventually found their first non-clinical position.

11.8 Inflexibility

The more flexible you are, the more opportunities there will be for you. We often get calls similar to this, "I live in rural Kansas and need a new career where I work close to home (at home preferable) and have no initial loss in income. I cannot relocate because of family concerns and I have no interest in going back to school. I hate anything to do with medical-legal work, managed care, or the government. These are the reasons I am miserable. Can you help me?" Are there non-clinical careers for such a person? Sure, but the opportunities are going to be very limited. Inflexibility in terms of willingness to modify your lifestyle, initial salary, and willingness to relocate makes a non-clinical career transition much more difficult. Be prepared to at least consider trade-offs.

11.9 Not Realizing the Breadth of Opportunities Available

There are *many* traditional non-clinical career paths available to physicians. These include:

- Pharma (safety, development, regulatory, marketing, and sales)
- Medical devices (safety, development, regulatory, marketing, and sales)
- Insurance (health, disability, and life)
- Medical administration
- Government (federal, state, and local)
- Occupational health
- Education
- Communications
- Marketing
- Informatics (IT)
- Consulting
- Entrepreneur
- Media
- Writing

In addition, just because you are a physician does not mean you are limited to the above traditional fields. Examples of physicians we have worked with who transitioned successfully into non-traditional careers include the following:

- An occupational medicine physician who started his own successful gourmet food company,
- A pediatrician who became a very successful financial advisor, and
- A physician who invented medical devices.

Physicians who are intelligent, hardworking, diligent, and have integrity and credibility can be an asset in almost any kind of business or industry.

11.10 Thinking You Are Too Old for a New Career

At our 2008 Non-Clinical Careers Conference, a physician asked one of our faculty members the following question, "I am 62 years old and looking to do something different for the next 10–15 years before I stop working. Would you consider an old fart like me?" The answer came from a physician who was responsible for hiring dozens of physicians at a large insurance company, "Absolutely. Look, in today's environment, it is typical for people to stay in a job two years or less on average. Given that fact, what do I care if you might retire in a few years? If I can get 2 good years out of you, I've made a good hire."

11.11 Thinking You Must Finish Your Internship and Residency to Have a Viable Non-Clinical Career

The sad fact is that private practice experience and board certification are generally not overly helpful in the long run for non-clinical careers. We have seen numerous examples of highly successful physicians who found out early on that a clinical career in medicine was probably not for them. Physicians who have left clinical medicine during their internships and residencies have gone on to hugely successful careers. On the flip side, a story we hear over and over again is the physician who wanted to leave during their training, but because they didn't want to disappoint their parents or spouse, stuck it out through training and through many years of unhappiness practicing clinical medicine. Post-transition, when we ask such physicians if they have any regrets, their most common answer is, "Yes, I should have left clinical medicine much, much sooner."

11.12 Not Recognizing Your Transferable and Valuable Skills

As a physician, you have numerous transferable and valuable skills. You must recognize these skills and be prepared to articulate them when selling yourself at a job interview. Make a detailed list of your core competencies and skills to use during your career transition and job interviews.

11.13 Unrealistic Short-Term Expectations and Not Thinking Long-Term

Depending on your situation (specialty, stage of career, geographic location, and the non-clinical career you have selected) you may have to take an initial pay cut associated with your first non-clinical position. A good number of physicians we have worked with have experienced this. You should think long-term, however. Many, if not most, such physicians meet or exceed their clinical earnings within two to three years and end up earning far more than they ever could have earned had they stayed in clinical medicine. For many physicians, it took many years of education, training, and experience to reach their current income level. It may not be realistic to expect to start your non-clinical position at the same income level.

11.14 Not Positioning Yourself Financially for a Career Change
Careful financial planning can greatly empower you to make a successful career change. Live well within your means and save as large of a cushion as possible to protect yourself from any initial drop in income. Accurately assess your financial situation and your financial needs to determine how long a career transition you can sustain without undue hardship for yourself and your family.

11.15 Being Unduly Concerned with What Your Parents Will Think
If you are staying in clinical medicine to not disappoint your parents, you are making a common mistake. From the doctors we work with we have found that the parents' initial shock of their star child no longer "being a doctor" is almost always transformed into pride in their child's new career and success and the immense satisfaction of seeing their child happy.

11.16 Not Taking Every Opportunity to Gain Non-Clinical Experience While Still Practicing Clinical Medicine
It is a mistake not to seize opportunities while practicing medicine to position yourself for a non-clinical career. For example, one of the physicians we have worked with positioned himself for a highly successful career in disability consulting by taking the opportunity to perform independent medical evaluations for insurers while he was a practicing neurologist. Another physician we have worked with positioned herself for a career in administration by publishing, speaking, and generally establishing her reputation in a particular topic she was very interested in. Another example of this is a physician who agreed to intern at a TV station and positioned herself to become a medical affairs TV reporter.

11.17 Leaping into a New Career That You Might Like Less than Your Current Clinical Position

It is a serious mistake to jump into the first non-clinical opportunity that presents itself without thorough due diligence. You do not want to end up in a job you actually like even less than your current clinical position. It took many years of hard work to become a physician. Physicians making a successful career transition realize that, done correctly, the transition to a non-clinical career may take 6 months to several years.

11.18 Not Getting the Buy-In of Your Spouse or Significant Other

Physicians who obtain the full support of their spouse or significant other are much more likely to make a successful transition to a non-clinical career.

Chapter 12 Conclusion: Roadmap to a Career Transition

12.1 Executive Summary

The most successful career transitions often follow a well-thought-out plan. A sample outline of such a plan is provided below.

12.2 Fifteen Steps to Your New Non-Clinical Career

The authors recommend taking the following steps if you are considering transitioning to a non-clinical career:

1. Understand up-front that a proper transition could take 2 to 5 years depending upon your situation. You can transition quicker than this, but this might be very costly in terms of short- and long-term compensation and job satisfaction.
2. Take a hard look at your current clinical job. Can you fix what you don't like by negotiating better employment terms, cutting down your hours, or changing jobs to a more attractive clinical position? For example, many doctors are now becoming hospitalists so that they can have a regular schedule. In addition, many young doctors are simply refusing to accept clinical positions with disruptive call schedules.[1] In our experience, many physicians can greatly improve their job satisfaction in clinical medicine by analyzing what they dislike the most (e.g., malpractice risk, dealing with insurers, and call) and modifying their current employment.

   Example 12.1: Physician stays in clinical medicine by switching clinical jobs
   A physician's main fear is losing everything due to a malpractice claim. He generally likes treating patients. He consults an attorney and does asset protection planning and takes a job at the VA where he has personal immunity from malpractice suits.

---

[1] "As Doctors Get a Life, Strain Shows," *The Wall Street Journal,* April 29, 2008.

Example 12.2: Physician who detests fighting with insurance companies
A physician whose main gripe is fighting with insurers decides that instead of giving up clinical medicine she will open a cash-based concierge practice in an affluent community.

Here is what one SEAK faculty member recommends:

Example 12.3: Try to fix your clinical practice before taking the leap
I'm empathetic with, probably, the struggle that [physicians considering a non-clinical career] may be going through. I want to tell them that there's a bright exciting world outside of clinical medicine, but I really believe that they have to do a self-inventory. They have to understand why they are not happy with what they are doing now and they also have to have a game plan...in what they think they would like to do. It's ok not to have all the answers, but they have to understand at a conscious level, why they are unhappy. If there's anything within their clinical practice that they can correct I would recommend them doing so before they take a leap. But, if they make the decision all I can say is come on board. It's been a very rewarding career that I've had ever since I left clinical medicine.

3. Start getting yourself in the financial position that gives you maximum flexibility for a career change. Live well within your means and save your pennies. Having a financial cushion could let you go back to school, start a business, buy a business, or maintain your lifestyle if you had to take an initial pay cut in your first non-clinical job.
4. Understand what you will need to do to extract yourself from your current situation in terms of managed care contracts, malpractice tails, patient notification, etc. Form a contingency plan for when you accept your first non-clinical opportunity.
5. Research the opportunities available for physicians with extreme diligence. If nothing truly interests you, keep looking. Talk to as many knowledgeable people as you can. Read everything you can. You do *not* want to run away from clinical practice, you want to move into something you truly want to do. Is there a non-clinical career for you that you can be passionate about?
6. Figure out what you can live with in terms of compensation, required travel, and relocation. Physicians should have high aspirations; they need to be realistic as well. Aspiring to a seven-figure income where you can work at home part-time may be fun but it is not realistic.

7. Get comfortable with yourself "no longer being a doctor." Are you happy in clinical practice? If not, this should not be deal breaker.

8. Get your spouse's buy-in on a career change. Don't worry about friends, parents, and family. If they love you they will support you and be proud of you. Educate your spouse and make him or her part of the process. The fact that non-clinical careers often mean less stress, regular hours, and better pay should be helpful. Be up-front, however, that non-clinical positions often have much less job security than clinical positions and may require relocation.

9. Once you've found a field you are interested in, research it to death online, through networking, and by reading everything you can in the field. Make sure the field is compatible with your requirements for short- and long-term compensation, travel, relocation, and with your skills and desires. Talk to as many people as you can.

10. Try to find a mentor who can give you information and guide you through the career-change process.

11. Start building your resume (see Section 9.20) to make yourself as attractive as possible to the industry you have targeted. Different industries will look for different skills and experience (see Chapter 3).

12. Draft a killer resume targeting the industry you have chosen (see Chapter 7).

13. Start looking for and applying for job opportunities through networking, recruiters, job postings, and blitzing an industry (see Section 9.18).

14. Negotiate and accept your job offer. Take the negotiation very seriously because there will be a lot at stake. If you do a good job negotiating you can make a lot more money. For more on negotiation, please see Chapter 10.

15. Work hard at your new career, take it seriously, and rapidly prove that you were being undercompensated as a clinician. Find the passion you may have been missing as a clinician and enjoy your new adventure.

Index

Index

189, 190, 195, 196, 197, 200, 203, 205, 206, 209, 215, 225–26, 232, 237
Communications industry, 45, 90–96, 122, 131, 234–35, 254
Community medicine, 158
Commute, 17, 33, 37–38, 152
Compensation, 1, 2, 7–13, 33, 34, 38–39, 45, 51–52, 61, 66–67, 69–70, 93, 98, 104–5, 106, 107, 108–10, 112, 113, 122, 126, 129, 136, 141, 151, 160, 167, 168, 188, 203, 205, 208, 219, 237, 239, 240, 241–45, 246, 251, 253, 256, 259, 260, 261
   negotiating, 247–48
Competencies, core, 185, 187, 196–202, 255
Competition, 58
Compliance, 49, 62, 63, 68, 77, 84, 87, 193
Composure, 200
Computer literacy, 75, 79, 88, 95, 102, 126, 162, 178, 191, 209
Concentra Physicians Review, 104
Conferences, 72, 77, 78, 79, 80, 92, 115, 125, 137, 139, 140, 141, 142, 143–44, 187, 216
Confidentiality, 233
Conflict management, 48, 197
Consensus building, 39, 48
Consultants, negotiating, 248
Consulting, 16, 22, 23, 45, 46–52, 67, 80, 84, 85, 86, 98, 101, 104, 132, 134, 143, 160, 171, 184, 219, 221, 223, 230, 231, 234, 235, 238, 244, 254, 256
   income, 9, 12, 47, 51–52
   informatics, 114–16
   niches, 47–50
   working from home, 23, 52
Contact information, 176–77
Contacts, 137, 139–40, 141, 143, 144, 145, 146–47, 149–50, 167, 169, 227
Contingency plan, 221, 260
Continuing education, 42, 45, 62, 80, 89, 90–96, 102, 115, 162, 163, 174, 187
   sample job posting, 95–96

Continuing medical education, 18, 64, 70, 71, 88, 94–95, 103, 110, 119, 162, 163
   reimbursement, 243
Contracts, 67, 239–49, 261
   covenants not to compete, 239, 244–45
   fringe benefits, 243
   negotiating, 245–48
   preparing to negotiate, 239–40
   termination provisions, 244
   terms of the offer, 241–45
Control, 13–20, 29, 36, 46
Copyrightable works, 244
Corporate culture, 1, 175, 192, 212
Corporate health and wellness, 45
Cost-cutting, 30, 99, 179, 180, 181, 184, 210
Covenants not to compete, 239, 244–45
Covey, Stephen, 217
Creativity, 22–25, 46, 53, 57, 93, 117, 133, 162, 199, 204, 211, 219
Credentialing, 100, 118, 119, 223
Credentials, 48, 207
Credibility, 40, 66, 127, 128, 162, 166, 167, 169, 170, 188, 189, 205, 218, 224, 237, 238, 254
Critical thinking, 190, 198
CSC, 114
Culture shock, 1, 27–30
Curriculum, 132
Customers, 59, 62, 76, 77, 78, 83, 84, 92, 94, 95, 100, 101, 180, 181, 198, 201
CV, 107, 173, 190, 229
   differs from resume, 173–74, 183–84

D

Databases, 74, 78, 79, 95
Deadlines, 196
Debt, 39
Deciding to leave practice, 33–35
Decision maker, 107, 141, 182, 224, 229, 230, 241, 246, 248
Decision tree, 239

Degrees, advanced, 33, 40, 43, 53, 58, 93, 94, 107, 112, 119, 122, 126, 155–72, 215, 233, 252
  advantages/disadvantages, 156–60, 165–71
  not completing, 158–59, 217–21
  on resume, 162, 182–83
  tuition, 155, 160, 162, 243
  where to pursue, 160–63
Deloitte, 114
Dental insurance, 243
Dermatology, 94
Detail-oriented, 198
Development, 72, 74, 80, 86, 95, 130, 165, 234, 254
Development, product, 73, 76, 79, 80, 83, 84, 85, 86, 89, 117, 181
Diabetes care, 84, 93
Direct reports, 212
Directory of Executive Recruiters, 232
Disability, 1, 2, 129, 210
Disability assessments, 104
Disability insurance, 28, 45, 97–98, 100–102, 243, 180, 254
  building resume, 236
  sample job posting, 101–2
Disability Management Services, 101
Discipline, 51
Discoveries, 244
Dissatisfaction, 1–7
Distributors, 60, 61
Documentation, 67, 68, 72, 87
Documentation review, 62
Doostang, 148
Drafting resumes, 174–76
Drug analyst, 24, 159
Drug development and safety, 25, 49, 63, 68, 72, 130, 131, 209, 234
  sample job posting, 82, 87–88
Dun and Bradstreet reports, 193

E
85 Broads, 148
Easing into work, 223–24
Eclipsys, 112
Economic conditions, 33, 44
Editor, medical, 132, 181
Education, 33, 35, 40, 43, 53, 58, 62, 63, 64, 65, 66, 70, 71, 72, 74, 75, 77, 79, 80, 85, 87, 88, 89, 90–96, 102, 103, 106, 110, 119, 122, 123, 130, 132, 140, 155–72, 174, 187, 215, 233, 254, 256
  leave training early, 40–41, 52, 158–59, 217–21, 229, 230, 255
  listing on resume, 182–83
  online, 161, 163
  sample job posting, 94–95, 95–96
  See also Advanced degrees
Education materials, 77
Ego, 17, 28, 188, 189–90, 232
  of interviewer, 195
Electronic medical records, 112, 113, 116, 125, 179, 180, 197
E-mail, 6, 107, 141, 142, 145, 146, 149, 191, 217, 253
Emergency medicine, 124
Emergency response, 106, 109, 125
Emotional trauma of career change, 33, 35
Employer, prospective
  allaying fears of, 187–91
  attributes sought by, 189–91
  blitzing, 215, 234–35, 261
  competencies sought by, 196–202
  human resources, 215, 224
  job description, 222
  needs of, 240–41
  negotiating with, 239–40, 245–48
  recruiters and, 230–33
  researching, 187, 192–93
  terms of the offer, 241–45
  timeframe, 241, 247
Employers, prior, 188, 209

Index